5500 QUESTIONS AND ANSWERS ON THE HOLY BIBLE

5500 QUESTIONS AND ANSWERS ON THE HOLY BIBLE

ZONDERVAN PUBLISHING HOUSE
OF THE ZONDERVAN CORPORATION
GRAND RAPIDS, MICHIGAN 49506

FOREWORD

The Bible is the most popular book in the world. Throughout the centuries it has been universally read and has been the subject of much controversy. Believers and unbelievers alike have diligently searched its pages, the one for proof of their beliefs, and the other to substantiate their doubts of the Divine Creator.

Men and women from all grades of society have been influenced to righteous living by its inspired words. Scholars have delved deep into its pages to find the meaning of life. Religious sects have looked to the Bible as reason for the hope that is within them. There are many other subjects taught in the Bible, such as patience, forbearance, honesty, virtue, truthfulness, brotherly love, charity, and hundreds of other graces of character.

It is a library of Scriptures comprising more than three score separate volumes. An important step toward understanding the Bible is to learn what is in it, to become acquainted in a general way with what each of its sixty-six books contributes to a better understanding of the Bible.

One of the most useful and suggestive methods of discovering how little one knows about the Bible is the use of questions and answers; a method that has been successfully followed by many inspired teachers of the Bible.

This is by far the largest collection of questions and answers on the Bible that has ever been assembled. It comprises questions and answers on *all* the books of the Bible. This book was formerly known as 4,500 Questions and Answers, but recently a new edition was made and more than a thousand questions and answers were added, making it now 5,500 Questions and Answers.

How to use these questions and answers. Let us suppose that your next Sunday-school lesson is from the book of Romans, chapter 8. You have been selected to tell the story of this chapter to your class. You have read the chapter in order to become acquainted with the "Law of the Spirit." You will be amazed to find that, among the twenty-four entries, there is a wealth of information of which you could not have known without these questions and answers. This method may be followed also by ministers and Christian workers in the preparation of sermons and addresses on Bible subjects.

These *Questions and Answers* have been prepared by eminent scholars of the Bible, and have been, and still are, a source of invaluable information for Bible students, both young and old.

JOSEPH HOWARD GRAY, D.D.

INTRODUCTION

The Bible is more than just a book. It is *the Book*, and without question, it is the greatest book in all the history of literature.

But, in the words of Dr. F. F. Bruce, renowned Biblical scholar: "The Bible was never intended to be a book for scholars and specialists only. From the beginning it was intended to be everybody's Book, and that is what it continues to be. The message which it contains is designed to meet a universal need; its central figure is rightly called the Saviour of the World. Although it was completed such a long time ago, the Bible never grows out-of-date, because the subjects with which it deals are those subjects which retain their relevance from one century to another, and concern us today as vitally as they concerned the people who first read the Bible."

An intimate knowledge of the Bible is essential to the personal recognition of its relevancy to the mid-twentieth century. And, this book, with its 5500 questions and answers, is designed to help every reader to a better understanding of the facts and the spirit of the Bible. Here is a rich sourcebook of study material for Bible study and group discussion in both church and home. Sunday school teachers and those preparing devotional talks for any occasion will find helpful background and resource material — conveniently arranged for instant reference.

Properly used, *5500 Questions and Answers* is a Bible study tool of infinite value.

THE PUBLISHERS

5500 QUESTIONS AND ANSWERS ON THE
HOLY BIBLE

FOR

BIBLE STUDENTS AND
SUNDAY SCHOOL TEACHERS

———o———

THE CREATION. (Gen. 1.)

1. When did God create the heaven and the earth?—In the beginning. Gen. 1:1.

2. Did he make them out of nothing?—He formed them out of the resources of his own being. We do not know how; but through faith we understand that the worlds were framed by the word of God, so that things which are seen were not made of things that do appear. Heb. 11:3.

3. Did God make all things complete at once?—No; for The earth was without form and void, and darkness was upon the face of the deep. Gen. 1:2.

4. How did he prepare the earth to be the abode of men?—By a series of changes extending through periods of time, called "days."

5. What was done on the first day?—The light was created and separated from the darkness. Isa. 45:7.

6. What was the work of the econd day?—The creation of an atmosphere, or firmament, and the separation of the waters under the firmament from those above it.

7. What of the third day?—The dry land appeared above the waters, and vegetable growth began.

8. What of the fourth day?— The sun, moon, and stars began to shine through the mists and lighten the earth. Now for the first time began the regular succession of day and night.

9. What of the fifth day?— Birds, fishes, reptiles, and insects sprang into being.

10. What of the sixth day?—The wild beasts and cattle were made. And lastly man was created.

11. How is man distinguished from all other animals?—By being made in the image of God. Gen. 1:27.

12. What is meant by his being made in the image of God?—By his being endued with a reasonable soul and the power of understanding. Eccles. 3:21; 12:7.

13. What favors did God bestow upon him?—He made him lord of all other created things.

14. Did this lordship impose upon him any duties?—Yes; he was to be fruitful, and multiply and replenish the earth, and subdue it.

15. Have these duties been discharged?—Only partially.

16. Why did God rest on the seventh day?—Because he then ceased to make any new kinds of things upon the earth.

THE FALL. (Gen. 2, 3.)

1. Where did God place man when he created him?—In the garden of Eden. Gen. 2:8.

2. Where was this garden?— Probably in Central Asia.

3. What description have we given to us of the garden?—God made to grow in it the tree of life, the tree of knowledge of good and

1

evil, and every tree that is pleasant to the sight and good for food. Gen. 2:9.

4. How was it watered?—By four rivers that flowed from a common source to the sea. Gen. 2:10-14.

5. Can any of those rivers be now traced?—The Euphrates, only, is well known; the others not certainly. Hiddekel is thought to be the Tigris.

6. Was man idle in the garden of Eden, or did God employ him there?—He was put into the garden to dress it and keep it. Gen. 2:15.

7. How was the garden refreshed before man was placed there to tend it?—By a mist from the earth. Gen. 2:6.

8. Did God permit man to pluck and eat the fruit of this garden?—He was allowed freely to eat of every tree with one exception. Gen. 2:16.

9. What was this exception?—The tree of knowledge of good and evil, under the penalty of death. Gen. 2:17.

10. Were they forbidden to eat of the tree of life?—They were not.

11. What do we conclude from this?—That they were intended to live forever.

12. Did man obey God's command?—He did not.

13. What did he do?—He ate the forbidden fruit.

14. Who was the first transgressor?—Eve.

15. How came it about?—The devil, in the form of a serpent, deceived her by a lie. Gen. 3:1-6.

16. What did the devil promise Eve?—That they should not surely die, but be as gods, knowing good and evil. Gen. 3:4, 5.

17. Was she disappointed?—Satan's words proved false, for there is no truth in him.

18. What foolish plan did they adopt to hide their shame?—They hid themselves amongst the trees of the garden.

19. Can any place conceal us from God's eye?—None.

20. What is it that makes us fear to meet God?—The consciousness that we have sinned, and that he knows it.

21. What do we do when we commit sin?—We generally try to hide our wrongdoings even from ourselves.

22. What ought we to do?—To confess and be truly sorry for our sin; to come to God, through Christ, for the pardon of it, and to forsake it.

23. Can we provide a covering for our sin?—No; for our very best deeds are imperfect and defiled.

24. Has God taken pity on us and given us a robe of righteousness?—He hath clothed me with the garments of salvation, he hath covered me with the robe of righteousness. Isa. 61:10.

25. Where is this further spoken of?—Even the righteousness of God which is by faith of Jesus Christ unto all, and upon all them that believe. Rom. 3:22.

26. How was it made known to our first parents?—It was included in the intimation of a Saviour, conveyed in the promise that the seed of the woman should bruise the serpent's head. Gen. 3:15.

27. How did God clothe their bodies?—In coats of skin. Gen. 3:21.

28. What is it supposed was done with the bodies of the animals thus slain?—That they were offered in sacrifice to God.

29. How did this represent the great atonement that Jesus afterward accomplished?—By the shedding of blood. Heb. 9:22.

30. Did God give them any direct promise of this blessed Person?—The promise was certain but obscure. Gen. 4:1.

31. Was the devil disappointed?—Yes; he failed in ruining man forever.

32. Who got the curse?—Satan, whose head or power was to be bruised or crushed. Gen. 3:15. Man also suffered in a less de-

2

gree, by being driven out of Eden, and condemned to laborious toil, and at last to bodily death. Gen. 3:17-19, 23, 24.

33. For whose sake was the ground cursed?—For man's sake. Gen. 3:17.

34. How was man to feel this?—By the weeds it brought forth and the labor it required.

35. Was there any special punishment to the woman for being first in the transgression?—Yes; personal suffering.

36. Was there not also a special mercy granted to her?—Yes; that she should be the ancestress of Christ. Gen. 3:15.

37. Did they continue in the garden of Eden?—No.

38. Why not?—Lest they should eat of the tree of life and live forever upon earth. Gen. 3:22.

39. Is the tree of life ever mentioned again in Scripture, and where?—In Rev. 22:1, 2, as standing by the river of the water of life, in the heavenly Jerusalem (Rev. 21:2); in the midst of the paradise of God. Rev. 2:7.

40. Who will again eat of it?—They that do God's commandments and that overcome in the battle with Satan and with sin. Rev. 22: 14; 2:7.

41. How did God guard the gate of Eden?—By cherubim or angels and a flaming sword. Gen. 3:24.

42. Where are the cherubim again mentioned in Scripture?—In the vision of Ezekiel, chapters 1 and 10, and in the account of the tabernacle and the temple, etc., twenty-one places altogether.

43. Why did Adam name his wife Eve?—Because she was the mother of all living—the word means "living." Gen. 3:20.

CAIN AND ABEL. (Gen. 4.)

1. What was the name of Adam's first child?—Cain. Gen. 4:1.

2. What is the meaning of the name?—Got, or obtained.

3. Whom did Eve suppose him to be?—The seed or child or Saviour promised.

4. Was she disappointed?—Yes; he became a wicked man and a murderer.

5. What name did she give her second son?—Abel, or Vanity.

6. What did this show?—That her expectations had been disappointed.

7. Did he prove as bad as his brother?—No; his works were righteous. 1 John 3:12.

8. What difference do we observe in the offerings of the two brothers?—Cain offered of the fruit of the ground, and Abel the firstlings of his flock. Gen. 4:3, 4.

9. How does this give us their characters?—The offerings were probably equally good in themselves; but Cain showed indifference or self-will, and Abel obedience and faith.

10. Will God receive us in any other way than the way he has appointed?—He will not.

11. How is that?—Jesus saith, I am the way, the truth, and the life; no man cometh unto the Father, but by me. John 14:6.

12. How did the slain lamb represent Jesus?—In its being without blemish and without spot (I Peter 1:19), and in having its blood shed in sacrifice for sin. Heb. 9: 22.

13. What did John the Baptist say of Jesus?—Behold the Lamb of God, which taketh away the sin of the world! John 1:29.

14. What proof did God give that Abel's sacrifice was accepted?—Probably the consuming it by fire from heaven, as Elijah's was consumed on Carmel. 1 Kings 18:38.

15. How did Cain act when he found that his own way did not please God?—He was very angry. Gen. 4:5.

16. How should he have acted?—He should have offered his gifts in penitence and faith. Gen. 4:7.

17. Did not sin lie at his own door then, seeing God had pro-

3

vided a way to remove it?—It did (Gen. 4:7), and led to greater guilt and sin.

18. What awful act did Cain's jealousy lead to?—The murder of Abel.

19. What fearful lie did he tell? —He told the all-seeing God that he knew not where his murdered brother was.

20. What did God say had cried to him?—His brother's blood.

21. In John 8:44, the devil is called a murderer. What is said of Cain in 1 John 3:12?—Not as Cain, who was of that wicked one and slew his brother. And wherefore slew he him? Because his own works were evil, and his brother's righteous.

22. Did Cain procure for himself Satan's portion—a curse?—See Gen. 4:11, 12.

23. What did Cain feel when God's curse lighted on him?—That his punishment was greater than he could bear, as anyone might kill him.

24. Did God in mercy mitigate Cain's punishment?—He set a mark upon him to prevent his being killed.

25. What is meant by Cain's going from God's presence?—He perhaps never heard him again, or saw him in the form he used to take, or felt his Spirit within him.

26. When God takes vengeance into his own hand will he let anyone else perform it?—God, to whom vengeance belongeth, says, Vengeance is mine; I will repay. Rom. 12:19; Psalm 94:1.

27. Is there a day of reckoning coming?—It is appointed unto men once to die, and after that the judgment. Heb. 9:27.

THE ANTEDILUVIAN PATRIARCHS. (Gen. 5.)

1. What is the allotted age of man?—In the time of Moses it was seventy or eighty years, though he himself lived to be one hundred and twenty.

2. Could we imagine it possible for men to have lived so long as the patriarchs?—Both the Bible and profane tradition intimate as much.

3. When did the term of human life grow shorter?—After the deluge.

4. How is it that Enoch's is so much shorter than that of the other antediluvians?—Because God took him to himself before he had lived half the usual time.

5. What does the apostle, in Heb. 11:5, say of Enoch?—By faith Enoch was translated, that he should not see death.

6. What remarkable prophecy attributed to Enoch does the apostle Jude repeat?—Behold, the Lord cometh with ten thousands of his saints.

7. To which coming of the Lord does it refer? To the first or second?—The second.

8. Is that second coming spoken of in other parts of the Bible? If so, where?—In 1 Thess. 4:16, 17, and fifty other places at least.

9. What was the object of Jesus' coming?—That the world through him might be saved. John 3:16, 17.

10. What will be the design of the Lord's second coming?—To judge the world.

11. What remarkable likeness is there between the prophecy of God's first prophet and God's last prophet?—Each foretold the coming of our Lord.

12. What did John say?—Behold, he cometh with clouds; and every eye shall see him, and they also which pierced him: and all kindreds of the earth shall wail because of him. Even so, Amen. Rev. 1:7.

13. Who guided those who wrote the Bible?—The Holy Ghost. 1 Peter 1:21.

14. Do we know when the Lord Jesus is coming?—Watch, therefore: for ye know not what hour your Lord doth come. Matt. 24:42

4

15. What effect should this uncertainty as to our knowledge have upon us?—Wherefore, beloved, seeing that ye look for such things, be diligent that ye may be found of him in peace, without spot and blameless. 2 Peter 3:10, 14.

16. Was Enoch ready when he was caught up?—Yes; quite.

17. With whom was he walking in communion?—With God.

18. What is said in Amos 3:3? —Can two walk together, except they be agreed?

19. Who should be companions? —Those whom we believe to be walking with God and who can help us to do so.

20. Should we delight in being alone with him?—We must be alone with him in death; and it is our wisdom and comfort to be much alone with him in life.

21. What solemn warning does God give in Heb. 3:7, 8?—As the Holy Ghost saith, To-day, if ye will hear his voice, harden not your hearts.

THE FLOOD. (Gen. 5, 6.)

1. What do we read of Cain's descendants in Gen. 4:17-23?— That Cain had a son Enoch, and built a city, etc.

2. Were they as good as they were skillful?—No, they shared the general corruption of mankind. Gen. 4:16; 6:5.

3. What was the name of the son that God gave Adam in the place of Abel, whom Cain slew? —Seth. Gen. 4:25.

4. Did the children of Seth keep themselves separate from Cain's children?—Yes. They called themselves by the name of the Lord. Gen. 4:26, margin.

5. When God looked down from heaven what did he see?—The great wickedness of man. Gen. 6: 5.

6. What did he resolve to do?— To destroy both man and beast. Gen. 6:7.

7. Did he find one faithful family?—Yes. Gen. 6:8, 18.

8. Whose was that?—Noah's.

9. What is Noah said to be in 2 Peter 2:5?—A preacher of righteousness.

10. When did Noah preach to these wicked people?—While the ark was preparing. 1 Peter 3:20.

11. What does the Book of Jonah show us?—That if man had repented God would have spared.

12. Did these sinners repent at the preaching of Noah?—No.

13. What was the consequence? —The flood came and took them all away. Matt. 24:39; Gen. 7: 21-23.

14. How were Noah and his family preserved?—In the ark, which Noah built at God's command.

15. What is a type?—A thing that represents another thing, or has some points of resemblance to it, and is intended to foreshow it.

16. Of whom was the ark in which Noah and his family were saved a type?—Of Christ.

17. How?—As an appointed means of saving man from destruction.

18. Of what was the flood a type?—Of the future destruction of the world. 2 Peter 3:6, 7.

19. Does this concern us at all? —Yes; as both living and dead will need a Saviour at that day.

20. What opportunity does God give us of fleeing into a place of safety?—He spares our lives, and gives us Bibles and preachers and teachers, to show us the way of salvation.

21. Has he provided a secure place of dependence? What is it? —God himself, in Christ, is our refuge. Psalm 119:114.

22. What does the Holy Spirit say to us in 2 Cor. 6:2?—Now is the accepted time; now is the day of salvation.

23. Can there be a time when even God shall forget to be gracious?—Yes; as when, in the parable of the ten virgins, the door was shut. Matt. 25:10.

5

NOAH. (Gen. 7-9.)

1. How long was the ark building?—Perhaps a great part of the time that Noah was preaching, or of the one hundred and twenty years mentioned in Gen. 6:3.

2. How old were Noah and his sons when they went into the ark?—Noah, six hundred years (Gen. 7:6), and his sons about one hundred. Gen. 5:32; 11:10.

3. Who shut them in?—God himself. Gen. 7:16.

4. What went into the ark with them?—(Besides their wives) seven, or two, of every living creature. Gen. 7:2, 3, 7-9, 13-16.

5. How long did it continue raining?—Forty days and nights. Gen. 7:12.

6. How long did the waters continue?—One hundred and fifty days. Gen. 7:24.

7. How did Noah ascertain when the waters had abated?—By sending out a dove, which returned with an olive leaf in its mouth, and which, when sent out again, did not return at all. Gen. 8:10-12.

8. Why did not the raven return to the ark?—It probably often went forth and returned, as the words "to and fro" are explained in the margin to mean. Gen. 8:7. But if it met with floating carcasses it might not come in for food.

9. Of what is that an emblem? —Perhaps of the carnal heart, content with the corrupt enjoyments of the world.

10. And is there anything to be learned from the opposite conduct of the dove?—The privilege of the soul, unsatisfied with the world, returning to Christ Jesus as its rest.

11. What does the Lord Jesus say in Matt. 11:28-30?—Come unto me, all ye that labor and are heavy laden, and I will give you rest.

12. What was Noah's first act when he came forth from the ark? —He built an altar and offered a sacrifice. Gen. 8:20.

13. What animals were used for burnt offerings?—A bullock, sheep, goat, turtledove, or young pigeon. Lev. 1.

14. Did God accept Noah's offering?—It pleased him as a sweet savor or smell. Gen. 8:21.

15. What promise did God give Noah at that time?—That he would not again curse the ground any more for man's sake, etc. Gen. 8:21-23; 9:2.

16, 17. Did God condescend to give him a token? What was it?— He said that the rainbow should be a token or remembrance of his covenant or promise. Gen. 9:8-17.

18. Does it remain?—Yes.

19. When does it appear?— Whenever the sun shines out during a rain.

20. Did God make any change in man's food at that time?—He gave him animal food, in addition to his former vegetable food. Gen. 9:3.

21. Under what restriction?— That the blood should not be used with the flesh. Gen. 9:4.

22. Why was not blood to be eaten?—Because it was a type of the blood of Christ and to restrain bloodthirsty cruelty to man or beast. Gen. 5:6.

23. What evil use did Noah afterward make of the fruits of the earth?—He once became drunk with wine. Gen. 9:21.

24. Does the Bible cover up and hide the sins of God's people?— No; it mentions them whenever it seemed in the wisdom of God to be desirable to do so.

25. What does the psalmist say of God's word in Psalm 119:140? —That it is "very pure."

26. Which of Noah's sons brought a curse on his posterity by his conduct to his father on this occasion?—Ham.

27. When was this curse fulfilled?—When the children of Israel took possession of the land of Canaan.

28. Show the fulfillment of Shem's blessing.—God's people, the Jews, and Christ himself descended from Shem.

29. Describe how Japheth has been enlarged?—By his descendants, the Aryan nations, who have colonized and possess all continents and islands of the sea.

30. How old was Noah when he died?—Nine hundred and fifty years. Gen. 9:29.

THE TOWER OF BABEL.
(Gen. 10, 11.)

1. What mighty nations have their origin given in these chapters?—The Chaldeans, Assyrians, and Canaanites.

2. Were the genealogies and histories of all these nations continued in the Bible?—No.

3. Why was one family singled out for this special honor?—Because out of it came Jesus Christ.

4. What great event happened in the days of Peleg?—The scattering of mankind over all the earth. Gen. 11:9.

5. Why did God thus divide or scatter men?—To restrain them from building the tower of Babel.

6. What motive had these men in building the tower?—To form a conspicuous gathering point, in defiance of the divine intention.

7. Of what did they compose it? —Of bricks, joined together with mortar of slime or mud that dried hard.

8. Are there any remains of the materials of which it was built yet in existence?—Yes; in the ruins of Babylon.

9. Where did Shem's family remove to?—Some of them from upper and middle Asia to Canaan.

10. Which of Abram's ancestors were alive when he was born?—Nahor and Terah.

11. How old was Shem when Abram was born?—Four hundred and fifty-two years. (B.C. 2448-1996.) Gen. 5:32; 11:27.

12. How many years did Shem live after Abram was born?—One hundred and forty-nine years. (B.C. 1996-1847.) Gen. 11:10, 11.

13. What was the name of Abram's father?—Terah. Gen. 11:26.

14. How many years was he contemporaneous with Noah?—One hundred and twenty-eight years. Gen. 5:29; 11:24.

15. Was Noah alive when Abram was born?—No; he died two years before. Gen. 9:29.

16. Was Adam alive when Noah was born?—No; he died one hundred and twenty-six years before.

17. Was Adam alive when Lamech was born?—Yes

18. How many years were they contemporaneous?—Fifty-six.

19. Were Adam and Abram contemporaries?—There were only Lamech, Noah, and Terah between them.

ABRAHAM. (Gen. 11-22.)

1. Where was Abram born?—In Ur of the Chaldees.

2. Where is Ur?—On the lower Euphrates, not far from the Persian Gulf.

3. Did his father die there?—No.

4. To what land did his father remove?—To Haran.

5. Which of Abram's brothers died before they left their native land?—Haran. Gen. 11:28.

6. Did he leave a son, and what was his name?—Lot. Gen. 11:27.

7. Did this grandson accompany Terah and Abram to Haran?—Yes. Gen. 11:31.

8. Where did Terah die?—In Haran. Gen. 11:32.

9. After that event, did Abram stay in Haran?—No.

10. Why did he remove?—Because God told him so to do.

11. What promise did God make him?—That he would make of him a great nation, and in him all the families of the earth should be blessed.

12. How old was Abram at that time?—Seventy-five years.

13. Who went with him?—Sarai his wife, and Lot, and their serv-

ants.

14. What relation was Lot to Abram?—His nephew.

15. Where are Haran and Canaan?—Haran is in Mesopotamia, between Nineveh and Tarsus; and Canaan is on the eastern shore of the Mediterranean Sea, between the mountains of Lebanon and Arabia.

16. Where did Abram first settle?—At Sichem, in the plain of Moreh, near Samaria. Gen. 12:6.

17. What remarkable circumstance in the history of Jacob happened there?—Jacob buried under an oak there the idols and earrings taken from his household. Gen. 35:4.

18. What acts of Joshua again distinguished this spot when he first subdued Canaan?—His assembling of the tribes of Israel to renew their covenant with God; his appointing Shechem one of the cities of refuge; his reading the law between Mounts Gerizim and Ebal. Josh. 24:1, 25, 26; 20:7; 8:33.

19. At what place did he rear the tabernacle, and at his death make a covenant with Israel?—At Shiloh, near Sichem. Josh. 18:1.

20. What event in the New Testament is recorded concerning this spot?—Christ's interview at Sychar with the woman of Samaria. John 4:5-42.

21. Did Abram continue to live at Sichem?—No; he removed to the neighborhood of Beth-el. Gen. 12:8, 9; 13:17.

22. From this place whither did Abram go?—To Egypt. Gen. 10:12.

23. Why?—Because there was a famine in the land.

24. What other famines occurred here?—See Gen. 26:1; 47:13; Ruth 1:1; 2 Sam. 21:1; 1 Kings 18:2; 2 Kings 6:25; 8:1; 25:3.

25. What sin was Abram guilty of in Egypt?—Of want of truthfulness respecting Sarai his wife. Gen. 12:11-20.

26. What does this teach us?—We have before proved, both Jews and Gentiles, that they are all under sin; as it is written, There is none righteous, no, not one. Rom. 3:9, 10.

27. Was Abram a rich or poor man?—He was very rich. Gen. 13:2.

28. In what did his wealth consist?—In cattle, in silver, and in gold. Gen. 13:2.

29. To what place did Abram go from Egypt?—To Beth-el.

30. Did Lot accompany him?—He did.

31. What did Abram do?—He called on the name of the Lord.

32. Had Lot prospered?—Very much. Gen. 13:5.

33. What was the result?—A quarrel between the herdmen of the two. Gen. 13:6, 7.

34. How did Abram behave on this occasion?—He proposed that they should part, and gave Lot the choice of the land. Gen. 13:8, 9.

35. Did Lot behave as well as Abram in this affair?—No; for he made no liberal offer in return.

36. Had Lot cause to repent of his choice?—He narrowly escaped with his life, but suffered the loss of his wife, many of his family, and much of his substance. Gen. 19:15-29; 2 Peter 2:7, 8.

37. What kind of people did he go to sojourn among?—Exceedingly wicked. Gen. 13:13.

38. After this separation how did God manifest himself to Abram?—He repeated to him his promises. Gen. 13:14-17.

39. What particular duty does the example of Abram teach?—Both family and private devotion.

40. What kings engaged in battle after Lot's separation from Abram?—See Gen. 14:1-17.

41. What news came to Abram concerning Lot?—That Lot and his goods had been carried away captive. Gen. 14:12, 13.

42. How did Abram act?—He armed his men and went in pur-

suit. Gen. 14:14.

43. What success did he have? —He recovered the prisoners and their goods. Gen. 14:15, 16.

44. Who met Abram on his return? Melchizedek, king of Salem. Gen. 14:18.

45. Where did Melchizedek live?—At Salem, afterward named Jerusalem. Gen. 13:18.

46. Is Melchizedek ever alluded to again in Scripture? Where?— Heb. 6:20; 7:1-3; Psalm 110:4.

47. Of whom was he a type?— Of Christ, in being both king and priest.

48. What did Abram do, when urged by the king of Sodom to take part of the spoil?—He declined taking anything but some food for his men. Gen. 14:21-24.

49. Why did he do this?—So that they might not say they had made Abram rich.

50. Who was the steward of Abram's house?—Eliezer of Damascus.

51. What did Abram ask of the Lord? The gift of an heir. Gen. 15:2, 3.

52. What did God promise him? —That his seed or descendants should be in number as the stars. Gen. 15:5.

53. Had Abram at this time any children?—No. Gen. 15:3.

54. To what did God compare the number of his seed?—To the dust of the earth. Gen. 13:16.

55. Did Abram believe the Lord?—Yes.

56. How was his faith accounted or reckoned to him?—For righteousness. Gen. 15:6.

57. Is faith, then, very precious in the estimation of God?—Yes; for his Son's sake.

58. What is faith?—Belief in Christ, accepting him as our Saviour, and obediently walking in his ways.

59. How much land did God promise to Abram?—From the river on the border of Egypt to the Euphrates. Gen. 15:18-21.

60. What sign did the Lord give

him that his seed should inherit this land?—See Gen. 15:5.

61. Who was Hagar?—One of Sarai's waiting maids. Gen. 16:1.

62. Of what nation was she?— Of Egypt.

63. Why did Abram take her to be his wife?—That Sarai might, by her, have children that would be reckoned as her own. Gen. 16:2.

64. Did Sarai use her kindly?— Hagar, when likely to have children, despised her mistress, and Sarai dealt hardly with her. Gen. 16:4-6.

65. What did Hagar do?—She ran away.

66. What did the angel of the Lord who met her direct her to do?—To return to Sarai and submit herself under her. Gen. 16:9.

67. What did God promise her? —That he would multiply her seed exceedingly; the Arabians sprang from her. Gen. 16:10.

68. After she returned, what event happened?—She bore a son.

69. What name was given to him?—Ishmael.

70. What was foretold concerning him?—See Gen. 16:12.

71. How old was Abram when Ishmael was born?—Eighty-six years.

72. When Abram was ninety-nine years of age, what further covenant did God enter into with him?—He renewed his promise that he should still have an heir, through Sarai his wife. Gen. 17:1-8.

73. To what did the Lord change their names?—From Abram, or "exalted father," to Abraham, or "father of a multitude;" and from Sarai, "contention," to Sarah, or "princess."

74. Did Abraham at once believe God?—The promise seemed too good to be true, and he besought God to allow Ishmael to be his heir. Gen. 17:17, 18.

75. Did God accept Abraham's prayer?—No; but he blessed Ishmael, and promised to make him a great nation. Gen. 17:20.

9

76. Who was to be the promised seed?—Isaac, who was not yet born, and with whom God established his covenant. Gen. 17:19.

77. How long did God fix for the fulfillment of his promise to Abraham and his wife?—A whole year. Gen. 17:21.

78. What was the sign of the covenant between God and Abraham?—Circumcision.

79. Was this intended to be a national or a religious rite?—Probably both.

80. How old was Ishmael when he was circumcised?—Thirteen.

81. Where was Mamre?—Near Hebron, in Judah. Gen. 13:18.

82. What remarkable event happened to Abraham there?—Three angels or heavenly visitors appeared to him in the form of men.

83. What is said of this visit in Heb. 13:2?—Be not forgetful to entertain strangers; for thereby some have entertained angels unawares.

84. Did Abraham know whom he was entertaining?—He took them at first for ordinary travelers, but found out, by what one of them said, that they were angels. Gen. 18:10, 14.

85. What is Abraham called in Isa. 41:8?—The friend of God. James 2:23.

86. How did Sarah displease the Lord at this time?—By laughing within herself at the unlikelihood of what he said.

87. What was she tempted to do when the Lord expressed his displeasure?—To deny that she had laughed.

88. When the three heavenly visitors had eaten with Abraham, did they all depart from him together?—One of the angels remained, and the other two went toward Sodom. Gen. 18:22.

89. Why did three angels appear to Abraham?—Probably as a mark of the divine favor, and to strengthen his faith in the promise of an heir.

90. Which of the angels remained?—The Angel of the Covenant, or the Son of God himself. John 8:56.

91. What became of the two angels?—They departed for Sodom.

92. How came Abraham to know the purpose of their visit to Sodom?—From what the Lord said to him. Gen. 18:20, 21.

93. Did Abraham venture to plead for the city? How?—By six times asking the Lord to spare it, as recorded in Gen. 18:23-32.

94. Did God permit him to go on as long as he would?—The Lord put no check upon his intercession, and consented to do all that he asked.

95. What should this teach us? —To persevere in prayer. Men ought always to pray and not to faint. Luke 18:1.

96. Where did Lot dwell?—In Sodom.

97. What happened to him one evening as he sat in the gate of the city?—Two angels came to him. Gen. 18:22; 19:1.

98. Why did he sit in the gate? —The gate was the place where judgments were rendered, and he was probably a judge. Gen. 19:9.

99. For what did the angels visit Sodom?—To destroy it and to rescue Lot.

100. Did they find it as wicked as they expected?—It could hardly have been worse than it was. Gen. 18:21.

101. What did Lot do when he saw them?—He invited them to go home with him, and entertained them. Gen. 19:2, 3.

102. Was such hospitality common?—It was, elsewhere.

103. Did the citizens treat the strangers courteously?—No; a mob of them gathered about Lot's house to assault him.

104. How did the angels punish the men who tried to get into Lot's door?—They struck them with blindness. Gen. 19:11

105. What did the angels do in the morning?—They hastened Lot,

10

because they were about to destroy the place.

106. Did Lot warn any of the people of the threatened destruction?—He spoke to his sons-in-law to escape at once.

107. How many of Lot's family believed the warning and fled with him?—His wife and two daughters. Gen. 19:16.

108. Did all these eventually escape?—The daughters escaped, but his wife looked back and became a pillar of salt. Gen. 19:26.

109. What is meant by a pillar of salt?—A perpetual memorial of the judgment of God. Luke 17:32.

110. When God commands, what ought we to do?—Obey the command at once.

111. What did the overthrow of Sodom and Gomorrah prefigure?—The destruction of Capernaum. Matt. 11:23.

112. What did the angel say to Lot when he pleaded for Zoar?—That he would not overthrow it. Gen. 19:20-22.

113. What does that teach us?—That God hears and answers prayer.

114. Whither did Lot go from Zoar?—To the mountain, where he dwelt in a cave. Gen. 19:30.

115. Who became the ancestress of the Moabites?—The firstborn daughter of Lot. Gen. 19:37.

116. Who of the Ammonites?—Lot's younger daughter. Gen. 19:38.

117. To what place did Abraham go from the plains of Mamre?—Toward the south, to Gerar. Gen. 20:1.

118. Into what disgraceful fault were Abraham and Sarah betrayed at Gerar?—Untruthfulness and distrust, in concealing that they were man and wife.

119. How did God preserve them?—By warning Abimelech in a dream. Gen. 20:6.

120. How did Abimelech behave?—He immediately restored to Abraham his wife and made him a handsome present. Gen. 20:14.

121. Did Sarah deserve the reproof which Abimelech gave her?—Yes.

122. How did the Lord put honor on Abraham?—He heard his prayer for Abimelech and his family. Gen. 20:17.

123. What did God do to Sarah?—He visited her with blessings. Gen. 21:1.

124. When did God do this?—At the end of the year, the time fixed. Gen. 21:2.

125. What did Abraham name the son that was born to him?—Isaac.

126. What does this name signify?—"Laughter," or "joy."

127. How old was Abraham at this time?—One hundred years. Gen. 21:5.

128. How did Sarah act when her son was born?—"God hath made me to laugh," she said, "so that all that hear will laugh with me." Gen. 21:6.

129. What circumstance occurred on the day Isaac was weaned?—Abraham made a great feast. Gen. 21:8.

130. What did Sarah see?—Ishmael mocking at Isaac. Gen. 21:9.

131. What did she wish Abraham to do?—To send away Hagar and Ishmael. Gen. 21:9, 10.

132. How did this request affect Abraham?—He was deeply grieved. Gen. 21:11.

133. Who confirmed Sarah's wish?—God himself, to carry out his purposes as to both Isaac and Ishmael. Gen. 21:12, 13.

134. How did Abraham act?—He sent them away provided with bread and water, and doubtless commended to the care of God. Gen. 21:14.

135. Where did Hagar go?—She wandered in the wilderness of Beer-sheba.

136. How did she fare?—All her drinking water was exhausted, and Ishmael fainted with thirst. Gen.

11

137. What did she do?—She laid him down in the shade of a bush, and sat a little distance off, wailing, for fear that he would die. Gen. 21:15, 16.

138. What relief came to her?—God heard her weeping, and called to her out of heaven and comforted her. Gen. 21:17, 18.

139. What did Hagar then do?—She found a spring of water close beside her, and she supplied her son with drink.

140. What became of Hagar and Ishmael?—They lived at last in the wilderness of Paran, in Arabia Petra. Gen. 21:21.

141. Who at the present day are the descendants of Ishmael?—The Arabs.

142. Who was Abraham's rightful heir, and child of promise?—Isaac. Gen. 21:1-3, 12.

143. What did Abimelech and Phicol say to Abraham?—They said that God was with Abraham in all that he did. Gen. 21:22.

144. What covenant did Abraham make with Abimelech?—Abraham agreed that he would not deal falsely with Abimelech, nor with his son, nor his son's son. Gen. 21:23-31.

145. What is the meaning of the word Beer-sheba?—The "well of the oath." Gen. 21:31.

146. Where was Abraham sojourning at this time?—In the land of the Philistines. Gen. 21:34.

147. Were the Philistines always friendly with Abraham's posterity?—They were frequently at war with the Israelites.

148. What was the greatest trial that Abraham's faith experienced?—The command of God to make a burnt offering of his only son Isaac, whom he loved.

149. What is said of this act in Heb. 11:17-19?—By faith Abraham, when he was tried, offered up Isaac; and he that had received the promises offered up his only begotten son, of whom it was said, That in Isaac shall thy seed be called; accounting that God was able to raise him up, even from the dead; from whence also he received him in a figure.

150. What proof did Abraham give of his prompt obedience?—He rose early in the morning and set out.

151. Did he tell his son what he was about to do with him?—No.

152. When Isaac inquired for the lamb, what was Abraham's reply?—That God would provide one. Gen. 22:8.

153. When Isaac knew his father's intention, did he resist it?—We do not know.

154. Was he able to have done so?—Yes, as he was twenty-five years old.

155. What is said of the Lord Jesus Christ when he was offered a sacrifice for sin?—That he did it of himself.

156. Did Abraham complete the sacrifice of Isaac?—No. His hand was stayed by an angel, and a ram caught by his horns in a thicket was substituted.

157. By what name did Abraham call the place where this occurred?—Jehovah-jireh, or, "the Lord will see or provide."

158. Is Mount Moriah mentioned again in the Scriptures?—Yes; in 2 Chron. 3:1.

159. What magnificent building stood on that mount?—Solomon's temple.

160. Why was this place chosen for that building?—Because here, on the threshing-floor of Araunah, the plague under King David was stayed.

161. What beautiful edifice now stands there?—The Mosque of Omar, a Mohammedan place of worship.

162. What do the Jews feel when they see this?—Doubtless deep grief, as they often visit a place near it called "the place of wailing."

163. What special covenant did the Lord renew with Abraham at this time?—That in Abraham's seed

should all the nations of the earth be blessed. Gen. 22:15-18.

164. Why is Nahor's posterity mentioned here?—Because one of them was Rebekah, Isaac's future wife.

ISAAC AND REBEKAH.
(Gen. 23, 24.)

1. How old was Sarah when she died?—One hundred and twenty-seven years.

2. Where did Abraham bury her?—In the cave of Machpelah, near Mamre, Hebron or Kirjatharba. Gen. 23:2, 19.

3. How did he obtain possession of this burying place?—By purchase from Ephron the Hittite. Gen. 23:3-18.

4. What did he give for it?—Four hundred shekels of silver (about $104).

5. What did that show?—That Abraham had no land of his own. Gen. 23:4.

6. How old was Isaac when his mother died?—About thirty-seven years.

7. How many years did he live before he married?—Forty.

8. How did his father obtain a wife for him?—He sent to his own kindred in Mesopotamia for the purpose.

9. Whom did Abraham send on this mission?—Eliezer of Damascus.

10. Who was this Eliezer of Damascus?—The steward of Abraham's house. Gen. 15:2.

11. How did this servant act?—With prudence, prayerfulness, diligence, and courtesy. Gen. 24:5-26.

12. Did he succeed in his mission?—He was led by God's providence to the house of Abraham's nephew, Bethuel. Gen. 24:15, 51.

13. Whom did he select?—The daughter of Bethuel—Rebekah.

14. What is said of Rebekah?—That she was a virgin, and was very beautiful. Gen. 24:16.

15. How did Rebekah act toward Eliezer?—She gave him drink from her pitcher, and drew water for his camels.

16. What did Eliezer give to Rebekah?—Golden earrings, bracelets, jewels of silver and gold, and raiment. Gen. 24:22, 30, 53.

17. What then did Rebekah do?—She ran and told them of her mother's house these things.

18. What did Rebekah's brother do?—He welcomed Eliezer, and gave him and his companions entertainment.

19. What was her brother's name?—Laban.

20. How did Eliezer describe his master's possessions?—That the Lord had greatly blessed him, and given him flocks and herds, silver and gold, etc. Gen. 24:35.

21. Was Rebekah willing to leave her home on his report?—She was. Gen. 24:58.

22. Did she find it all true?—Doubtless she did. Gen. 13:2.

23. Who came out to meet her?—Isaac himself. Gen. 24:62, 63.

24. Where did he take her, and how did he feel toward her?—To his mother's tent, and she became his wife, and he loved her. Gen. 24:67.

25. Eliezer followed his master's instructions; what does this teach?—That we are to obey God.

26. If we thus obey will success always attend our efforts?—Yes; in God's way.

JACOB AND ESAU.
(Gen. 25-27.)

1. Whom did Abraham marry after Sarah's death?—Keturah. Gen. 25:1.

2. How many children had she?—Six.

3. How did he portion them?—He made them gifts.

4. To whom did he leave his great riches?—To Isaac.

5. How old was Abraham when he died?—One hundred and seventy-five years.

6. Who buried him?—Isaac and Ishmael.

13

7. Where did Isaac now dwell?
—At Lahai-roi.

8. By what title are Ishmael's twelve sons called?—Princes.

9. Where did they dwell?—In Arabia, from Havilah to Shur.

10. What was Isaac's occupation?—That of a herdsman and shepherd.

11. How many sons had Isaac? —Two, Esau and Jacob. Gen. 25: 26.

12. Were they born before Abraham's death?—Yes.

13. How many years before that event?—Fifteen.

14. What was the difference personally between those two boys?—Esau was red or hairy, and Jacob smooth. Gen. 25:25; 27:11.

15. Did they grow up alike?— No; Esau was a skillful hunter, and Jacob a quiet man, fond of home. Gen. 25:27.

16. How did the parents of Esau and Jacob feel toward them?— Isaac loved Esau, but Rebekah loved Jacob. Gen. 25:28.

17. How did God feel toward these two sons?—He rejected Esau, but chose Jacob. Mal. 1:2, 3.

18. Which was the firstborn?— Esau.

19. Did he value his birthright? —He regarded it as of little worth, and sold it to Jacob for a mess of pottage. Heb. 12:16.

20. To what place did Isaac remove from Lahai-roi?—To Gerar. Gen. 26:6.

21. Why did he go thither?— Because of a famine in the land.

22. What covenant did God renew with Isaac?—The covenant he had made with Abraham. Gen. 26:2-5.

23. What direction did God give Isaac as to his place of sojourn?— That he should not go down into Egypt, but dwell among the Philistines at Gerar. Gen. 26:2, 3.

24. What deception did Isaac practice?—He passed off his wife as his sister.

25. When Rebekah was discovered to be his wife what did Abimelech do?—He charged all his people to leave Isaac and his wife alone.

26. How did the Philistines behave toward Isaac?—They envied his prosperity and persecuted him. Gen. 26:14-21.

27. Did he return evil for evil? —No; he removed more than once out of their way.

28. What was Isaac's character? —He was a peacemaker. Gen. 26: 14-31.

29. Whom did Esau choose as his wives?—Judith and Bashemath, Hittites. Gen. 26:34.

30. Did his parents approve his choice?—No; they were grieved by it.

31. What was it the custom of the ancient patriarchs to do before their death?—To bless their children.

32. Which son did Isaac consider his firstborn?—Esau. Gen. 27: 1-4.

33. How had he forfeited his birthright?—By selling it to his brother. Gen. 25:29-34.

34. Did Jacob allow Esau to obtain the blessing of the birthright? —No; he pretended to be Esau, to prevent it. Gen. 27:20-29.

35. Did he go the right way to work?—No; he should have left it to God to secure him the blessing in his own time and way.

36. Who shared his sin with him?—His mother.

37. How did Esau feel when he found that he had lost his blessing? —He was greatly distressed.

38. Had he not voluntarily sold it to Jacob some years before?— Yes; about forty-five years before.

39. Whom had he then to blame?—Chiefly himself.

40. How was Esau affected toward Jacob?—He intended to kill him. Gen. 27:41.

41. What did Rebekah do?—She told Jacob to flee to Haran, to her brother Laban, until Esau's anger

14

was cooled down.

42. What excuse did she make to Isaac for wanting to send Jacob away?—She pretended to be afraid that Jacob would marry a Hittite woman. Gen. 27:46.

43. What was Jacob's general character?—One of artifice and deceit.

JACOB. (Gen. 28-35.)

1. Did God then choose Jacob for his natural goodness?—No; there is no one whom he chooses on this account.

2. What should this teach us?—That as we all have sinned it is only by the faith that unites us to Christ that we can be righteous before God.

3. What did Isaac do after Jacob obtained the blessing?—He again blessed him, and charged him not to take to wife a daughter of Canaan. Gen. 28:1.

4. Whither did he send him?—To Padan-aram, to the house of his grandfather, Bethuel. Gen. 28:2.

5. When Jacob went away what did Esau do?—He married Mahalath, a daughter of Ishmael.

6. Where did Jacob lodge the first night of his journey?—At a place called Luz, afterward named Beth-el. Gen. 28:19.

7. What remarkable thing occurred there?—He had a vision by night, and a renewal of God's promise and blessing. Gen. 28:10-15.

8. Did he understand it?—Not fully; but he seems to have been inspired with fear and awe.

9. Do we see the meaning?—We, happily, are taught to see Christ as the ladder of communication between heaven and earth.

10. What did Jacob say when he awaked?—"Surely the Lord is in this place, and I knew it not." Gen. 28:16.

11. What did he do in the morning?—He took the stone upon which he had lain, and set it up for a pillar, and poured upon it an offering of oil.

12. What promise did Jacob make?—That the Lord should be his God and that he would devote to him a tenth of all that he should give him. Gen. 28:20-22.

13. Whom did Jacob first see when he got to Syria?—The servants of Laban, and then Rachel, his daughter. Gen. 29:3-5, 9.

14. How many daughters did Laban have?—Two, Leah and Rachel.

15. How did his uncle Laban receive him?—With kindness and affection. Gen. 29:13, 14.

16. What did he promise him?—That he should have Rachel for his wife, in return for seven years' service.

17. Did Laban afterward fulfill his promise?—No; he gave him Leah instead.

18. How many wives had Jacob?—Two, Rachel and Leah. See Gen. 16:2.

19. How many years did Jacob serve Laban before he allowed him to have any cattle for his wages?—Fourteen years. Gen. 30:26-30.

20. How long did Jacob remain altogether in the service of his father-in-law?—Twenty years. Gen. 31:41.

21. Did Laban drive a hard bargain with Jacob?—He certainly did; but Jacob outwitted him. Gen. 30:28-43.

22. Did Jacob in this way succeed in obtaining large possessions of flocks and herds?—Yes. Gen. 30:43.

23. How did the sons of Laban feel when they observed this?—They were displeased at the success of his plan.

24. What did God direct Jacob to do?—To return to Canaan, the land of his fathers.

25. What did Jacob and his wives resolve to do?—To obey the command of God. Gen. 31:3, 14-16.

26. What wicked act was Rachel guilty of?—Of stealing her father's images. Gen. 31:19.

15

27. What did it prove?—That she and her father still worshiped heathen gods.

28. What did Laban do when he found Jacob had left him?—He pursued him.

29. How did God protect Jacob from Laban's anger?—By warning Laban in a dream.

30. How did the interview between Laban and Jacob terminate?—It ended peacefully and well. Gen. 31:44, 55.

31. What is the meaning of the word Mahanaim?—Two hosts, or camps. Gen. 32:1, 2.

32. Why was the place so called? —Because a company of angels met Jacob there.

33. How ought Jacob to have felt when he saw this angelic guard?—That he was secure against all harm.

34. How did he feel when he heard his brother Esau was coming to meet him?—He was greatly afraid and distressed. Gen. 32:7.

35. How did Jacob act?—He divided his people and flocks into two bands. Gen. 32:7, 8.

36. What occurred to Jacob before he went over the brook?—A heavenly Being wrestled with him during the night.

37. How long did the angel wrestle with Jacob?—Until break of day.

38. Why did Jacob and the angel wrestle together?—That Jacob might learn by this experience that neither Laban nor Esau should have any power to injure him.

39. When the angel found that he could not prevail what did he do to Jacob?—He touched the hollow of his thigh, and the sinew shrank.

40. Did Jacob then relax his hold on the angel?—He did not; and he still refused to let him go until the angel blessed him.

41. What did the angel then say?—He said that Jacob should no longer be called Jacob, but Israel—"a prince of God;" because as a prince he had power with

God and with men, and had prevailed.

42. Who was the mysterious being that wrestled with Jacob?— From Hosea (12:4) we learn that it was an angel, doubtless the angel of the covenant.

43. What name did Jacob give to the place where this occurred? —Peniel, or "the face of God."

44. Why did he so call it?—Because he said that he had seen God face to face. Gen. 32:30.

45. What spiritual act does this typify?—Prayer, in which, if real, we have communion or intercourse of spirit with God.

46. How did Jacob and Esau meet?—In brotherly affection and peace. Gen. 33:4.

47. Where did Jacob pitch his tent and make booths for his cattle when he got into Canaan?—At Succoth. Gen. 33:17.

48. Name the two instances in Scripture where this purchase is afterward referred to.—His purchase at Shalem, a city of Shechem, is referred to in John 4:5, 6 and Acts 7:15, 16. Gen. 33:18, 19.

49. Between what two mountains was Shechem situated?—Gerizim and Ebal.

50. Where was the tabernacle first reared in the land of Canaan? —At Gilgal, on the Jordan.

51. Where did Joshua make his solemn covenant with Israel before his death?—At Shechem. Josh. 24:1.

52. Where was the first idol temple built in Israel?—In Shechem. 1 Kings 12:25-33.

53. Of what act of treachery were Simeon and Levi guilty to Shechem, the founder of this city? —They wickedly slew him. Gen. 34:13, 25, 26.

54. What did God at this time desire Jacob to do?—To go and live at Beth-el. Gen. 35:1.

55. How did Jacob prepare for this journey?—By calling upon his people to put away their idols,

16

and be clean and change their garments.

56. How did God preserve him from the anger of the inhabitants of the land?—By making the inhabitants afraid of him and of his God.

57. What sorrowful event happened at Beth-el?—The death of Rebekah's nurse. Gen. 35:8.

58. What peculiar name did God confer, and what special blessing did he give to Jacob at this place?—The name of Israel and the gift of the land of Canaan. Gen. 35:9-12.

59. What great loss did Jacob sustain when near Bethlehem?— The death of Rachel. Gen. 35:19.

60. How many children had Jacob at this time?—Twelve. Gen. 35:22-26.

61. How far south did Jacob travel?—To Mamre, near Hebron.

62. Who resided there?—Isaac.

63. How many years did Jacob live with his father before his father died?—About three years.

64. Who united together to bury Isaac?—Esau and Jacob.

JACOB AND HIS SONS.
(Gen. 37.)

1. To which son did Jacob show a great partiality?—To Joseph. Gen. 37:3.

2. Why did Jacob feel this, and how did he show it?—Because he was the son of his old age, and by making him a coat, with sleeves, similar to the garments worn by princes.

3. What character did the other sons of Jacob display?—An envious and malicious one.

4. Why did they hate Joseph?— Because of the preference shown to him by his father, but still more because of his innocent and ingenuous character. Gen. 37:2.

5. Why did Joseph dream prophetic dreams?—Because thus early God desired to give him intimations of his future lifework, and to make known to him the ultimate destinies of his nation.

6. How did Joseph's father feel when he heard one of the dreams? —He was surprised at the dream, but doubtless felt it was from God. Gen. 37:11.

7. How did Joseph get into his brethren's power?—On Jacob sending him to them to see if they were well. Gen. 37:14.

8. How old was Joseph at this time?—About seventeen years of age.

9. What was done with Joseph? —He was thrown into a pit, and afterward sold to a caravan of Midianites, or Ishmaelites, passing that way. Gen. 37:24.

10. Why was he thus disposed of?—Because they thought that thus they would get rid of him.

11. For how much was he sold? —For twenty pieces of silver, or about $11.

12. What story did they make up to their father?—That they had found his coat bloody, and that he had been killed by a wild beast.

13. What difference was there in Reuben's behavior toward Joseph from the rest of his brethren? —He dissuaded them from killing him. Gen. 37:21, 22.

14. How did Jacob receive the news?—He mourned and refused to be comforted.

15. How did the Ishmaelites dispose of Joseph?—They took him out of the pit, and carried him down into Egypt. Gen. 37:28.

16. What connection was there between Abraham and the Midianites?—Midian was a son of Keturah, his second wife. Gen. 25:1, 2.

17. What connection was there between Moses and the Midianites? —He lived among them, and took his wife thence. Exod. 2:15, 21.

18. What connection was there between Balaam and the Midianites?—He lived among them, and was killed in battle by the Israelites.

19. What event in Gideon's history was connected with the Midianites?—The appearance to him of

17

an angel of the Lord before he fought against and overthrew them Judg. 6:11.

JOSEPH IN EGYPT.
(Gen. 39-41.)

1. To whom did the Ishmaelites sell Joseph?—To Potiphar, captain of Pharaoh's guard. Gen. 39:1.

2. What office did Potiphar appoint Joseph to fill?—Overseer of his house. Gen. 39:4.

3. How was God's favor manifested to Joseph in this situation? —By everything prospering under his care. Gen. 39:2-5.

4. Was he not deprived of his situation by false accusation?— Yes; through the wickedness of his master's wife. Gen. 39:7-18.

5. What unjust punishment was suffered by Joseph?—He was put in prison.

6. How was he treated in prison?—They hurt his feet with fetters; he was laid in iron. Psalm 105:18.

7. Did the Lord forsake him?— He was with him, and showed him mercy.

8. How did the keeper of the prison behave to Joseph?—He gave him the entire charge of the prison.

9. What kind of prison was this?—A prison in which state prisoners were kept.

10. What remarkable circumstance occurred to two of those prisoners?—They had dreams which troubled them.

11. How did Joseph assist them in their perplexity?—He interpreted their dreams. Gen. 40.

12. What became of the butler and the baker?—The chief butler was restored, and the chief baker was hanged, as Joseph had foretold.

13. How did Pharaoh's butler behave to Joseph?—Like many others in their prosperity. He forgot his promise to get Joseph released.

14. What brought his dream again to his mind?—A dream which Pharaoh had. Gen. 41:1-13.

15. What was Pharoah's dream? —See Gen. 41:1-7.

16. Could the magicians of Egypt interpret Pharaoh's dream? —They could not. Gen. 41:8.

17. For whom did he send?— For Joseph, whom the butler had named.

18. Did Joseph take the honor of interpretation to himself, or confess God's power before the king? —He said, It is not in me; God shall give Pharaoh an answer of peace. Gen. 41:16.

19. What was Joseph's interpretation of the dream?—See Gen. 41:26-32.

20. How old was Joseph at this time?—Thirty years. Gen. 41:46.

21. What advice did Joseph give to Pharaoh?—He advised Pharaoh to appoint a commissioner to gather all the surplus grain of the kingdom during the next seven years and lay it up in granaries for food during the seven years of famine.

22. Does it not seem presumptuous for a slave thus to advise the king?—It does; but the customs of that time allowed a freer intercourse between slaves and their masters than was allowed in later ages.

23. What name did Pharaoh give Joseph, and what is the meaning of it?—Zaphnath-paaneah, a "revealer of secrets," or "the man to whom secrets are revealed."

24. What were the names of Joseph's wife and of his two sons? —Asenath, Manasseh, and Ephraim. Gen. 41:45, 51, 52.

25. What did Joseph do during the seven years of plenty?—He laid up the food in the cities. Gen. 41:48.

26. When the people cried to Pharaoh for bread to whom did he send them?—To Joseph. Gen. 41:55.

27. Was this great famine confined to the land of Egypt?—It was not. Gen. 41:56, 57.

18

JACOB AND HIS SONS IN EGYPT. (Gen. 42-50.)

1. Where were Jacob and his family living at this time?—In Canaan. Gen. 42:5.

2. Did the famine extend to the land of Canaan?—It did. Gen. 42:5.

3. How did they procure bread?—Ten of Jacob's sons went to buy corn in Egypt. Gen. 42:3.

4. How did Joseph behave to his brethren when he saw them?—He made himself strange to them and spoke roughly to them. Gen. 42:7.

5. Did they recognize him?—No. Gen. 42:8.

6. What did Joseph affect to think they were?—Spies.

7. What proof did he require that they were not spies?—He demanded that they bring down their youngest brother Benjamin, as evidence of their truthfulness.

8. How did Jacob feel when they returned and told him the news?—He felt that all things were against him, and that he should lose Benjamin also. Gen. 42:36, 38; Rom. 8:28.

9. Did they take Benjamin with them on their second journey?—They did. Gen. 43:15.

10. What presents did they take to Joseph?—Fruits, honey, spices, myrrh, nuts, almonds, and balm. Gen. 43:11.

11. How did Joseph feel when he saw Benjamin stand among his brethren?—His heart yearned over his brother, and he retired to weep. Gen. 43:30, 31.

12. What closer relationship was there between Joseph and Benjamin than between Joseph and his other brothers?—They had the same mother—Rachel. Gen. 30:22-24; 35:16-18

13. What effect did Joseph's kindness have on them?—They wondered at it. Gen. 43:33.

14. What was Joseph's intention in all this treatment?—He wished to bring them to a sense of their former wickedness, to humble them.

15. Did it have the effect he desired?—It had. Gen. 42:21; 44:16.

16. How did Judah behave at this trying time?—He begged that Benjamin might be allowed to go back with the rest, and offered to remain himself behind as surety for his return. Gen. 44:18, 33.

17. How was Joseph's heart affected by all this?—He could bear it no longer, but wept aloud, and told them he was Joseph their brother. Gen 45:1-4.

18. How did they feel when they knew this mighty prince was their own brother?—They could not answer him for fear. Gen. 45:3.

19. What proofs did he give them of his relationship?—He gave proofs of his love and power by the rich presents he made them, and the promise of a home and plenty in Egypt. Gen. 45:17-23.

20. Did Joseph and his father ever meet again?—They met in Egypt, whither Jacob and all his family had come. Gen. 46:29.

21. How?—Joseph went up in his chariot to meet his father, as far as to Goshen. Gen. 46:29.

22. Where in the land of Egypt did Jacob and his family dwell?—In the land of Goshen. Gen. 47:1.

23. Had the Egyptians any particular antipathy to shepherds?—They disliked shepherds and cattle dealers from foreign lands, probably for the reason that the Hyksos or Shepherd Kings were foreign invaders, and thus held possession of the government.

24. What family did Jacob have at this time?—Counting Joseph and his two sons there were in all seventy souls. Gen. 46:27; see also Acts 7:14.

25. Was Jacob introduced to Pharaoh?—Yes, and gave him his blessing. Gen. 47:7.

26. What proof have we in Jacob's remark to Pharaoh of the truth of Psalm 90:9, 10?—The

longest life is but short to look back on.

27. How did the famine affect the Egyptians?—They were compelled to buy food of the government.

28. Did the policy benefit Egypt? —It unified the nation; it established a certain rate for taxes; it brought the people into more direct connection with the king, and gave the government more power to construct public works and establish defenses against foreign and domestic foes.

29. How long did Joseph live to administer the affairs of the nation?—Eighty years.

30. How long did Jacob live in Egypt?—Seventeen years. Gen. 47:28.

31. What did Jacob in his extreme old age desire of his son Joseph?—That after his death he might be carried to the grave of his fathers and there entombed.

32. Did Joseph promise to do this?—He did, and confirmed his promise with an oath.

33. What peculiar blessing did Jacob on his deathbed give to the sons of Joseph?—He placed his right hand on the younger instead of the elder. Gen. 48:17-19.

34. How was Joshua in this a type of Jesus?—As Joshua led the Israelites in the wilderness and into the promised land, so Jesus is the guide of his people upon earth and the means of their entrance into heaven. Heb. 4:8.

35. In his prophetical blessing of his twelve sons to whom did he give the birthright?—To Joseph (Gen. 48:8); but of Judah was to come the chief ruler. 1 Chron. 5: 1, 2.

36. What was the special blessing of Judah?—That out of his family the Messiah should come. Gen. 49:10.

37. How was this fulfilled?—Our Lord sprang out of Judah. Heb. 7:14.

38. After the death of Jacob what was first done to his body? —It was embalmed, after the manner of the Egyptians.

39. How long was required to complete the embalming?—Forty days.

40. When the days of mourning were completed what did Joseph do?—He obtained permission from the king to carry the body of his father to Canaan. Gen. 50:4-9.

41. Where was Jacob buried?— In the cave of Machpelah. Gen. 50:13.

42. What fears had Joseph's brethren after Jacob's death?—That Joseph would illtreat them and punish them. Gen. 50:15.

43. How did Joseph behave to them?—He comforted them and spoke kindly to them.

44. At what age did Joseph die? —At the age of one hundred and ten years. Gen. 50:26.

45. When was Joseph buried? —Not until the Israelites reached Canaan, above two hundred years after his death.

JOSEPH'S HISTORY.

1. What great peculiarity marks the Bible narratives?—They contain the history of human redemption, God's methods of dealing with men, and the progressive knowledge of the truth as unfolded by the prophets. Throughout the entire Scriptures there is a constant reference to our Lord Jesus Christ.

2. Is it not, then, our duty to seek for Jesus even so far back as the fall of man?—Moses wrote of him, and the first promise made to man was that he should destroy the devil and all his works. Gen. 3:15; John 1:45; Luke 24:27.

3. Who wrote Genesis?—Moses.

4. How was Joseph a type of Jesus, when he was at home clothed in a beautiful robe, the darling of his father?—In that Jesus shared his Father's glory and enjoyed his love.

5. How was Joseph a type in going out to look after the welfare of his brethren?—In Jesus graciously visiting his brethren in

human nature.

6. How in their treatment of him?—In the being sold by Judas and delivered to death by the Jews.

7. How in his dreams?—In his prophecies of his future kingdom and glory. Matt. 25:31, 32.

8. How in the false accusations brought against him?—In his freedom from blame. Matt. 26:59, 60.

9. How in being committed to prison?—They laid hands on Jesus and took him. Matt. 26:50.

10. How in leaving that prison and being exalted?—God hath made that same Jesus, whom ye have crucified, both Lord and Christ. Acts 2:36.

11. How in his feeding and blessing his brethren and all who came to him?—In being the Bread of Life.

12. How in Pharaoh transferring all his power to him?—The Father committed all judgment unto the Son. John 5:22.

13. How in his returning good for evil?—Jesus died for his persecutors, forgave their transgressions, and prayed for them to the last.

THE ISRAELITES IN EGYPT.
(Exod. 1.)

1. How did the Egyptians behave to the children of Israel after the death of Joseph?—They enslaved and oppressed them. Exod. 1:8-14.

2. Why were they reduced to bondage?—Because of the great increase in their numbers, joined to the well-known predictions of their future power.

3. Did the children of Israel greatly increase and multiply?—They did. Exod. 1:12.

4. Why should this have made the Egyptians afraid?—Lest they should join their enemies. Exod. 1:10.

5. How were the children of Israel employed by the Egyptians?—In making bricks and other field service, and in building treasure cities. Exod. 1:14.

6. What cruel device did Pharaoh resolve on to destroy the male children of Israel?—To employ the Hebrew nurses to do so. Exod. 1:16.

7. Who was this Pharaoh?—He is thought by some to be Amenophis; by others, Rameses II.

8. When this edict failed what did Pharaoh do?—He ordered all the male infants of the Hebrews to be cast into the river Nile.

9. Who was Moses?—The second son of Amram and Jochebed of the tribe of Levi. Exod 2:1; 6:20.

10. What plan did his mother adopt to spare his life?—She hid him in a floating basket among the rushes growing by a riverside. Exod. 2:2, 3.

11. How did her design succeed?—The child was found by some of the maids of Pharaoh's daughter, who took charge of it. Acts 7:20; Exod. 2:5-10.

12. Whom had his mother set to watch the little ark?—His sister Miriam. Exod. 2:4; 15:20.

13. When the princess sought a nurse for the child whom did Miriam fetch?—His mother. Exod. 2:7-9.

14. What blessing did this insure to Moses?—The tenderest care, and perhaps also the knowledge of the true God.

15. How was Moses trained by Pharaoh's daughter?—He was adopted as her own son and instructed in all the learning of the Egyptians. Acts 7:21, 22.

16. With whom did Moses join himself—with the Egyptians or the Hebrews?—With the Hebrews. Heb. 11:24, 25.

17. What did Moses do to deliver them?—He delivered one of the Hebrews whom he saw cruelly beaten by an Egyptian taskmaster, by killing the Egyptian. Acts 7:25.

18. Did the Hebrews receive him graciously?—No; they accused him of murder. Acts 7:27, 28.

21

19. What was Moses obliged to do?—To leave Egypt. Exod 2:11-15.

20. To what land did he flee?—To Midian.

21. What did Moses do in Midian?—He watered the flocks for Jethro's daughters. Exod. 2:16-17.

22. What did the shepherd maidens do?—They reported the fact to their father.

23. What then occurred to Moses?—Reuel (or Jethro) entertained him, and gave him his daughter Zipporah to wife. Exod. 2:21; 18:3, 4.

24. How long did he stay there?—Forty years. Acts 7:30.

25. What was his employment in Midian?—He kept the flock of Jethro, his father-in-law. Exod. 3:1.

26. Where did he feed the flock?—On the back side of the desert, as far as Horeb.

27. How many sons had he?—Two, Gershom and Eliezer. Exod. 2:22; 18:3, 4.

THE BURNING BUSH.
(Exod. 3, 4.)

1. While there what wondrous sight attracted the attention of Moses?—A burning bush, unconsumed. Exod. 3:2.

2. When Moses saw this strange sight what did he do?—He turned aside, to see why the bush was not burnt. Exod. 3:3.

3. Who called to him out of the midst of the bush?—The Angel of the Lord. Exod. 3:2.

4. What was Moses told to do?—To remove his sandals, because the place where he stood was holy ground.

5. What commission did the Lord give to Moses?—To go to Pharaoh and bring the Israelites out of Egypt. Exod. 3:10.

6. Was Moses willing to undertake it?—He was not.

7. What excuses did he make?—He said they would not believe that God had appeared to him. Exod. 4:1.

8. How did the Lord show him that it was not his own might or power in which he was to go to Pharaoh?—He changed Moses' rod into a serpent, and made his hands leprous, and restored them again. Exod. 4:2-8.

9. Did this remove his scruples?—No; for he objected that he was too poor a speaker to deliver God's message. Exod. 4:10.

10. How did the Lord answer this objection?—He promised to teach him what to say. Exod. 4:12.

11. What did Moses then reply?—He said, "O my Lord, send, I pray thee, by the hand of him whom thou wilt send," that is, some one else.

12. Did the Lord release him from this commission?—No; but he joined Aaron his brother with him; he also made Aaron to be the chief spokesman. Exod. 4:14, 15.

13. What passed between Moses and Jethro on the subject?—Jethro approved his return to Egypt, and dismissed him in peace.

14. What solemn rite had Moses neglected to perform on his son in the land of Midian?—Circumcision. Exod. 4:24.

15. What punishment had God enjoined on those who neglected it?—The uncircumcised man child shall be cut off from his people; he hath broken my covenant (by loss of privileges or by death). Gen. 17:14.

16. Did not the son of Moses narrowly escape?—He was, perhaps, in imminent danger of punishment with Moses himself. Exod. 4:24-26.

17. Who met Moses on his return to Egypt?—Aaron, by command of God. Exod. 4:27.

18. What did they do when they first came into Egypt?—They gathered the elders of the children of Israel together, and told them all that the Lord had said, and did the signs commanded them.

19. How did the Israelites re-

ceive the message?—They believed it, and worshiped God. Exod. 4:31.

THE DEMAND UPON
PHARAOH. (Exod. 5-7.)

1. Who was the king of Egypt now?—Pharaoh.

2. Was it the same Pharaoh who had ordered the little children to be killed?—No; it was one who lived one hundred and forty years later.

3. Did he treat the children of Israel more mercifully than the former king?—Though he did not order their male offspring to be put to death like the former king, he was very cruel to them.

4. How did he receive Moses and Aaron when they went in to him?—He abused them for interfering with the people's work. Exod. 5:2-4.

5. What was the result?—Heavier work was laid upon them. Exod. 5:6-9.

6. What complaint did the officers of the children of Israel make to Pharaoh?—They said that no straw was given them, and yet they were compelled to make bricks the same as before. Exod. 5:15.

7. What did Pharaoh do?—He refused to relieve them. Exod. 5:17, 18.

8. Whom did the children of Israel blame for this?—Moses and Aaron. Exod. 5:20, 21.

9. What did Moses do?—He returned unto the Lord, and spread out his complaints before him. Exod. 5:22.

10. What was the Lord's answer?—See Exod. 6:6-8.

11. How did the Israelites receive this message?—They would not listen to it because of the anguish of their spirit and their cruel bondage. Exod. 6:9.

12. When Moses recited this to the Lord what did the Lord say? —He told Moses and Aaron to go back to the Israelites and to Pharaoh. Exod. 6:11, 13.

13. What message were they to bring?—That the Israelites were to leave Egypt, and that Pharaoh should let them go.

14. Of what tribe were Moses and Aaron?—Of the tribe of Levi. Exod. 6:16-20.

15. What were the names of their parents?—Amram their father, and Jochebed their mother. Exod. 6:20.

16. How old were Moses and Aaron when they went in unto Pharaoh?—Moses was eighty years old, and Aaron eighty-three. Exod. 7:7.

17. What did the Lord bid them do?—He bade them work a miracle, if Pharaoh should demand one, in token of their authority.

18. What miracle did they perform?—Aaron threw his rod on the ground, and it became a serpent. Exod. 7:10.

19. Could the magicians of Egypt perform the same miracle? —They seemed to do so. But Aaron's rod swallowed up the others.

20. What effect did this miracle have upon Pharaoh?—He hardened his heart, and would not listen to their demands. Exod. 7:13.

21. What was Moses then directed to do?—To bring a plague upon Egypt. Exod. 7:17.

THE TEN PLAGUES.
(Exod. 7-11.)

1. What was the first plague?— The river Nile was turned into blood, and the fish in it died. Exod. 7:20.

2. In what respect was this a peculiar trial to the Egyptians?— Because the yearly overflowing of the Nile was most valuable for their land, and much of their food was fish.

3. How long did the plague continue?—Seven days.

4. What were the second and third plagues?—Frogs and lice. Exod. 8.

5. How far were the magicians able to follow Moses and Aaron? —So far as to turn water into

23

blood and to bring frogs. Exod. 7, 8.

6. What did they say when they could go no farther?—That the miracles of Moses were the finger of God. Exod. 8:19.

7. What effect did these plagues have upon Pharaoh?—He still remained inflexible to the demands of Moses. Exod. 8:8, 15.

8. What was the next plague? —Swarms of flies or hurtful insects. Exod. 7:24.

9. How did God mark the distinction between the Egyptians and Israelites in this?—He suffered none in the land of Goshen, where the Israelites dwelt.

10. Did this influence Pharaoh to let the Israelites go?—No (Exod. 8:32), though he again gave way a little. Exod. 8:28.

11. What was the fifth plague? —A murrain upon cattle, horses, asses, camels, and sheep. Exod. 9.

12. What plague did God send next?—Boils and blains upon men and beasts. Exod. 9:9.

13. Did any of these move the haughty king?—No. Exod. 9:7, 12.

14. What merciful provision did God make in the seventh plague for those who believed in his word?—He warned them to remove their cattle to a place of shelter. Exod. 9:19.

15. Why was this plague peculiarly terrible to the Egyptians?— Because they were not accustomed to either hail or rain. Deut. 11: 10, 11.

16. Why was it that all these judgments had no effect on Pharaoh?—Because his heart was hardened. Exod. 8:15, 32; 9:34, 35.

17. What was the eighth plague? —Locusts. Exod. 10.

18. What appearance must the land of Egypt have presented at this time?—The land was darkened by them and every green thing eaten up. Exod. 10:15.

19. What advice had the servants of Pharaoh given him when the plague was threatened?—To let the Israelites go. Exod. 10:7.

20. Did Pharaoh consent?—He agreed that the men might go, to offer sacrifices to Jehovah, as Moses had said.

21. Was Moses willing to accept this compromise?—No. See Exod. 10:9.

22. Did Pharaoh expect them to return?—If the entire population of Israel went, with their flocks and cattle, he feared they would never return.

23. What was the ninth plague? —Thick darkness for three days. Exod. 10:21-23.

24. What solemn interview had Moses with Pharaoh during this awful darkness?—When Pharaoh bade Moses see his face no more. Exod. 10:28.

25. What was the last plague?— The destruction of the firstborn of men and cattle throughout all the land of Egypt.

26. Why had Pharaoh been so unwilling to let the Israelites go? —In the first place, to show his contempt of Jehovah and his messengers; and, secondly, because of the valuable service the Israelites were rendering to him.

27. Why did not the Israelites rise in rebellion and throw off the Egyptian yoke?—Their spirit had been broken by servitude; they had not a single weapon of war; they had no trained soldiers nor any military leaders; and they were under guard constantly.

THE PASSOVER. (Exod. 12-14.)

1. What did God command the Israelites to do before he brought the last plague on the Egyptians? —To institute the passover sacrifice and feast. Exod. 12.

2. Of whom was the lamb a type?—Of Christ the Lamb of God, slain from the foundation of the world. John 1:29; Rev. 13:8.

3. In how many ways was the paschal lamb a type of him whom it prefigured?—In its gentleness and unblemished innocence, and

24

in its being slain without a bone being slain; and in other respects besides.

4. What divine ordinance in the Christian Church takes the place of the passover?—The Lord's Supper.

5. When was it instituted?—The evening before our blessed Saviour suffered.

6. What does it set forth?—The sacrifice of the death of Christ and the benefits we receive thereby.

7. What is the meaning of the word passover?—It refers to the destroying angel passing over the blood-sprinkled doorposts of the children of Israel. Exod. 12:23.

8. How were the Israelites preserved from the destroying angel? —By striking the lintels and doorposts of their houses with the blood of the slain lamb. Exod. 12:22.

9. Why was not the blood sprinkled on the threshold?—Lest any should trample on so sacred a thing.

10. How was the bread to be prepared?—Without leaven or yeast to raise it. Exod. 12:15.

11. What does the apostle Paul declare this to be a type of?—Of purity and sincerity. 1 Cor. 5:7, 8.

12. What did the bitter herbs signify?—The bitterness of Egyptian bondage, true sorrow for sin, and Christ's cup of suffering. Psalm 69:20, 21.

13. If any Israelite had despised the means of safety what would have been the consequence?—He would have lost his firstborn child.

14. How was the passover to be observed?—Each family was to slay a lamb or kid not over one year old, and prepare and roast it whole in the evening. It was to be eaten the same night, with the loins girded, shoes on the feet and staff in the hand, and in haste, with the unleavened bread and the bitter herbs.

15. When was the lamb selected?—On the tenth day of the month Abib, the first month of the

year. Deut. 16:1.

16. When killed?—On the fourteenth day, in the evening.

17. If the family was too small to eat the lamb what was done? —Two or three neighbors might join together in the feast.

18. If any of the lamb was left over what disposition was made of it?—It was burned with fire.

19. How were the years now to be reckoned?—The month Abib was made the beginning of the year. The year formerly began in the fall; now it was to begin in the spring.

20. How did Pharaoh act when he found the threatened vengeance of God had descended on him?— He ordered the Israelites to depart. Exod. 12:31, 32.

21. Were the Egyptians willing for the Israelites to depart?—They were, and they gave them the things necessary for their journey.

22. In what way did the Israelites obey the king's mandate?— They hurried away with their flocks and herds and hastily prepared food. Exod. 12:37-39.

23. Did they remember Joseph's wish at this time?—They took his bones with them. Exod. 13:19.

24. Did Pharaoh quietly allow them to go?—He pursued them to bring them back. Exod. 14:5-9.

25. How did the children of Israel feel when they heard that Pharaoh was pursuing them?— They were terribly afraid. Exod. 14:10.

26. What had the Israelites to guide them as to the way they should take?—A pillar of cloud and fire. Exod. 14:19, 20, 24.

27. What speech did Israel make to Moses when they saw the sea before them and the host of Pharaoh behind?—That it would have been better for them to remain in Egypt. Exod. 14:11, 12.

28. How did God deliver them? —He made a way for them through the sea. Exod. 14:16.

29. How many of the Israelites departed from Egypt?—Six hun-

dred thousand men on foot, besides children; in all about three million souls. Exod. 12:37.

30. Who went with them?—A mixed multitude, and flocks and herds in large numbers. Exod. 12:38.

31. Did they carry out of Egypt much wealth?—They got from the Egyptians great quantities of silver and gold and raiment. Exod. 12: 35, 36.

32. Did they proceed easily and rapidly through the sea?—They went through on dry land.

33. At what point did they cross?—They crossed an arm of the Red Sea, probably at some point between Suez and the Bitter Lakes.

34. How did the Lord hinder the Egyptians?—They drove heavily in their chariots.

35. How did God keep the hosts separate all the night?—By the pillar of cloud, which kept the Egyptians in darkness and prevented them from moving on. Exod. 14: 20.

36. Ought we ever to doubt a God who can help his people in any difficulty?—If God be for us, who can be against us?—Rom. 8: 31.

37. What happened as soon as Israel was safely over the sea?— The Egyptians were overwhelmed by the returning waters. Exod. 14:27, 28.

THE SONG OF MOSES.
(Exod. 15:1-21.)

1. What does Paul call this passage of the Red Sea?—A baptism to Moses.

2. What is baptism?—A dedication to God, with the application of water. See 1 Peter 3:21.

3. What did the Israelites do when they had passed over the sea?—They sang a song of rejoicing. Exod. 15:1.

4. Is this song ever referred to again?—See Rev. 15:2, 3.

5. Did the women take part in these rejoicings?—Miriam and the women went out with timbrels and dances. Exod. 15:20.

6. Were women public teachers among the Israelites?—Some of them were. Miriam was a prophetess; so was Deborah; so was Anna; so were the four daughters of Philip.

7. What will be the end of all God's enemies?—To be subdued by Christ. Acts 2:34, 35.

8. Which is the last enemy that is to be destroyed?—Death. 1 Cor. 15:26.

9. What song may the Christian sing even now in prospect of that victory?—Death is swallowed up in victory. 1 Cor. 15:54-57.

10. Through whom is the conquest obtained?—Heb. 2:14, 15; 1 Cor. 15:57.

THEIR JOURNEY BEGUN.
(Exod. 15:22-27.)

1. How many days did Israel travel in the wilderness before they found water?—Three. Exod. 15: 22.

2. What wilderness was this?— The wilderness of Shur.

3. When they found water, of what kind was it?—Bitter. Exod. 15:23.

4. How did the children of Israel bear this disappointment?— They murmured against Moses. Exod. 15:24.

5. To what is this world often compared?—To a wilderness.

6. What do the journeyings of Israel teach us?—To follow God's guidance, and to submit to all his dealings with us on our heavenward way.

7. What does God's word say in Micah 2:10?—Arise ye, and depart; for this is not your rest.

8. What one thing can turn the bitter waters of earthly sorrow into sweetness?—Seeing a father's hand overruling all our affairs.

9. Where did Israel next encamp?—At Elim. Exod. 15:27.

10. What blessing had the Lord in store for them there?—Plenty of

26

water.

11. Whither did they journey from Elim?—Toward Sinai, in the wilderness of Sin. Exod. 16:1.

12. About what did they murmur?—About their lack of food. Exod. 16:2, 3.

13. What relief was promised?—God promised to give them bread out of heaven. Exod. 16:4.

14. What more did God promise them?—Flesh meat. Exod. 16:12.

15. Of what kind?—Quails.

16. Why did they not slaughter their sheep and cattle?—They probably did to some extent; but they expected soon to reach Canaan, and wanted to preserve all that it was possible to keep, to stock their new possessions.

17. Is it not God's way ever to bring good out of evil?—Yes. See Deut. 8:16.

THE MANNA. (Exod. 16:4-36.)

1. How were the Israelites fed in the wilderness?—With manna.

2. What was manna?—A small round thing, like a coriander seed, white, and the taste of it was like wafers made with honey. It was of vegetable origin, but was miraculously sent by God, and able to be made into bread. Exod. 16: 14, 15, 23, 31.

3. Is manna still obtained in Arabia?—A vegetable product, so called, is obtained from the tamarisk shrub, and other plants.

4. How often were they to gather it?—Every day except the Sabbath day.

5. What provision did the Lord make for sanctifying the Sabbath day, and resting on it?—A double quantity of manna the day before. Exod. 16:22-30.

6. Were the children of Israel obedient to the Lord in this arrangement?—Some of them went out to gather on the Sabbath day, but found none. Exod. 16:27.

7. Who is the true bread that came down from heaven?—The Lord Jesus Christ. John 6:51.

8. Were the Israelites satisfied with God's provision?—They said, "Our soul loatheth this light bread." Num. 21:5.

9. Was any of this manna preserved for a memorial?—A pot containing an omer of it was kept for many years in the Ark of the Covenant. It was finally destroyed or lost at the capture of Jerusalem.

10. How much is an omer?—The tenth part of an ephah, or something over two quarts.

11. How long were the Israelites fed with manna?—During the whole time of their wandering in the wilderness, about forty years. Exod. 16:35; Josh. 5:12.

THE SMITTEN ROCK.
(Exod. 17:1-17.)

1. What are those who travel in deserts constantly liable to?—The want of water.

2. Where did the Israelites encamp?—At Rephidim.

3. How were they afflicted here?—They suffered from thirst. Exod. 17:3.

4. What did they do?—They murmured against Moses, and tempted the Lord.

5. How were they supplied with water?—From a stream that flowed from a rock in Horeb on Moses striking it with his rod. Exod. 17:6.

6. Of whom is the smitten rock a type?—That rock was Christ. 1 Cor. 4:10.

7. What did Jesus say to the woman of Samaria?—Whosoever drinketh of the water that I shall give him shall never thirst; but the water that I shall give him shall be in him a well of water springing up into everlasting life. John 4:14.

8. What did Moses call the place?—Massah, "temptation," and Meribah, "strife." See Psalm 95: 8; Heb. 3:8.

THE BATTLE WITH AMALEK. (Exod. 17:8-16.)

1. What is prayer?—The earnest desire of the heart, taught by the

27

Holy Spirit and presented through Jesus Christ to God.

2. Why do we pray to God?—Because he is willing and able to help us.

3. How did God teach Israel this at Rephidim?—By giving them victory over the Amalekites in answer to Moses' prayer. Exod. 17: 8-11.

4. Who were the Amalekites?—A nomadic tribe inhabiting the peninsula of Sinai and the wilderness between the southern hill ranges of Palestine and the borders of Egypt.

5. Was it not cruel and cowardly to come out and fight Israel when they were so weak?—Yes. They thought this was their opportunity, but they did not know that God was on Israel's side.

6. Was not God angry with them for this?—God sentenced them to constant war, and at last to destruction. Exod. 17:14, 16.

7. When were they destroyed?—Saul crippled their power, and David completed their destruction. 1 Sam. 15, 27, 30.

8. In their contest with Moses which army obtained victory?—That of the Israelites.

9. How was this?—By the continued prayer of Moses. Exod. 17: 12.

10. How did he pray?—By lifting up his hands. 1 Tim. 2:8.

11. When his hands grew heavy through weariness what was done?—Aaron and Hur stayed up his hands, one on each side, until the sun went down.

12. Of whom was Moses a type when he thus interceded for Israel?—Of Christ, who ever lives to make intercession for us in heaven.

13. How did Moses commemorate this victory?—By writing a memorial of it in a book, and by building an altar which he called Jehovah-nissi.

14. What is the meaning of Jehovah-nissi?—"The Lord my banner." Exod. 17:15.

THE VISIT OF JETHRO.
(Exod. 18.)

1. Who came to see Moses at this place?—His father-in-law, Jethro.

2. Why did he come?—Because he had heard of all that God had done for Moses and for Israel.

3. Whom did he bring with him?—Zipporah, the wife of Moses, and their two sons, whom Moses left behind when he returned to Egypt. Exod. 18:6.

4. How did Moses receive Jethro?—With the greatest courtesy. Exod. 18:7, 8.

5. How was Jethro affected by this narrative?—He rejoiced greatly and blessed the Lord for his goodness to Israel. Exod. 18:9-12.

6. What advice did Jethro give to Moses?—He advised him to appoint associate judges and to reserve only the weightier causes for himself to decide. Exod. 18:19-22.

7. Did Moses follow this counsel?—Yes. Exod. 18:24-26; Deut. 1:13-17.

8. How long did Jethro remain with Moses?—Only a few days. Exod. 18:27.

THE GIVING OF THE LAW.
(Exod. 19, 20.)

1. Where did the children of Israel next encamp?—In the wilderness of Sinai. Exod. 19:2.

2. How were the people to prepare themselves for the coming of Lord on Mount Sinai?—They were to sanctify themselves for two days, and wash their clothes, and to be ready against the third day. Exod. 17:10, 11.

3. How was the man or beast that touched the mountain to be punished?—By being stoned to death or shot through. Exod. 19: 12, 13.

4. What signs accompanied the descent of the Lord on the mount?—There were thunders and lightnings and a thick cloud, and the voice of the trumpet exceeding loud. Exod. 19:16; Heb. 12:18-21.

5. Were the people allowed to

come near to the mount?—They were not to come up into the mount, nor to break through the bounds to gaze. Exod. 19:21.

6. Was Moses allowed to go up into the mount?—He and Aaron were allowed after the Lord had called Moses up. Exod. 19:20, 24.

7. What commandments were spoken in the hearing of the people?—The Ten Commandments. Exod. 20.

8. How were these commandments given?—By the mouth of God's angels. Acts 7:38, 53.

9. What is the substance of these commandments?—See Matt. 22:37-40; Mark 12:29-31.

10. Were any other commands given?—Yes, but not in the same manner. The other commands were given through Moses, who was directed to write them in a book. Exod. 21.

11. What are the various classes of laws?—They are religious, civil, and sanitary.

12. How are the religious laws distinguished?—As moral and ceremonial.

13. Are they applicable to all times, persons, and places?—The moral law is of perpetual application; the ceremonial or ritual law was temporary.

14. Why was the ceremonial law given?—The law was our schoolmaster to bring us unto Christ. Gal. 3:24.

15. Did Jesus abolish the ritual laws?—He fulfilled them. Col 2:14; Acts 15:10.

16. Do ceremonial laws exist in the Christian Church?—The Lord prescribed none, but there are such laws enacted by the authority of the Church itself.

17. Have these laws any spiritual value?—They serve to lead the devotions of the people and to assist them in their acts of worship.

18. Are the civil laws of Moses in force now?—The foundation of all our modern civil laws is the Mosaic code.

19. To what do these laws relate?—To all matters of business, commercial enterprises, crimes and misdemeanors, and to the rights of persons and of property.

20. What penalties were imposed for the violation of these laws?—Death, fines, corporal punishment, or confinement. Exod. 21-23.

21. How was the punishment of death inflicted?—By stoning, burning at the stake, beheading, impalement, etc.

22. To what did the sanitary laws specially refer?—To cases of leprosy or other forms of contagious disease, to unwholesome dwellings, and to articles of diet.

MOSES IN THE MOUNT.
(Exod. 24-32.)

1. Who were called up into the mountain before the Lord?—Moses and Aaron, Nadab and Abihu, and seventy of the elders of Israel. Exod. 24:1.

2. What did they see?—They saw a manifestation of the God of Israel; under his feet there seemed to be a paved work of a sapphire stone, as it were the body of heaven in its clearness. Exod. 24:10.

3. Which of them was allowed to come near to God?—Moses. Exod. 24:13.

4. Who were left in charge of the congregation while Moses was gone?—Aaron and Hur. Exod. 24:14.

5. When Moses went forth with God's message to the Israelites what did they promise to do?—All the words which God had said. Exod. 24:3.

6. Were they able to perform their promise?—No.

7. Why?—From the sinfulness of their own hearts.

8. Are we able to keep God's holy law now?—Not of ourselves; the natural man receiveth not the things of the Spirit of God, because the carnal mind is enmity against God. 1 Cor. 2:14; Rom. 8:7.

9. What refuge, then, have we

from God's wrath?—Christ hath redeemed us from the curse of the law, being made a curse for us. Gal. 3:13.

THE STONE TABLES OF THE LAW BROKEN. (Exod. 32.)

1. How long was Moses upon the mount with God?—Forty days and nights. Exod. 24:18.

2. What directions were given to Moses while on the mount?—Directions concerning the tabernacle, its furniture, the altars, and the consecration of the priests.

3. What awful proof did Israel give of their inability to keep the law, of their forgetfulness of God, and of their own evil hearts, while Moses was on the mount?—They made and worshiped a golden calf. Exod. 32:1-6.

4. When was Moses made acquainted with their sin?—God told him while he was on the mount. Exod. 32:7, 8.

5. Did he plead for them with God?—Yes; and his prayer was heard. Exod. 32:11-14.

6. Who was waiting on the side of the mount for Moses when he came down?—Joshua. Exod. 32:17.

7. What sight did they see?—The calf, and the people dancing about it. Exod. 32:19.

8. What did Moses do?—He broke the stone tables, as they had broken the law, and he destroyed the golden calf. Exod. 32:19, 20.

9. Who was the leader of the Israelites in this transgression?—Aaron. Exod. 32:2, 5.

10. Was his excuse a reasonable one?—No.

11. Why was this painful history recorded?—For our instruction. 1 Cor. 10:1-12.

THE SECOND GIVING OF THE LAW. (Exod. 32:30-35; 33, 34.)

1. Who interceded for Israel at this awful time?—Moses. Exod. 32: 30-32.

2. What testimony did Moses bear against them?—That they had sinned a great sin. Exod. 32:30.

3. What punishment was inflicted on the idolatrous Israelites? —A plague fell upon them. Exod. 32:35.

4. What proof did the Lord give to Moses that he had accepted him?—Allowing him to see something of his glory and proclaiming to him his name. Exod. 33:16; 34:7.

5. How was the law given the second time?—By Moses taking two new tables of stone up the mount and God's writing upon them the Ten Commandments. Exod. 34: 1, 4, 28.

6. How long was Moses in the mount this time?—Forty days and forty nights. Deut. 10:10.

7. What wonderful manifestation on the face of Moses showed that he had been with God and that God had spoken to him face to face?—The skin of his face shone brightly. Exod. 33:11; 34: 29, 30.

8. How did the children of Israel feel when they saw this?—They were afraid to come near him. Exod. 34:30.

THE TABERNACLE.
(Exod. 35-40.)

1. How did Moses obtain the instruction to make the tabernacle? —From God himself and a pattern shown him on the mount. Exod. 25:9, 40.

2. What is a tabernacle?—A tent.

3. Whom did God specially endow with skill to perform this work?—Bezaleel and Aholiab and other wise-hearted men. Exod. 36:1.

4. Where did Moses get the materials?—From the free offerings of the people. Exod. 35:21; 36:3-7.

5. Did the women assist?—Yes; in spinning. Exod. 35:22, 25, 26.

6. What solemn injunction did Moses receive?—To make the tabernacle and its furniture according to the patterns God had

30

shown him. Exod. 25:40; 26:30; Heb. 8:5.

7. What expression, used eight times in the fortieth chapter of Exodus, shows that Moses fulfilled the work that God gave him to do?—As the Lord commanded Moses.

8. When was the tabernacle reared?—On the first day of the first month in the second year of the sojourn in the wilderness. Exod. 40:17.

9. Where was the tabernacle placed?—Without the camp. Exod. 33:7.

10. Who were allowed to enter it?—Only Moses and Aaron and other priests. Exod. 40:31, 32.

11. How was the tabernacle consecrated?—With holy anointing oil; Exod. 30:26.

12. Was its furniture consecrated in the same way?—It was. Exod. 30:26, 27.

13. Of what was the holy oil compounded?—See Exod. 30:23-25.

14. Might this oil be used for common purposes?—No. Exod. 30:32, 33.

15. What else was used in the consecration of the tabernacle?—Perfumes. Exod. 30:35-38.

16. Are our bodies compared to a tabernacle and temple?—Yes; to a tabernacle, to be taken down, in 2 Cor. 5:1; and to a temple of the Holy Ghost, to be kept holy, in 1 Cor. 6:19.

17. In what respect was the tabernacle in the wilderness a type of Jesus?—As the way to the Father's presence. Heb. 9:8, 9, 11, 12.

18. What was its outward appearance?—Plain, from its badgerskins covering. Exod. 26:14; Isa. 53:2, 3.

19. Was the inside different?—Yes; it was richly adorned with gold and silver and embroidery Exod. 31 and 36.

20. What token did God give of his accepting the tabernacle?—A cloud covered it, and the glory of the Lord filled it. Exod. 40:34.

21. Did this cloud remain upon it?—It did; but when the cloud was lifted from it the Israelites went onward in their journeys.

22. What did this cloud signify?—The continual presence of God with his people, as protector and guide.

23. How often did the priests enter the tabernacle?—Daily, for their priestly ministrations.

24. What was in the tabernacle?—The ark of the covenant; the seven-branched golden lampstand, the golden altar of incense, and the table of showbread.

25. When was incense burned on this altar?—Every morning. Exod. 30:7.

26. What does the smoke of the incense represent?—The prayers of the saints. Psalm 141:2; Rev. 8:3.

27. Were the lamps kept constantly burning on the lampstand?—They were. Exod. 27:20.

28. What kind of oil was used in them?—Pure olive oil.

29. For what was the brazen altar constructed?—For the sacrificial fires which consumed the victims.

30. Who first kindled the fire on this altar?—God himself. Lev. 9:24.

31. Of what is fire a type?—It is the element of purification. Ezek. 21:31, 32; 22:31; Heb. 12:29.

32. What do we deserve?—God's wrath.

33. Who was the Sin-bearer in our stead?—Christ Jesus. Isa. 53:5.

34. Suppose any Israelite had refused to bring his offering to this altar, what would have been the consequence?—He would have remained unclean, and would have been deprived of the privilege of worshiping.

35. Suppose we refuse to lay our sins on Jesus, what will be the consequence?—They will remain upon ourselves, and the wrath of God will abide upon us.

31

36. What stood next to the brazen altar in the outer court?—The laver. Exod. 38:8.

37. What was its use?—For the priests to wash their feet. Exod. 30:18-21.

38. Of what was the laver made? —Of copper or bronze melted from the plates of polished metal, which the women used as mirrors.

39. How does Paul speak of these mirrors?—He says we see through (or in) them, darkly. 1 Cor. 13:12.

40. Of what is the laver significant?—The washing of regeneration.

41. Where was the brazen altar of burnt offering placed?—In the outer court of the tabernacle.

42. What was the size of the tabernacle?—Thirty cubits long, ten broad, and ten high. We may reckon the cubit at twenty-one inches.

43. How large was the court surrounding it?—One hundred cubits from east to west, and fifty broad from north to south.

44. Was this court inclosed?—It was, with a row of twenty pillars on each side, five cubits high and five cubits apart. There were ten pillars on the western side, but only six on the eastern. Upon these were hung curtains, stretched from pillar to pillar.

45. What material was used for the curtains?—At the eastern end, where was the entrance, the curtain was blue, purple, scarlet, and white fine twined linen. Exod. 27:9-18.

46. Of what was the Ark of the Covenant made?—Of acacia wood.

47. How large was it?—Two and a half cubits long, one and a half broad, and one and a half deep, plated over with gold, inside and out.

48. How did it represent the glory of Jesus?—By the mercy seat and cherubim above it. Exod. 25:17, 22.

49. To what use was it put?— It was the sacred deposit chest of the nation, and contained the two tables of stone, for which reason it is called the "Ark of the Covenant;" and since it contained also Aaron's priestly rod which budded, and a pot of manna, it is named the "Ark of the Testimony." Heb. 9:3, 4; 1 Kings 8:6.

50. Of what was the budding rod a type?—The resurrection of the dead. 1 Cor. 15:42.

51. What was this incorruptible manna a type of?—Being born again, not of corruptible seed, but of incorruptible, by the word of God, which liveth and abideth forever. 1 Peter 1:23; Acts 2:31, 32.

52. Where in the revelation is this incorruptible manna alluded to?—To him that overcometh will I give to eat of the hidden manna. Rev. 2:17.

53. What was the mercy seat? —The lid of the chest, placed above it, plated with pure gold, and sustaining two golden emblematical figures, one at each end.

54. Where was the ark placed? —In the inner part of the tabernacle, separated from the rest of the tabernacle with embroidered curtains.

55. Who were permitted to go in and minister in the holy place? —The priests went always into the first tabernacle, accomplishing the service of God. Heb. 9:6.

56. Who alone might go into the most holy place?—The high priest.

57. How often might he go in? —Once every year. Heb. 9:7.

58. Of what is the most holy place a type?—Of the immediate presence of God.

59. Who has entered there?— Jesus the Son of God. Heb. 4:14.

60. What happened to the veil of the temple when the Lord Jesus was crucified?—It was rent in two from the top to the bottom.

61. What did this show?—That the way into heaven was now open. Heb. 10:19-22.

THE SACRIFICES AND OFFERINGS

(Lev. and Num. 19.)

1. What is the principal thing treated of in the Book of Leviticus?—The different sacrifices and oblations, the consecration of the priests, the various kinds of uncleanness and their purification, the festivals, vows, tithes, and things devoted.

2. Name the four principal offerings.—The burnt offering, the sin offering, the trespass offering, and the peace offering.

3. What characterized the burnt offering?—It was the male animal, without blemish, from the herd or the flock, or a turtledove or young pigeon; the blood of the beast being sprinkled about, and its body cut up and burnt on the altar. Lev. 1.

4. In what did the sin offering and the trespass offering differ from the burnt offering?—In the sin offering having the blood sprinkled and poured out on and under the altar, and having the fat, and not the whole animal, burnt upon it; and in the trespass offering being allowed to be of the female sex, and being on account of special rather than general sin. The sin offering referred rather to atonement, and the burnt offering to self-dedication. Lev. 4, 5, 6.

5. What was the peace offering? —The peace offering was an expression of thankfulness to God for his gifts. Lev. 3; 7:11-38.

6. What difference was there between the meat offering and the burnt offering?—The meat offering, of flour, oil, and wine, was also a sacrifice of thanksgiving. Lev. 2.

7. What was prefigured by all these sacrifices?—The great sacrifice and atonement made for us by our Lord Jesus Christ upon Calvary.

8. What is said in Heb. 10:1-18?—The sacrifice of Christ's body, once offered, hath forever taken away sins.

9. Where was Moses when God gave him the instruction about sacrifices?—On Mount Sinai. Exod. 24:18; 32:15.

10. Were any of these sacrifices eaten by the offerer?—The whole burnt offering was consumed on the altar; the ashes were then carried out of the camp into a clean place. Other sacrifices, after being offered, were returned to the offerer for food, a portion being reserved for the priest. 1 Sam. 2:13.

11. What was done with the blood of the victims thus sacrificed?—A few drops were sprinkled on the altar, and the rest was shed upon the ground at the side of the altar.

12. What was done with the fat?—It was burned on the altar. Lev. 3:16.

13. Could the blood or the fat be used, when beasts were slain for food only?—The blood was to be shed on the ground and then covered with earth, but the fat could be used for any other purpose, except eating. Lev. 7:23, 24.

14. Name some of the ceremonies which took place on the great day of atonement.—Aaron the high priest made sin offerings for himself and for the people, and sprinkled the blood upon the mercy seat in the most holy place; confessed the sins of the people over the scapegoat, and sent it away into the wilderness, and offered burnt offerings for himself and for the people. Lev. 16.

15. What is the meaning of the word "atonement?"—Reconciliation, or setting at one again, by sacrifice in another's stead.

16. Who atoned for our sins?— Jesus Christ, who suffered in our place the punishment of our sins.

17. How did the scapegoat set this forth?—It bore away the sins of Israel, as Christ bears ours. Lev. 16:22.

18. What was done with the scapegoat?—It was led away by

33

the hands of a fit man into the wilderness and turned loose. Lev. 16:21.

19. What is the significance of the two goats, one slain and one sent away?—They were equally a vicarious offering procuring the pardon of sin. They make but a single sacrifice, though only one of them was slain. They prefigured the human and divine natures of Christ; the slain goat showing his death, and the scapegoat his resurrection.

20. What is the difference between an oblation and a sacrifice?—In a sacrifice life was taken, and blood was shed. An oblation consisted of such offerings as vegetables and fruits, or articles made of them, as oil and wine.

21. What were drink offerings?—They usually consisted of wine. They were never used separately, but part was poured on the head of the victim, or on the food offering, to consecrate it, and part was allotted to the priests.

22. What was used with every meat offering?—Salt. Lev. 2:13.

23. What was the ceremony connected with the red heifer?—The heifer was slain and burnt, and its blood was sprinkled before the tabernacle.

24. What was the appointed use of the ashes of the red heifer?—They were mixed with water and sprinkled upon persons who had become unclean, and as a token of purification for sin.

25. Who was again prefigured here?—Christ was evidently typified in these proceedings. 1 Peter 1:2.

26. Where was the fire obtained to burn the sacrifices and the incense?—From the sacred altar. It was kindled by God himself when the tabernacle was consecrated, and was to be kept continually burning. No other fire was to be used by the Israelites in their worship. Lev. 9:23, 24; 6:13.

27. Might not fire be obtained for this purpose elsewhere?—No.

28. What was the sin of Nadab and Abihu?—They lighted their censers with strange fire.

29. Did God accept their service thus rendered?—He did not.

30. How were they punished?—Fire came forth from the Lord and consumed them.

31. What does this teach us?—That the ordinances of God must not be changed by any human authority. God demands exact obedience.

THE SABBATH AND THE NATIONAL FEASTS.
(Exod. 23; Lev. 23.)

1. What is the subject of these chapters?—The Hebrew feasts.

2. What is the first feast named?—The Sabbath. Lev. 23:1.

3. Why is the Sabbath called a feast?—Because it was a holy day, a day of rest and enjoyment.

4. Of what is the Sabbath a type?—Of the rest and enjoyment of heaven. Heb. 4:8-11.

5. How often was the Sabbath kept?—One day in every seven.

6. Why?—Because the Lord made the heaven and the earth in six days, and rested on the seventh; wherefore the Lord blessed the seventh day and hallowed it. Exod. 20:11.

7. What day do Christians keep as the Sabbath?—The first day of the week.

8. Why was the change made from the seventh day to the first?—In honor of the Lord's resurrection on the first day.

9. Was this change sanctioned by the Lord?—It undoubtedly was; besides, it had been predicted. Ezek. 43:27.

10. Did the apostles authorize this change?—They probably observed the seventh day because of their Jewish education and prejudices, and the first because of their affection for Jesus; but they seem to have required the observance of the first day only of their Gentile converts.

11. What name was given to the first day by the early Chris-

tians?—The Lord's Day. Rev. 1 10.

12. What was the Sabbatical year?—Every seventh year, the fields, orchards, and vineyards were not allowed to be cropped; all were required to rest without tillage. What grew of itself was to be given to the poor. Exod. 23:10, 11.

13. Who were required to keep the Sabbath?—Every man, woman, and child in the nation.

14. When was the keeping of the Sabbath first enjoined?—In the garden of Eden, when God first sanctified it or set it apart for holy use. (See also Exod. 16 and 20.)

15. Does God unite gladness and joy with the keeping of his Sabbaths?—He does. Isa. 58:13, 14.

16. How should the Sabbath be kept?—Quietly, with religious services, and with acts of mercy and thanksgiving.

17. If the Sabbath is not a delight to us what is the cause?—We have either no religion at all or not enough to make us happy.

18. How can our souls, even in this world, "enter into rest?"—We may enjoy the rest of a steadfast faith, an anchored hope, and an abiding peace.

19. Which was the second feast or festival spoken of?—The feast of the passover or of unleavened bread. Lev. 23:5, 6; Exod. 23:15.

20. When was that kept?—One whole week, beginning with the fourteenth day of the first month, about our March or April.

21. How was it kept?—By the sacrifice of a lamb, the use of unleavened bread and bitter herbs.

22. When was this instituted?—When the Israelites came out of Egypt.

23. What did the passover teach them, and what must it teach us?—To remember their deliverance by blood, and to look for our own deliverance by the same means.

24. What feast or festival came next?—The offering of the first fruits of the harvest, when the sickle was first put to the grain.

25. What ceremony were they to perform with the first sheaf?—The priest was to wave it before the Lord. Lev. 23:10, 11.

26. What did "waving" it mean?—An act of worship of the Lord of the whole earth.

27. Whom did that first sheaf represent?—Now is Christ risen from the dead, and become the first fruits of them that slept. 1 Cor. 15:20.

28. Did Jesus compare himself to wheat when speaking of his death?—Verily, verily, I say unto you, Except a corn of wheat fall into the ground and die, it abideth alone: but if it die, it bringeth forth much fruit. John 12:24.

29. What were the Israelites to do fifty days after they had brought in the first fruits?—To offer a new meat offering to the Lord. Lev. 23:15-21.

30. Of what was this a type?—Of the outpouring of the Holy Ghost at Pentecost. Acts 2.

31. What festival was held on the first day of the seventh month?—The feast of trumpets. Lev. 15: 23-25.

32. Of what was this a type?—Of the call to repentance and of the preaching of the Gospel.

33. How many days after this festival of trumpets was the great day of atonement kept?—On the ninth day.

34. What remarkable ceremonies took place on this day?—See Lev. 16.

35. Are we not very prone to excuse ourselves when looking into our own sinful hearts?—The heart is deceitful above all things, and desperately wicked: who can know it? Jer. 17:9.

36. Where shall we best discover God's estimate of sin?—In those parts of Scripture which contain his denunciations against it, his punishments of it, and his provision for its pardon and removal.

35

37. What other ceremony took place on this day, mentioned in this chapter and not in the sixteenth chapter?—The blowing of trumpets on the first day of the month. Lev. 23:24.

38. Who were to blow the trumpets?—The priests. Num. 10:8.

39. Where is this more fully described?—Lev. 25:9.

40. What was the jubilee?—It was a festival celebrated every fiftieth year, counting from the entrance of the Israelites into Canaan. Lev. 25:10.

41. How are we interested in it?—Because it represents the redemption of sinners from the bondage of sin and the restoration of God's people to their blood-bought inheritance. "Blessed is the people that know the joyful sound!" Psalm 89:15; Isa. 61:1, 2.

42. How many days after the day of atonement did the feast of tabernacles occur?—Five days. Lev. 23:34.

43. What ceremonies marked this festival?—The offering of sacrifices and the dwelling in booths.

44. How many days was it kept?—Eight days.

45. Where were the booths constructed?—On the flat roofs of the houses and in the lanes and streets of the city where the festival was held.

46. Why was this feast instituted?—To remind the nation of the journeyings of their fathers in the desert, when they dwelt in booths, and of their present blessings. Lev. 23:43.

47. What does the twenty-ninth chapter of Numbers tell of?—Of the offerings at the feasts of trumpets and tabernacles and on the day of atonement.

48. Is the feast of tabernacles ever mentioned in the New Testament?—Now the Jews' feast of tabernacles was at hand. In the last day, that great day of the feast, Jesus stood and cried, saying, If any man thirst, let him come unto me and drink. John 7:2, 37.

49. At what time of the year was King Solomon's temple dedicated?—Solomon kept the feast seven days in the seventh month. 2 Chron. 7:8.

50. When was the second temple dedicated?—The children of the captivity kept the passover upon the fourteenth day of the first month. Ezra 6:19.

51. Where was Solomon's temple of God built?—In Jerusalem.

52. What is now God's temple? —The human body. 1 Cor. 3:16, 17.

53. What is to be God's temple hereafter?—God himself, and the Lamb. Rev. 21:22.

54. In what place?—In the holy city, the new Jerusalem. Rev. 21:2.

55. Where is the new Jerusalem to be?—In the new earth. Rev. 21:1.

56. Who are to be the inhabitants of that city?—They which are written in the Lamb's book of life. Rev. 21:27.

57. Are our names written there? —Each one may know for himself. 1 John 3:14; Rom. 8:16.

THE NUMBERING OF THE ISRAELITES AND DEPARTURE FROM SINAI.
(Num. 1:4, 7-10.)

1. What do these chapters describe?—The numbering of the people, the duties of the priests and Levites, the offerings for the tabernacle, the marchings of the Israelites, etc.

2. How long had the children of Israel remained at Sinai?— About eleven months.

3. What are some of the most remarkable events that occurred there?—The giving of the law, the worship of the golden calf, the making of the tabernacle, and the punishment of Nadab and Abihu.

4. How long after they left Egypt was the tabernacle first set up?—About ten months. Exod. 40:2.

36

5. What rite did they celebrate on the fourteenth of the first month?—The passover. Num. 9:1-5.

6. What did God command Moses to do on the first of the second month?—To number the people. Num. 1:1-3.

7. Whom did God accept for his service instead of the firstborn?—The Levites. Num. 3:12; 8:16.

8. Did the numbers tally exactly?—The firstborn were two hundred and seventy-three more. Num. 3:46.

9. How was the difference arranged?—Five shekels (about $2.60) each was paid to Aaron for them. Num. 8.

10. How were the children of Israel to encamp and to march on their journey?—Each tribe was to march and encamp by itself in a fixed order and place, the Levites in the midst. Num. 2.

11. Who provided the wagons to carry the tabernacle?—The princes or heads of the tribes. Num. 7:2, 3.

12. Why had not the sons of Kohath any wagons allotted to them?—Because their burdens were carried on their shoulders according to the law.

13. What part of the tabernacle did they carry?—The holy things. Num. 4:2-15.

14. What did each of the princes of Israel offer as a gift to the service of the tabernacle?—Gold and silver vessels, and animals for sacrifice. Num. 7.

15. What direction did the Lord give Moses as to making trumpets?—That they should be of silver, and be used for assembling and for marching in journeys or in war. Num. 10:1-10.

16. On which day did the cloud move?—On the twentieth day of the second month of the second year. Num. 10:11.

17. Of what was the moving of the cloud to inform the Israelites?—That they were to proceed on their journey. Num. 9:17.

18. When the first alarm of the trumpets was given which tribes marched first?—Judah, Issachar, and Zebulun.

19. How many encamped on the east of the tabernacle?—The above three. Num. 2:3-9.

20. What immediately followed these three tribes?—The tabernacle. Num. 10:17; 7:7, 8.

21. Which three tribes followed these wagons?—Reuben, Simeon, and Gad. Num. 10:18-20.

22. What part of the tabernacle next went?—The sanctuary. Num. 10:12.

23. Name the six tribes that followed.—Ephraim, Manasseh, and Benjamin; Dan, Asher, and Naphtali.

24. Whom did Moses entreat to accompany them?—Hobab, his father-in-law. Num. 10:29.

25. Did he at first refuse?—He did. Num. 10:30.

26. What proofs have we afterward that he changed his mind and went with the Israelites into the Promised Land?—The children of the Kenite, Moses' father-in-law, went up out of the city of palm trees with the children of Judah into the wilderness of Judah, and dwelt among the people. Judg. 1:16.

27. To what family did Jonadab, mentioned in 2 Kings 10 and Jer. 35, belong?—To the Kenites, that came of Hemath, the father of Rechab. 1 Chron. 2:55; 2 Kings 10:15.

28. When all was ready for marching what prayer did Moses offer?—Rise up, Lord, and let thine enemies be scattered; and let them that hate thee flee before thee. Num. 10:35.

29. And what when the ark rested again?—Return, O Lord, unto the many thousands of Israel. Num. 10:36.

TRANSGRESSIONS. (Num. 11.)

1. By what were the children of Israel in the wilderness chiefly distinguished?—By their repeated re-

bellions against God. Heb. 3:8-12; Psalm 106:7, 8, 13-46.

2. Of what should their sad history warn us?—Of the sad consequences of sin.

3. On what did the Lord feed Israel while at Sinai?—On manna.

4. How did they behave toward God while on their journey?—They ungratefully desired a change of food. Num. 11:1-6.

5. But did God hear their cry for flesh food?—He did, and sent them quails in abundance. Num. 11:31.

6. How were they punished for their murmurings?—Many of them were destroyed by fire and others by the plague.

7. Did not Moses feel their continual provocation too much for him?—He complained to God of the burden it was to him. Num. 11:11-15.

8. How did the Lord assist him?—By the appointment of seventy elders. Num. 11:16, 17.

9. How did Joshua show his affection for his master and zeal for his honor?—By telling him of Eldad and Medad. Num. 11:26-28.

10. What was the reply of Moses?—Enviest thou for my sake? would God that all the Lord's people were prophets, and that the Lord would put his Spirit upon them!

11. Were not all of the nation intended to be prophets?—They were. 1 Chron. 16:22; Psalm 105:15.

12. When the Israelites got the food they coveted how did they act?—They probably indulged in it to excess. Num. 11:20.

13. Is gluttony reproved in the Bible?—It is, in several places. Prov. 23:2; 1 Peter 4:3.

14. What lessons should we reap from their transgressions?—Now these things were our examples, to the intent we should not lust after evil things, as they also lusted. 1 Cor. 10:5, 6.

MIRIAM'S SIN AND PUNISHMENT. (Num. 12.)

1. What proof have we here that Rom. 3:10 is true?—The sin of Miriam and Aaron shows that there is none righteous; no, not one.

2. What was the sin of Miriam and Aaron?—They claimed equal authority with Moses himself. Num. 12:2.

3. What special favor had God given to Moses?—More intimate communion with himself and a nearer view of his glory. Num. 12:8.

4. Ought anyone to aspire to offices in the Church which God has not called him to fill?—He ought not, except to covet earnestly the best gifts.

5. Is aspiration for better things wrong?—Clearly not. Col. 3:1, 2.

6. Is personal ambition consistent with the Christian life?—No. Jer. 45:5.

7. What special proof did God give of his displeasure?—He made Miriam a leper. Num. 12:10.

8. Who pleaded for Miriam?—Aaron with Moses, and Moses with God. Num. 12:11, 13.

9. How did the Lord mitigate her punishment?—By removing her disease in seven days. Num. 12:14, 15.

10. Of what was her punishment the type?—Of the loathsomeness of sin in the eyes of God.

11. In what way did the Lord permit the whole camp to sympathize with Miriam?—By not requiring them to go on their way until she was restored.

THE REPORT OF THE SPIES. (Num. 13, 14.)

1. Where were the children of Israel at this time?—In the wilderness of Paran. Exod. 12:16; 13:3.

2. Was it far from the land of Canaan?—One end of it was near to the wilderness of Judea.

3. What did God command Moses to do?—To send spies to search the land of Canaan. Num. 13:2.

4. Whom did Moses select for this errand?—Heads of the tribes.

5. How many were there?—

Twelve.

6. What change did he make in the name of one of them?—He called Oshea, son of Nun, Jehoshua or Joshua. Num. 13:16.

7. Give the meaning of the name before and after the change, and then say of whom he was the type.—"Help" before, and "help of Jehovah" or "Saviour" after—a type of Christ the Saviour.

8. How long were the spies in searching the land?—Forty days.

9. What report did they bring? —That the land flowed with milk and honey, but that the inhabitants were giants and the cities great and walled. Num. 13:26-28, 31-33.

10. What is meant by flowing with milk and honey?—Having excellent pasturage, and abundance of fruit and honey. Judg. 14:8.

11. How did the spies show the goodness of the land?—By the fruits which they brought back.

12. What fruits were they?— Grapes, pomegranates, and figs. Num. 13:23.

13. How far did the spies go?— As far as to Hamath.

14. Did all the twelve join in the cowardly report?—All but Caleb and Joshua. Num. 13:30; 14:6-9.

15. What effect did this have on the people?—They were in great distress, and proposed returning to Egypt. Num. 14:1-4.

16. How did Moses and Aaron act?—They fell on their faces in humiliation and intercessory prayer. Num. 14:5.

17. What did Caleb and Joshua say?—That the Lord was with Israel, and that they had nothing to fear from the inhabitants of the land. Num. 14:6-9.

18. Who appeared at the moment when they were about to be stoned?—God himself in his glory. Num. 14:10.

19. What did he propose to Moses?—To disinherit Israel and to make of Moses a mightier nation than theirs. Num. 14:11, 12.

20. Did Moses accept this great honor?—No; he pleaded for their pardon instead.

21. What special mercy did the Lord promise to Caleb and Joshua? —That they alone should enter the land of Canaan. Num. 14:30.

22. How did he punish the ten rebels?—They died of the plague. Num. 14:37.

23. What punishment did the Lord lay on the whole congregation?—That of wandering forty years in the wilderness till all who came out of Egypt had died. Num. 14:33.

24. Of what foolish act were they guilty next day?—Some of them entered the land against the command of God.

25. What was the result of their attempt?—They were attacked and driven back.

26. Had they been warned of their defeat?—Yes. Num. 14:43.

27. Were they well armed for battle?—They were not.

28. Why?—Because the Lord was not among them.

29. Are the strongest battalions the most successful in battle?— Not always. Eccles. 9:11.

THE SABBATH-BREAKER, THE SIN OF KORAH, AND THE BUDDING ROD. (Num. 15-17.)

1. Of what sin was a man found guilty about this time?—Of gathering sticks upon the Sabbath day. Num. 15:32.

2. What did they do with him? —They brought him to Moses. Num. 15:33.

3. How was he punished?—He was stoned to death by God's command. Num. 15:35, 36.

4. Had not God already declared his mind about this sin?—Yes. See Exod. 31:14.

5. Did he there say how the man was to be put to death?—He did not.

6. Does this not show us that Moses acted in everything immediately under the Lord's direction?—

39

It does. Num. 15:34, 35.

7. What did the Lord order the people to make, that they might keep in remembrance his commandments?—A blue-fringed ribbon on the borders of their garments. Num. 15:38-40.

8. Who was Korah?—A Levite. Num. 16:8.

9. Of what tribe were Dathan, Abiram, and On?—Of the tribe of Reuben. Num. 16:1.

10. What sin did they commit? —They rebelled against the authority of Moses and Aaron. Num. 16:3.

11. Who were leagued with them?—Two hundred and fifty princes of the assembly. Num. 16:2.

12. Had they not lately had a warning of this very sin in Miriam's case?—The very same. Num. 12.

13. What did Moses propose for these men to do, to prove whether God accepted them as priests or not?—That they should come to the tabernacle, burning incense, to see if God would accept them. Num. 16:7, 18.

14. In what way did God at once manifest his displeasure?—By commanding Moses and Aaron and the congregation to separate themselves from Korah, Dathan, and Abiram, and their habitations (Num. 16:20-24), when the earth opened and swallowed them up. Num. 16:31, 33.

15. What became of the other two hundred and fifty men that transgressed?—A fire from the Lord consumed them. Num. 16:35.

16. Did this still the murmurings of the people?—No; for they charged Moses and Aaron with killing the people of the Lord. Num. 16:41.

17. How did God vindicate the honor of his own appointed priesthood?—Above fourteen thousand died of the plague. Num. 16:49.

18. What did Moses command Aaron to do when he knew that

judgment was about to fall on the people?—To burn incense and make an atonement. Num. 16:46.

19. How did he know of this judgment?—The Lord told him. Num. 16:45.

20. Did God accept the service and own the act?—He immediately stopped the plague. Num. 16:47, 48.

21. Of whom was Aaron the type?—Of Christ, the High Priest of our profession.

22. What was done with the censers of the rebels?—They were beaten into plates to cover the altar, as a memorial of their sin. Num. 16:38-40.

23. How did the Lord himself show whom he had chosen?—By causing Aaron's rod to bud. Exod. 17:1-10.

24. Of what was the budding rod a type?—Of the resurrection and eternal life of Christ.

25. And what proof has he given to us that Jesus "is able to save to the uttermost" all that put their trust in him?—By raising him from the dead. Acts 17:31.

26. Why is resurrection a proof that Jesus is the Son of God?— Because he laid down his life and took it again by his divine power. Rom. 1:4.

27. Who alone was able to atone for sin?—The Lamb of God. John 1:29; 3:16.

THE SIN OF MOSES AND AARON; AARON'S AND MIRIAM'S DEATH. (Num. 20.)

1. Where did Miriam die?—At Kadesh, in the desert of Zin. Num. 20:1.

2. What trial of their faith did the children of Israel have here? —The want of water. Num. 20:2.

3. How did they behave?—They reproached Moses for it. Num. 20: 2-5.

4. What did the Lord command Moses to do?—To speak to the rock before the people, and it should give forth water.

5. How did Moses in this matter dishonor the Lord?—He spoke

as if he and Aaron, by their own power, would bring the water out; and he also struck the rock. Num. 20:10, 11.

6. What punishment did he and Aaron bring upon themselves for their sins?—They were not allowed to enter the Promised Land. Num. 20:12.

7. How many times did Moses mention this in his after writings? —Five times. Num. 27:14; Deut. 1:37; 3:26; 31:2; 32:51.

8. Did the Lord alter his purpose?—No.

9. How did the Edomites behave at this time to the children of Israel?—They refused them a passage through their land. Num. 20:14-21.

10. From whom had the Edomites descended?—From "Esau, who was Edom." Gen. 36:1.

11. Why were they called by this name?—Esau was called Edom, or "red," from the red pottage he got from Jacob. Gen. 25:30.

12. What event happened at Mount Hor?—The death of Aaron. Num. 20:22-29.

13. What solemnity attended it? —The removal, first of his priestly robes, and putting them on Eleazar his son.

14. What mark of respect did the children of Israel pay to the memory of Aaron?—They mourned for him thirty days.

15. Was the usual period of mourning thirty days?—It was. See Gen. 50:3; Deut. 21:13.

16. What ceremonies accompanied the mourning?—Generally it was accompanied with loud crying and music. See Gen. 50:10; Eccles. 12:5; Matt. 9:23; 11:17.

17. What is the meaning of consecrated?—Set apart for the service of God.

18. How was Aaron a type of Jesus in this?—Jesus was anointed by the Holy Ghost, sanctified or set apart for his atoning and interceding work.

19. What is the meaning of the name Christ?—Anointed.

20. Where is Jesus spoken of as intercessor?—In Heb. 7:22, 24, 25.

21. Which of the apostles had a vision of Jesus dressed in priestly garments?—John, in Rev. 1:12, 13.

22. How is the Lord Jesus described in Heb. 4:14, 16?—As a great High Priest.

23. Who succeeded Aaron as high priest?—Eleazar.

24. At what age could a priest enter upon his office?—The Levites began to serve at the age of twenty-five (or thirty) years, and in David's time at twenty; the priests probably the same. Num. 8:24; 4:3; 1 Chron. 23:24, 27.

25. Is the perfume of Aaron's garments ever spoken of in connection with Christ's kingdom?— Yes; in Psalm 45:8.

26. Were perfumes much sought after among the Hebrews?—They were. See Prov. 7:17; 27:9; Isa. 57:9; John 12:3.

27. In how many respects does the priesthood of the Lord Jesus excel the priesthood of Aaron?— In its divinity and duration, Christ being God and a priest forever.

28. To what order of priesthood is the priesthood of the Lord Jesus Christ compared?—The priesthood of the order of Melchizedek. Heb. 5:6, 7.

THE BRAZEN SERPENT.
(Num. 21:1-9.)

1. Who came and fought with Israel?—King Arad, the Canaanite.

2. Which army was victorious? —The Israelites.

3. How came it about?—Because they made a vow unto God to destroy the Canaanites if he gave them the victory.

4. Did they destroy the Canaanites?—They utterly destroyed them and their cities.

5. Which way did the Israelites go from Mount Hor?—By the way of the Red Sea.

41

6. Why were the people obliged to take such a long way round?—To avoid the land of Edom. Num. 20:21.

7. How did they meet this trouble?—They were much discouraged.

8. How did the Lord punish them?—By means of fiery serpents.

9. What remedy was Moses commanded to prepare?—A serpent of brass upon a pole, that the people might look upon it and live.

10. Of whom was this a type? —Of Christ.

11. How?—The sinner must look to Christ for salvation. Isa. 45:22.

12. What became of the brazen serpent?—It was preserved until the days of Hezekiah, who called it Nehushtan; it was broken to pieces by his order. 2 Kings 18:4.

13. Of what wicked spirits are the serpents a type?—Of that old serpent the devil. Rev. 12:9.

14. Are we all in the same danger?—We are.

15. What is our remedy?—To look unto Christ by faith.

16. May we not be saved some other way?—No. Acts 4:12.

17. What is faith?—The substance of things hoped for, the evidence of things not seen. Heb. 11:1.

BALAAM. (Num. 21:10-35; 22-25; 31:1-8.)

1. How far had the children of Israel got on their journey?—To the wilderness before Moab.

2. Where was Moab?—On the east side of the Jordan.

3. What interesting event had occurred at Beer?—A supply of water, followed by a song of praise.

4. What two mighty kings did the children of Israel conquer and slay at this time?—Sihon, king of the Amorites, and Og, king of Bashan. Num. 21:23, 24, 33-35.

5. What is said of Og in Deuteronomy?—Only Og, king of Bashan, remained of the remnant of giants. See Deut. 3:11.

6. How many times in the Psalms are these conquests spoken of?—Twice: Psalm 135:11 and 136:19, 20.

7. What was the name of the king of Moab?—Balak. Num. 22:4.

8. How did he feel when he saw the host of Israel?—He was greatly alarmed. Num. 22:2-6.

9. Who was Balaam?—A heathen priest or prophet, who sometimes received revelations from God. Num. 22:5; 24:1, 2.

10. Why did Balak desire so much to see him?—To get him to curse the Israelites, so that he might overcome them. Num. 22:6.

11. Did Balaam desire to go?—Yes, as the rewards that were offered him tempted his covetousness. Jude 11.

12. What hindered him?—The command of God. Num. 22:12.

13. Did God permit him to have his own way?—Yes. Num. 22:20.

14. Did that show that God was pleased with the errand?—No; but it gave him an opportunity of showing his power over him in a more public and striking manner. Num. 23:7-12.

15. How did God show his disapprobation?—By sending his angel to stop him on his way. Num. 22:22.

16. What reproof was given to him, and how?—See 2 Peter 2:16.

17. Did God send Balaam back, or permit him to go on?—He let him go on. Num. 22:35.

18. Had Balaam any power when he got there?—Only to say what God told him. Num. 22:38.

19. Did he try by divination to accomplish Balak's wish?—Yes, while the sacrifices were burned on the altar. Num. 23:3, 15, 23; 24:1.

20. Did it succeed?—No; God made him utter a blessing instead of a curse. Num. 23:8-10, 20-24; 24:2-9.

21. How did Balak feel when he found he had brought a blessing

42

instead of a curse on his enemies? —He was angry with Balaam. Num. 24:10.

22. When Balaam found that he could not prevail by enchantment, did he yield himself to the power of God?—Yes. Num. 24:13, 14.

23. What prophecy did he utter of the glory of the Lord Jesus?— I shall see him, but not now; I shall behold him, but not nigh; there shall come a Star out of Jacob, and a Scepter shall rise out of Israel. Num. 24:17.

24. When did this star appear? —At the birth of Jesus.

25. Had this star been looked for?—Yes, by the astronomers of the East.

26. Did they know what it foretokened?—Yes. Matt. 2:1, 2.

27. How did they know it?— From the prophecies, of which Balaam's was one, which had long been circulated throughout the entire East.

28. How did Moses obtain these prophecies of Balaam?—It is believed that Balaam committed them to writing, and brought them to Moses—for a reward.

29. Can wicked men utter true prophecies?—They can if controlled by the Spirit of God. See Judg. 7:14; John 11:49-52.

30. How did Balaam show he was a bad man?—By his counsel to Balak to tempt the children of Israel to sin. Num. 31:16.

31. What was Balaam's end?— He was killed by the Israelites in battle with the Midianites. Num. 31:8.

32. What sin did the children of Israel commit?—They joined in the impure worship of the Moabites. Num. 25:2.

33. Through whom were they enticed?—By the Moabite women.

34. How were they punished? —Many of these idolaters were slain by the judges of Israel; others perished by the plague. Num. 25:5, 9.

35. How was the plague stayed? —By the zeal of Phinehas. Num. 25:8-11.

36. What blessings were bestowed on Phinehas for this?—God gave him a covenant of peace, and confirmed to him and his descendants the priesthood forever.

37. What was Moses directed to do?—To vex the Midianites and to smite them. Num. 25:17.

THE CITIES OF REFUGE.

(Num. 26 and 27; 31-35.)

1. What does chapter 26 record?—The numbering of the Israelites.

2. What was the sum of the males of twenty years old and upward?—Six hundred and one thousand seven hundred and thirty.

3. Had they increased or diminished since they were numbered at Sinai?—There was a small decrease (1,820 persons).

4. What was the number of the Levites of a month old and upward at this time?—Twenty-three thousand.

5. Had they increased or diminished since the former census? —There was an increase of seven hundred and twenty-seven.

6. Were there many of those numbered at Sinai yet living?— There were not, except those who were then children.

7. How many men were left of those who came out of Egypt with Moses?—Only two, Caleb and Joshua. Num. 26:65.

8. How was this?—God had said that all the rest should die in the wilderness. Num. 26:65.

9. What lesson should it teach us?—To beware of unbelief. Heb. 3:7-19.

10. What kind of arrangement did the Lord make for one family when all the men of it were dead? —That the property of the father should go to his daughters. Num. 27:1-11.

11. What petition did Moses present to the Lord at the end of chapter 27?—That he would provide him a successor. Num. 21:15-17.

43

12. Whom did the Lord appoint?—Joshua.

13. Of which tribe was Joshua?—Ephraim. 1 Chron. 7:22-27.

14. How often was the continual burnt offering to be offered?—Day by day, morning and evening. Num. 28:3, 4.

15. At what other times were there to be statedly additional offerings?—Every Sabbath, at the beginning of each month at the passover, and at all the solemn feasts.

16. Were vows always to be fulfilled?—Where made freely, and without constraint, they were.

17. What does chapter 31 describe?—The defeat of the Midianites.

18. How was the spoil to be purified?—By fire or by water.

19. To what is the judgment of the last day compared?—1 Cor. 3:13-15.

20. Which of the children of Israel had their inheritance on the east of the Jordan?—Reuben, Gad, and half the tribe of Manasseh. Num. 32.

21. What do chapters 33 and 34 describe?—The several stages of the journey through the wilderness, the boundaries of Canaan, and the officers appointed to divide it.

22. How many cities out of the tribes of Israel were to be given to the Levites?—Forty-eight. Num. 35:7.

23. For what purpose were six of these cities to be separated?—For cities of refuge. Num. 35:6.

24. Who had the privilege of fleeing thither?—Any one who had accidentally killed another. Num. 35:11, 12, 24-28.

25. Was there any protection to be afforded to the murderer?—No. Num. 35:16-21.

26. In what relationship did the "avenger of blood" stand to the slain person?—Next of kin.

27. How many witnesses were necessary to prove the wicked deed?—Two.

28. What event released the manslayer from the city of refuge, and permitted him to go at large again without fear of death?—The death of the high priest. Num. 35:25.

29. Where were those cities of refuge?—Three on the east of Jordan and three on the west. Deut. 4:41-43.

30. Were they in valleys or on hills?—On hills.

31. Why was this?—So as to be more easily seen.

32. Of whom is the manslayer a type?—Of Satan, the great enemy of souls.

33. How can we be said to be manslayers?—By permitting sin to destroy us. Hosea 13:9.

34. Who is represented by the way to the cities of refuge?—Jesus Christ. John 14:6.

35. Of what is the avenger a type?—Of the law, which requires us to do or die. Rom. 3:9-19; Gal. 3:22-24.

36. Are we all conscious of our danger?—Sinners are dead in sin, and both wise and foolish often slumber and sleep.

37. Who must arouse us?—Christ, by his awakening and enlightening Spirit. John 16:7-9; Eph. 5:13, 14.

38. Are there any hindrances in the way?—None from Christ himself.

39. What tribes petitioned Moses to be allowed to settle on the east side of Jordan?—Reuben and Gad (Num. 32:2-5). With them was joined half the tribe of Manasseh.

40. Did Moses approve of their request?—He did not, for he did not wish them to settle down in ease until Canaan was subdued.

41. What did they then engage to do?—To go over the Jordan with the other tribes, and assist them in driving out the inhabitants.

42. Did Moses then consent?—He did. Num. 32:20-22.

44

43. What were they to do with their families and their flocks?—Build cities and folds for their protection.

44. How many encampments did the Israelites make in passing from Egypt to Canaan?—Sixty-one.

45. What were the boundaries of Palestine?—The river of Egypt (a small stream emptying into the Mediterranean, on the southwest) and the deserts of Arabia on the south; the plains of Jordan on the east; the Lebanon ranges of mountains and the river Euphrates on the north and northeast; and the Mediterranean Sea on the west.

46. How many were appointed to divide the land among the tribes?—One prince out of every tribe.

47. Whom might an heiress of landed property marry?—Only a husband in the tribe of her father.

48. What was the object of this law?—That the several tribes might retain their own inheritance undivided.

DEUTERONOMY.
(Deuteronomy.)

1. How many chapters are there in Deuteronomy?—Thirty-four.

2. Why is the book so called?—Because it is largely a "repetition of the law."

3. By whom was it written?—By Moses.

4. Where?—In the plains of Moab.

5. When?—A little before Moses' death. Deut. 2:3.

6. Where were Moses and the children of Israel at this time?—In Moab, on the east of Jordan. Deut. 1:1, 4, 5.

7. Of what is the book a summary?—Of much of the history and the laws contained in the three foregoing books.

8. Of whom does Moses speak in Deut. 18:15-19 as "the prophet?"—Of Jesus Christ. Acts 3:20-22.

9. What beautiful ceremony does he bid them perform when they should get into the Promised Land?—To bring a basket of first fruits to the priest as a thank offering to God. Deut. 26:1-11.

10. What were the names of the two mountains on which the blessing and the curse were to be pronounced?—Gerizim and Ebal. Deut. 27:1-8, 11-13.

11. What fearful prophecy and warning did Moses utter?—Curses of pestilence, drought, war, famine, and other evils for disobedience of God's law. Deut. 28-30.

12. In what way (chapter 31) did the Lord signally set apart Joshua to the office of leader?—By appearing to him in the tabernacle in the pillar of cloud. Deut. 31:14, 15.

13. In what way did Moses preserve what he said to them?—By writing it and delivering it to the priest (Deut. 31:9), to be put in the ark of the covenant. Deut. 31:24-26.

14. What special song was he commanded to write and rehearse before them?—That contained in Deut. 32:1-43; 31:19.

15. Who assisted him in the task?—Joshua. Deut. 32:44.

16. What did the Lord command Moses to do immediately after he had finished this work?—To ascend Mount Nebo and die. Deut. 32:48-52

17. In pronouncing his dying blessing on the tribes of Israel, which did he single out for peculiar honor?—Levi and Ephraim and Manasseh.

18. What spot on earth was appointed by God to be the place of the death of Moses?—The top of Pisgah. Deut. 34:1.

19. What splendid prospect did the Lord give him ere he died?—A great part or the whole of the land of Canaan. Deut. 32:2-4.

20. In what did Moses differ from any other prophet?—In God's speaking to him (as if) face to face. Deut. 34:10.

21. How old was Moses when

45

he died?—One hundred and twenty years. Deut. 34:7.

22. What special power was manifested in the preservation of his bodily strength?—The power of God, who prolonged his life and strength.

23. Where was Moses buried?—Near the spot where he died, in a valley in the land of Moab.

24. By whom?—By God himself, or by angels commissioned for the purpose. Jude 9.

25. Has his tomb ever been found?—It has not.

26. Why was it hidden?—Perhaps that it might not become an object of idolatrous reverence.

27. In what four particulars may Moses be regarded as a type of Jesus?—As a leader, as a legislator, as a priest, and as a prophet.

JOSHUA. (Josh. 1-4.)

1. Who was Joshua?—The son of Nun, of the tribe of Ephraim.

2. What was Joshua's first commission?—To go over the Jordan. Josh. 1:2.

3. What encouragement did God give to him?—Be strong and of a good courage; be not afraid, neither be thou dismayed: for the Lord thy God is with thee withersoever thou goest. Josh. 1:9.

4. What order did Joshua make?—He directed the officers to go throughout the host, and command the people to prepare victuals.

5. Why was this done?—Because on the route they would not be able to gather manna.

6. Was manna yet their only food?—The Israelites had already subdued their enemies on the east of the Jordan, and had taken provisions such as corn, oxen, and sheep from them; and they probably joined this to the manna.

7. Where were they now?—At Shittim, on the east side of the Jordan.

8. Did the tribes who had already obtained their inheritance agree to cross the Jordan with the other tribes?—They did. Josh. 1:

16.

9. Of what is Canaan regarded as a type?—Of heaven.

10. Of what the wilderness?—Of the world.

11. Of what the river Jordan?—Of death.

12. What glorious prospect have believers in Christ?—A land of everlasting rest and happiness.

13. Did the Israelites have such a view?—No; for they were obliged to contend for the possession of the Promised Land.

14. Did they finally obtain rest?—Their rest from war was never of long duration. They drove out their enemies only by degrees, and were often subdued by them. Heb. 4:1-11.

15. Where is rest only to be found? In the Lord Jesus Christ here, and with him hereafter.

THE TAKING OF JERICHO—THE SCARLET LINE.
(Josh. 2, 5, 6.)

1. Where did the city of Jericho stand?—Near the west side of the Jordan.

2. How did Joshua endeavor to ascertain the strength of the city?—By sending two spies.

3. How were these men treated in Jericho?—They were sheltered in the house of Rahab.

4. Who was Rahab?—Probably the keeper of an inn.

5. Were women innkeepers among the ancients?—It so appears from history. See Judg. 16:1.

6. Why did the king of Jericho suspect these men?—It was told him they were spies.

7. What did the king then do?—He ordered Rahab to deliver them up. Josh. 2:3.

8. Did she obey the order?—No; she secreted them (Josh. 2:4) until the officers of the king went out of the city to search for them.

9. What promise did they make to the woman who had hid them?—To save the lives and property of her family on the taking of the

46

city. Josh. 2:12-14.

10. Did she avail herself of the token they gave?—She did. Josh. 2:17-21.

11. How did the spies escape?—When it was dark she let them down by a cord through a window in the city wall, and told them to get to the mountain lest the pursuers should overtake them. Josh. 2:22.

12. What message did they bring back to Joshua?—They said: Truly the Lord hath delivered into our hands all the land; for even all the inhabitants of the country do faint because of us. Josh. 2:24.

13. What effect had this report on the people?—They were much encouraged.

14. How did the Israelites cross the Jordan?—Early in the morning they removed from Shittim and came to Jordan. When all was ready the priests carried the ark into the river, and as soon as they touched the water the waters which came from above ceased their flow, while those below emptied into the Dead Sea.

15. When all had crossed, what did Joshua do?—He directed twelve men, one from each tribe, to carry out twelve great stones from the bed of the river and set them up in the place where they lodged, for a memorial. Joshua also piled up twelve great stones in the river, where the priests stood. When all was done he commanded the priests to come up out of Jordan; and as soon as they touched the western bank the waters of the river returned to their course.

16. Was the Jordan at that time at low water?—No; it was at flood height. Josh. 3:15.

17. Where was the first encampment in Canaan?—At Gilgal. Here the memorial stones were set up.

18. What solemn rite was renewed at Gilgal?—The rite of circumcision.

19. At what time did the Israelites encamp in Gilgal?—In time to keep the passover on the fourteenth day of the first month.

20. After the passover feast was eaten what happened?—The Israelites ate of the old corn of the land, unleavened cakes, and parched corn.

21. Did the manna now cease?—It did, on the morrow after they had eaten of the old corn.

22. What remarkable event happened on the plains of Jericho?—The appearance of a heavenly Being to Joshua.

23. Who was it that appeared to Joshua?—The Angel of the Covenant.

24. Did Joshua perceive at first who it was?—No; he merely saw an armed man.

25. How did he find it out?—By his saying he was captain of the Lord's host.

26. What directions did the Lord give him as to the taking of the city?—To march round it with the ark and blowing of trumpets, and at last with a shout. Josh. 6:3-5.

27. Did he and Israel obey the Lord?—Yes. Josh. 6:8-16, 20.

28. What was the result?—The wall fell down flat, and the city was taken and destroyed. Josh. 6: 20, 21, 24.

29. Did Rahab perish with the slain?—She was brought away safely. Josh. 6:23.

30. What was her preservation?—Her faith and the scarlet-cord token that she had been directed to use. Heb. 11:31.

31. Of what is the destruction of Jericho a type?—Of the destruction of all the enemies of God.

32. Are we interested in this?—Yes; as sinners.

33. How?—We are exposed to God's wrath, and deeply interested to know how we may be saved.

34. What does the Bible tell us must be our safeguard in the day of wrath?—Rev. 7:13, 14.

35. Can we trust that word?—He is faithful that promised. Heb. 10:23.

36. Had Rahab any reason to re-

gret her faith in the word of the spies?—No.

37. Are there many ways of escape, or only one?—There is none other name under heaven given among men, whereby we must be saved. Acts 4:12.

38. Perhaps Rahab had been scoffed at for her scarlet line; did that deter her from trusting in it?—No.

39. Should the laugh and jeer of the world hinder us from trusting to the blood of Jesus for safety?—They should not.

40. Was Rahab alone saved?—Her near relatives and her goods were saved with her. Josh. 6:22, 23.

41. Were they admitted into the congregation of Israel?—They were left without the camp. Rahab herself was married to Salmon, an ancestor of David. Matt. 1:5.

42. If we knew a place of safety should we not tell others of the same?—Yes.

43. How can we do so?—By preaching and exemplifying the truth.

ACHAN'S SIN, AND THE TAKING OF AI. (Josh. 7, 8.)

1. What special command was given to Israel at the destruction of Jericho?—To bring the silver and the gold into the treasury of the Lord. Josh. 6:18, 19.

2. Who transgressed this command?—Achan.

3. What punishment did this sin bring on all Israel?—A defeat by the men of Ai. Josh. 7.

4. How was the offender discovered?—By drawing lots under the guidance of God. Josh. 7:16-18.

5. To what honored tribe did he belong?—Judah. Josh. 7:1.

6. Did this preserve him?—No; honor and privilege often increase guilt.

7. What awful punishment was necessary to cleanse Israel from the sin Achan had brought on them?—The destruction of himself and his family and goods by ston-

ing and by fire. Josh. 7:24, 25.

8. What view of God's character does this history give us?—His hatred of sin. Our God is a consuming fire. Heb. 12:29.

9. Will the riches of the sinner avail when God brings him into judgment?—Nothing at all.

10. Can we hide our sins from God?—No. Psalm 139:1-3.

11. When Achan's sin was wiped away did God again give victory to Israel?—The city of Ai was taken and destroyed. Josh. 8:28.

12. What was done with the cattle and spoil?—The Israelites took it for a prey to themselves. Josh. 8:27.

13. Who bore the wrath of God and the punishment due to our sin?—Our Lord Jesus Christ.

14. Can God again smile on us?—Yes; in Christ Jesus, in whom he is "well pleased."

15. After the destruction of Ai what solemn act of obedience did Joshua perform?—He wrote the law upon stone and read its blessings and its curses on Mounts Gerizim and Ebal. Josh. 8:30-35.

16. What acts of worship were here performed?—An altar of whole stones was erected, and they offered upon it burnt offerings and sacrificed peace offerings. Josh. 8:31.

17. Where in the land of Canaan were those two mountains situated?—Near Samaria.

18. For what was Joshua remarkable as well as for courage?—For obedience to the will of God.

THE GIBEONITES (Josh. 9.)

1. How did the Gibeonites act when they saw the victories of the Israelites?—They sent to Joshua messengers, who pretended that the Gibeonites did not live in Canaan, so that Joshua might be at liberty to spare them.

2. Did they deceive Joshua and the elders of Israel?—Yes. Josh. 9:15.

3. How came Joshua to fail in

48

this particular?—Because he had not asked God's direction. Josh. 9:14.

4. Who is the only Person that never failed?—Christ, who knows the hearts of men.

5. Were the Gibeonites spared?—Yes.

6. Why?—Because of the league made with them, confirmed by oath. Josh. 9:16, 19.

7. Did the people approve of this league?—All the congregation murmured against the princes.

8. Was the Lord jealous when an oath was made in his name?—Yes, very. Num. 30:2.

9. What proof have we of this in the case of the Gibeonites in the after history of Israel?—2 Sam. 21:1, 2.

10. To what service were the Gibeonites appointed?—To be hewers of wood and drawers of water. Josh. 9:21.

THE BATTLE OF THE FIVE KINGS. (Josh. 10.)

1. What did the rest of the kings of Canaan do when they found that the Gibeonites had made peace with Israel?—Five of them joined in war against Gibeon.

2. To whom did the Gibeonites appeal?—To Joshua. Josh. 10:6.

3. Who fought for and with Israel?—God did. Josh. 10:10, 11.

4. What signal proofs did the Lord give of this in the battle with those kings?—Showering heavy hailstones upon their enemies, and miraculously prolonging the light of the sun and the moon upon the scene of battle and pursuit. Josh. 10:11-14.

5. Where did the five kings hide themselves?—In a cave at Makkedah.

6. What did Joshua do to secure them?—He closed the mouth of the cave with great stones and set men to watch it.

7. After the battle was over what did he do with the kings?—He hanged them on trees.

8. Where were their bodies buried?—In the cave where they had hid.

9. What other places did Joshua subdue in this campaign?—Makkedah, Libnah, Lachish, Eglon, Hebron, and Debir.

10. How extensive was the territory conquered?—It extended from Kadesh-barnea to Gaza, over all the country of Goshen, even to Gibeon.

11. Where did the host gather after these conquests?—At the camp in Gilgal.

12. Was the conquered territory parceled out among the Israelites?—Not yet.

THE FINAL BATTLE WITH THE KINGS OF CANAAN. (Josh. 11.)

1. What commandment had the Lord given relative to the destruction of the Canaanites?—Exod. 34:11-13; Deut. 7:1, 2.

2. Why did the Lord thus deal with these nations?—Their wickedness had now reached its height. Gen. 15:16.

3. How is the host that mustered against Joshua described?—As being numerous as the sand upon the seashore. Josh. 11:4.

4. What great advantage had they over Israel?—The possession of chariots and horses.

5. And yet which conquered?—The Israelites, completely. Josh. 11:8.

6. How was this?—If God be for us, who can be against us? Rom. 8:31; Psalm 118:6-9.

7. What did Joshua do with the city of Hazor?—He burnt it with fire.

8. Why Hazor in particular?—Because it was the head of all the kingdoms he had fought with.

9. Was this the last battle that Joshua fought?—No; he had a long war afterward, till he took the whole land. Josh. 11:15-23.

10. Did Joshua make peace with any of these cities?—He did not. Josh. 11:19.

49

11. Who were the Anakims?—The children of Anak.

12. Were they all exterminated? —A few were left in Gaza, Ashdod, and Gath. Josh. 11:22.

DIVIDING THE LAND, AND DEATH OF JOSHUA. (Josh. 12-24.)

1. What did Joshua begin so soon as the land had rest from war?—To divide it among the tribes.

2. Where was the tabernacle set up?—At Shiloh. Josh. 18:1.

3. In which tribe was this?—Ephraim.

4. How many men did Joshua appoint to survey the land?—Three men from each of the last seven tribes. Josh. 18:4.

5. How was it divided?—By lot before the Lord. Josh. 18:6.

6. How were their portions registered?—In a book. Josh. 18:9.

7. Describe the position of all the tribes on the map.—Asher, half-Manasseh, Ephraim, and Dan down the west coast, but Ephraim reaching to the Jordan; Naphtali, Zebulun, Issachar, Benjamin, and Judah by the west border of the sea of Chinnereth, the Jordan, and the Dead Sea; and Simeon below; half-Manasseh, Gad, and Reuben on the east borders.

8. In which tribe had Joshua his inheritance?—Ephraim.

9. Why?—Because of his own choice. Josh. 19:49, 50.

10. What portion had Caleb?—Hebron. Josh. 14:12-14.

11. Why?—Because he chose it, and Joshua confirmed his choice.

12. What was the next thing they did after dividing the land? —They appointed the cities of refuge.

13. Which tribe was it that had no portion of the land set apart for them?—Levi.

14. How were they provided for?—Forty-eight cities were assigned to them by the tribes.

15. How many tribes had their inheritance on the east of Jordan?

—Reuben, Gad, and half-Manasseh. Num. 32:33.

16. What part of these tribes passed over Jordan with their brethren?—The armed men. Josh. 1:14.

17. When did they return home to their families again?—After the end of the war and the division of the land. Josh. 22.

18. What unexpected act did they do which alarmed their brethren?—They built an altar of their own to the Lord. Josh. 22:10.

19. How did they explain it?—They built it to remind them and their children after them of their connection with the true altar. Josh. 22:26, 27.

20. Was it satisfactory?—Quite. Josh. 22:30, 33.

21. To what age had Joshua lived?—About one hundred and nine years.

22. What was the last act he performed?—He gave the elders of Israel (Josh. 23) a short history of their nation and a solemn exhortation to renew their covenant with God. Josh. 24.

23. What solemn covenant did Israel enter into with him?—That they would serve idols no more. Josh. 24:16-24.

24. Where did they make this covenant?—At Shechem. Josh. 24:1.

25. Where was Shechem?—In Ephraim, or Samaria.

26. What token of remembrance did Joshua set up there?—A stone of witness. Josh. 24:26, 27.

27. How old was Joshua when he died?—One hundred and ten years.

28. Where was he buried?—In Mount Ephraim. Josh. 24:30.

29. What other illustrious person was buried in Mount Ephraim?—Eleazar. Josh. 24:33.

30. How many kings had Moses subdued on the east of the Jordan?—Two; Sihon, king of the Amorites, and Og, king of Bashan.

31. How many did Joshua overcome on the west side?—Thirty-

one. Josh. 12:9-24.

32. Was all the land subjugated?—No. Josh. 13:1-6.

33. What celebrated prophet was slain during these wars?—Balaam. Josh. 13:22.

34. How do we count twelve tribes, since Levi was omitted?—The tribe of Joseph was divided between his two sons, Ephraim and Manasseh, Jacob having adopted them for his own. These tribes are sometimes called half-tribes.

35. What was done with the embalmed body of Joseph?—It was buried in Shechem, according to Joseph's own request before he died in Egypt. Josh. 24:32; Gen. 50:25.

36. How long did the Israelites serve the Lord?—All the days of Joshua and all the days of the elders that survived Joshua. Josh. 24:31.

THE JUDGES—BOCHIM, OR ISRAEL'S FAILURE. (Judg. 1, 2.)

1. When Joshua was dead which tribe was directed by the Lord to fight against the Canaanites?—Judah. Judg. 1:2.

2. What tribe went up with Judah?—Simeon.

3. What success did they have?—The Canaanites and Perizzites were delivered into their hands.

4. What did they do to the King Adoni-bezek?—They cut off his thumbs and his great toes, as he had himself done to seventy other kings.

5. Where did the family of Moses' father-in-law settle?—In the wilderness of Judah in the south of Arad. Judg. 1:16.

6. Did the Israelites dispossess all the Canaanites on their borders?—They did not. Judg. 1:19-36.

7. What is the meaning of the word Bochim?—"Weepers." Judg. 2:5, margin.

8. Why was the place so called?—Because the Israelites wept there.

9. What caused the weeping of Israel?—Sorrow for the sin for which an angel rebuked them. Judg. 2:1-4.

10. How had they transgressed?—By neglecting their covenant to make no league with the Canaanites.

11. Of what further sin were they guilty?—Of worshiping Baal and Ashtaroth and of forming marriage alliances with the Canaanites. Judg. 2:13; 3:6, 7.

12. What punishment was inflicted upon them?—They were delivered into the hands of their enemies. Judg. 2:14.

13. Did they repent?—They added still more to their sins.

14. Did the Lord deal mercifully with them?—Their oppression excited his pity.

15. Did the Lord deliver them?—Not until they cried unto him.

16. To whom must we look for deliverance when the sins of our hearts, like the foes in Canaan, rise against us?—To Christ our Saviour.

OTHNIEL, EHUD, SHAMGAR, DEBORAH, AND BARAK. (Judg. 3-5.)

1. Whom did the Lord first raise up as Israel's deliverer?—Othniel. Judg. 3:9.

2. To what great warrior was he related?—To Caleb, who was probably his brother.

3. How many years had the land rest?—Forty. Judg. 3:11.

4. When the children of Israel did evil again to whom did the Lord deliver them?—To Eglon, king of Moab. Judg. 3:12-14.

5. When they again repented did God hear their prayer?—Yes.

6. Whom did he raise up to save them?—Ehud, a Benjamite. Judg. 3:15.

7. What was there remarkable about him?—He was left-handed.

8. How did this bring about the king of Moab's death?—It enabled Ehud to stab him in an unexpected manner. Judg. 3:21.

51

9. What did Ehud bring from the Israelites to Eglon?—The tribute money.

10. What did he say to the king?—That he had a secret message for him.

11. Was this a pretense?—It certainly was.

12. After the king was assassinated, how did Ehud escape?—By a private door and stairway.

13. Did Israel avail themselves of his death to go against the Moabites?—Yes. Judg. 3:27, 28.

14. How many did they slay?—About ten thousand men. Judg. 3:29.

15. How long had the land rest from war?—Eighty years.

16. How long had the Israelites then been subject to Eglon?—Eighteen years.

17. Who was Israel's third deliverer?—Shamgar. Judg. 3:31.

18. What marvelous feat of strength is recorded of him?—He slew six hundred Philistines with an oxgoad.

19. Into whose hands were the Israelites next delivered for their apostasy?—Into the hands of Jabin. Judg. 4:2.

20. Where did he reign?—In Hazor.

21. Had Hazor been rebuilt?—It was probably rebuilt not long after its destruction by Joshua.

22. Why?—Because the Israelites failed to occupy and keep the site as their own.

23. Was it an important fortress?—It seems to have been, for Solomon again built it. 1 Kings 9:15.

24. How long did Jabin oppress the Israelites?—Twenty years.

25. Who was the captain of Jabin's host?—Sisera.

26. Who was judge of Israel at this time, and prophetess also?—Deborah. Judg. 4:4.

27. Who was Barak?—A leader of the tribes of Zebulun and Naphtali. Judg. 4:6, 10.

28. Which appeared to have the most courage, Deborah or Barak?—Deborah. Judg. 4:8.

29. How was Barak reproved for his faintheartedness?—By being told that the enemy's general would be given into the hands of a woman. Judg. 4:9.

30. What kind of army did the Canaanitish general muster?—Nine hundred chariots of iron formed part of it. Judg. 4:13.

31. How came it that Israel conquered such a host?—The power of God was with them. Judg. 4:14, 15.

32. Who was Jael?—The wife of Heber. Judg. 4:17.

33. From what family had Heber, Jael's husband, descended?—The Kenites and Hobab. Judg. 4:11.

34. Was that an Israelitish family?—No; the Kenites were one of the families or nations promised to Abraham's seed, but Hobab's family was settled in Israel.

35. Was this why Sisera took shelter in their tent?—He took shelter with them because they were at peace with Jabin his master. Judg. 4:17.

36. Which side of the battle did Heber favor?—That of the Israelites. Judg. 4:11.

37. What proof did his wife give of this?—She killed Sisera. Judg. 4:21.

38. Can we justify this assassination?—We cannot.

39. Which side did the Lord take?—The Israelites. Judg 4:14, 15, 22.

40. Who delivered Sisera into Jael's hand?—The Lord himself. Judg. 4:9.

41. Who helps us if we desire to conquer our evil passions?—The grace of God is sufficient for us.

42. To what evil in our hearts can we compare Sisera with his nine hundred chariots of iron?—To our chief evil passion or temptation.

43. To whom did Deborah and Barak give the glory of the victory in their beautiful song?—To God.

Judg. 5:2.

44. What fearful curse did they pronounce on those who would not assist in this battle?—Read Judg. 5:23.

45. And what will be our condemnation if we are indifferent to those momentous concerns?—We shall suffer with the enemies of God.

46. After this victory how long did the land have rest?—Forty years. Judg. 5:31.

GIDEON. (Judg. 6-8.)

1. How came it, after this, that Israel got into trouble again?—They did evil in the sight of the Lord. Judg. 6:1.

2. Whom did the Lord permit to be their scourge at this time?—The Midianites and the Amalekites. Judg. 6:3.

3. To what miserable plight were the Israelites reduced?—They were left without food. Judg. 6:4.

4. On which side of Israel did these two nations lie?—The Midianites on the southeast, and the Amalekites on the southwest.

5. Where was Gaza?—In the land of the Philistines.

6. What means did the children of Israel at last use to free themselves from their great affliction?—They cried unto the Lord. Judg. 6:7.

7. Did the Lord hear them?—He sent a prophet to them, and afterward a deliverer, Gideon. Judg. 6:7-12.

8. Who was Gideon, and of what tribe and family?—A warrior, of the tribe of Manasseh, and family of the Abiezrites.

9. Who appeared to him?—An angel (Judg. 6:11), or rather the Angel of the Covenant—the Son of God. Judg. 6:14.

10. What was he doing?—Threshing wheat.

11. Did he at first know who addressed him?—No. Judg. 6:13, 17.

12. How did he find it out?—By

the angel's causing fire out of the rock to consume the food set before him (Judg. 6:21), and also by the language he used. Judg. 6:16.

13. What were his feelings?—Those of deep humility and conscious sinfulness. Judg. 6:22.

14. Had he any cause for fear?—Not if he were conscious of his integrity.

15. What makes man in general afraid of God?—The consciousness of unrepented sin. Gen. 3:9, 10.

16. What has the Lord provided to remove our fear?—The accepted sacrifice of Christ.

17. Who has power to speak "peace" to the soul?—Christ alone.

18. What was Gideon's first act of faith?—To throw down the altar of Baal. Judg. 6:25-30.

19. Was he put to death for fulfilling God's will?—No. Judg. 6:31, 32.

20. How was his own father's heart influenced by the act?—He took his son's part.

21. How does God reward those who honor his word?—He says, "Them that honor me I will honor."

22. What name of honor did Gideon get for this act?—Jerubbaal, or, "let Baal plead" against him. Judg. 6:32.

23. Describe the army that was at this time gathered against Israel.—The Midianites, Amalekites, and other eastern nations. Judg. 6:33.

24. What mighty power rested on Gideon at this time?—The Spirit of the Lord. Judg. 6:34.

25. Was he entirely without fear?—No; for he asked God to give him a private token of his power. Judg. 6:36-40.

26. How did he prove that God was a hearer and answerer of prayer?—By the sign of the wet fleece on the dry ground, and of the dry fleece on the wet ground.

27. Does God hear and answer prayer now?—The effectual fervent prayer of a righteous man availeth

53

much. James 5:16.

28. When Gideon blew his trumpet, how many came after him?—Thirty-two thousand. Judg. 6:34; 7:3.

29. Did the Lord intend to use so many to destroy the enemy?—No, not even ten thousand.

30. What sign did the Lord give to Gideon whereby he should know how many and which he had chosen?—Their two different ways of drinking water on a particular occasion. Judg. 7:4, 5.

31. How many remained with Gideon after this selection?—Three hundred men.

32. How was this a test of their fitness?—It showed their tolerance of thirst, and their watchfulness so as not to be surprised by the enemy.

33. Must this not have been a great trial to Gideon's faith?—No doubt it was. 1 Peter 1:7.

34. Did it fail?—No; for God strengthened it. Judg. 7:7, 9, 14; Heb. 11:32-34.

35. What did Gideon and his servant hear when they went down at night to spy the camp of the Midianites?—A dream told by one of the soldiers. Judg. 7:13, 14.

36. What effect had this man's dream on Gideon?—He praised God, and immediately prepared his men. Judg. 7:15, 16.

37. What effect did it have on his own people?—The same as on Gideon himself. Judg. 7:14, 20.

38. Is the Lord ever at a loss for means to effect his purpose?—Never.

39. What plan was adopted to surprise the enemy?—The blowing of trumpets and exposing a line of lights all around the enemy's camp in the middle of the night. Judg. 7:16-20.

40. Did it answer?—Yes; it was of God.

41. In what way?—The Lord set every man's sword against his fellow, even throughout the whole host. Judg. 7:22.

42. Does God always work by means?—He does.

43. Who tells us that he is "the light of the world?"—Jesus Christ, in John 8:12.

44. Whom does God appoint to hold up that light?—His ministers especially, by their preaching and their example.

45. Are not all Christians charged to do it?—They are. Matt. 5:14.

46. Whose mighty power is it that must accompany the word for, it to be effectual?—The Spirit of truth. John 16:13.

47. On whom must we depend if we are to overcome and conquer our spiritual foes?—On the same almighty power.

48. Did Gideon offer sacrifices to God, himself, without a priest? —He did.

49. Was this against the law?—It was an exceptional sacrifice, ordered by God himself. Judg. 6:26.

50. Were sacrifices like this common?—They were not; but a number of like instances are recorded in the Scriptures.

51. Was Gideon conqueror?—Yes, completely. Judg. 7:22-25.

52. Shall we be?—We certainly shall. Rom. 8:31.

53. How was Gideon treated after this victory by his fellowcountrymen when he was faint and weary?—They refused food to him and his men. Judg. 8:4-6.

54. Did they afterward desire to honor him?—They wished him to be their king. Judg. 8:22.

55. Would he accept their kingly office?—He declined it, as God had not yet appointed that form of government for Israel. Judg. 8:23.

56. Yet what did he desire of them?—The golden earrings taken from their enemies. Judg. 8:24-26.

57. What effect did this have on his family?—Gideon made the earrings into an ephod, which brought temptation and punishment upon his family. Judg. 8:27.

ABIMELECH. (Judg. 9.)

1. Who was Abimelech?—A son

54

of Gideon by a concubine. Judg. 9:1.

2. Was his course an honorable one, like that of his father?—No; he basely plotted to be made king. Judg. 9:2.

3. Of what awful crime was he guilty?—He slew his brethren. Judg. 9:5.

4. Did any escape?—Jotham alone.

5. What fable did Jotham utter? —That of the trees choosing a king. Judg. 9:8-15.

6. Can you explain the meaning of this fable as it respects Abimelech?—The bramble represents the character and end of Abimelech. Judg. 9:51-57.

7. Of what are the olive, vine, and fig tree types?—Of useful, amiable, wise, and humble-minded men.

8. How was it fulfilled?—In the foolish choice of Abimelech by the Shechemites, in the violent quarrels between them, and the destruction of both. Judg. 9:15, 20, 23, 49, 52, 54.

9. Where did all this shameful scene take place?—At Shechem.

10. What remarkable events had rendered this spot peculiarly hallowed?—The visit of Abraham on reaching Canaan, the reading of the law (Josh. 9), and the renewal of the covenant. Josh. 24.

11. How did it stand with regard to the two mountains of blessing and cursing spoken of in Deut. 27 and in Josh. 8?—In a narrow plain between them.

12. How near was it to Shiloh, where the tabernacle was pitched? —About twenty miles.

13. Of what was an idol temple built on this spot a proof?—That the Israelites had not yet entirely destroyed idolatry. Judg. 9:4-6.

14. Has Jotham's fable any lesson for us?—Yes; that the men who seek office are often the least worthy of it.

15. Who in Scripture are compared to fruit trees?—God's own people. Psalm 1:3; 92:12-14.

16. Who are represented by the bramble?—Vain and worthless men.

17. What is expected of fruit trees?—That they should bring forth fruit.

18. What is the bramble good for?—To be burned. Isa. 30:12; 2 Sam. 23:6, 7; Eccles. 7:6.

19. How is the hypocrite known from the true Christian?—Ye shall know them by their fruits. Matt. 7:16.

20. What should our prayer be? —Search me, O God, and know my heart. Psalm 139:23.

TOLA, JAIR, JEPHTHAH, IBZAN, ELON, AND ABDON.
(Judg. 10-12.)

1. What was the name of the next judge of Israel?—Tola. Judg. 10:1.

2. How long did he judge Israel?—Twenty-three years.

3. Who succeeded him?—Jair.

4. How is his family described? —As riding on ass colts as deputy judges. Judg. 5:10; 10:4.

5. From whom did he get this inheritance?—The children of Machir the son of Manasseh went to Gilead and took it and dispossessed the Amorite which was in it. And Moses gave Gilead unto Machir the son of Manasseh; and he dwelt therein. And Jair the son of Manasseh went and took the small towns thereof, and called them Haboth-jair. Num. 32:39-41.

6. How long did he judge Israel?—Twenty-two years.

7. Did the land have peace during the rule of these two judges? —No mention is made of any hostile incursions.

8. Did the Israelites continue to worship God?—They lapsed into idolatry.

9. How many false gods are enumerated which Israel at this time worshiped?—Baalim and Ashtaroth and the gods of five nations besides. Judg. 10:6.

10. What had God commanded Israel with respect to this awful

sin?—Neither shall ye set up any image of stone in your land. See Exod. 20:3-5; Lev. 26:1.

11. How did he punish them?—By delivering them into the hands of the Philistines and Ammonites for eighteen years. Judg. 10:7, 8.

12. When they prayed to the Lord did he heed them?—No. Josh. 10:10-13.

13. Did he at once deliver them?—He said, Go and cry unto the gods which ye have chosen: let them deliver you. Judg. 10:14.

14. Did this convince them of their sin?—Yes; they confessed their guilt. Judg. 10:15.

15. When God had convinced them of their sin did they repent?—Yes.

16. Was their repentance genuine?—Yes, for they put away the strange gods from among them, and served the Lord.

17. How did the Lord feel for them?—His soul was grieved for their misery.

18. What did the Ammonites do when the Israelites revolted?—They encamped in Gilead.

19. Where did the Israelites assemble?—They encamped in Mizpeh.

20. Did they have a leader to direct the armies?—They had not.

21. Who was Jephthah?—A great warrior of Gilead. Judg. 11:1.

22. On which side of the land of Israel was the land of the Ammonites?—On the east.

23. Where was Gilead?—In the neighboring tribe of Gad.

24. Why did the men of Gilead choose Jephthah to be their captain?—Because he was likely to lead them to victory.

25. On what conditions did Jephthah accept the office?—That he should be their head on his return. Judg. 11:9.

26. What vow did Jephthah make before he went to battle?—That if he were victorious whoever came forth first out of his house to meet him on his return should be

the Lord's, and that he would offer it to the Lord a burnt offering besides. Judg. 11:30, 31.

27. Who came out first to meet him?—His daughter and only child. Judg. 11:34.

28. What did Jephthah feel and say when he saw his only child?—He was deeply distressed, and told her of his vow. Judg. 11:35.

29. What was her answer?—That as God had given him victory he must do to her according to his vow. Judg. 11:36.

30. What law of God was there to regulate what Jephthah said under these circumstances?—That the subject of the vow might be redeemed by a payment in money. Lev. 27:2-5.

31. What difference was there between a "vow" and a "devoted thing?"—A thing devoted by som more solemn consecration than a vow could not be redeemed.

32. For how much did Jephthah redeem his daughter if he did not slay her for an offering?—About $5 or $15, according to her age.

33. What reason have we to think that he redeemed her?—Because her friends went every year to lament her separation from them, or to talk with her. Judg. 11:40, margin.

34. Why was it a great grief for any woman in Israel to be childless?—Because she might be the foremother of the Messiah. Gen. 3:15.

35. Did Jephthah value the honor which he had sought, of being the head of his tribe, after this mournful event?—Probably not, as it had cost him the society of his only child.

36. Can any honor or pleasure in this world give satisfaction in itself?—No; nothing in the world that is passing away.

37. What proof did Jephthah give of his knowledge of the Scripture history when he met the king of Ammon before the battle?—He told him how it was that the Israelites became possessed

of the land that the king was unlawfully claiming from them. Judg. 11:12-28.

38. Where must our strength lie when we go against our spiritual foes?—In the Lord and the power of his might. Eph. 6:10.

39. What weapons did the Lord Jesus Christ use when he met Satan?—The sword of the Spirit, which is the word of God. Eph. 6:17.

40. What is "the word of God" called in Heb. 4:12?—Quick (or living) and powerful, and sharper than any two-edged sword.

41. By what shall we be judged at the last day?—The word that Christ has spoken.

42. Why were the men of Ephraim offended at Jephthah?—Because they were not called to go with Jephthah to the fight against Ammon. Judg. 12:1.

43. What did they threaten to do unto him?—To burn his house with fire.

44. What did Jephthah do?—He gathered the fighting men of Gilead, and fought with Ephraim.

45. What method did Jephthah's men take at the passages of Jordan to discover the Ephraimites?—They required them to say "Shibboleth;" and if they pronounced it "Sibboleth" they slew them.

46. How many of them were slain?—Forty-two thousand.

47. How long did Jephthah judge Israel?—Sixty years.

48. Who judged Israel after Jephthah?—Ibzan.

49. For how long?—Seven years.

50. Who succeeded Ibzan?—Elon.

51. How long did he judge Israel?—Ten years.

52. Who followed Elon?—Abdon.

53. How many sons and nephews had he?—Seventy sons and nephews or grandsons.

54. What distinguished them from others?—They rode on ass colts.

55. Was a large family considered a great honor in Israel?—Yes.

56. What higher honor had Jephthah than even being the ancestor of the Messiah?—The honor of being named in the roll of heroes and martyrs. Heb. 11:32.

SAMSON. (Judg. 13-17.)

1. Into whose hands did the Lord next deliver Israel for their sins?—The Philistines. Judg. 13:1.

2. For how long?—Forty years.

3. Who was Samson?—One of the tribe of Dan. Judg. 13:1.

4. What remarkable circumstance took place before his birth?—The angel of the Lord appeared to his mother. Judg. 13:2-5.

5. What was the name of Samson's father?—Manoah. Judg. 13:2.

6. Did he have doubts lest his wife had been mistaken?—Perhaps so. Judg. 13:8.

7. Did the angel appear a second time?—He did.

8. Did he alter anything he had said before?—No.

9. What should this teach us?—This truth: I am the Lord, I change not. Mal. 3:6.

10. Which seemed to have the greater faith, Manoah or his wife?—His wife.

11. How do you prove this?—By Judg. 13:22, 23.

12. How did Manoah and his wife know that their visitor was an angel?—By the words he spoke, and by his ascending in the flame. Judg. 13:18-20.

13. Did Manoah offer a sacrifice to God?—He offered a kid on an altar.

14. Did the angel ever appear to them again after the birth of Samson?—No.

15. What was there remarkable about Samson?—His very great strength.

16. What was a Nazarite?—A person "separated unto the Lord." Num. 6:2-21.

17. What special gift rested on

Samson?—The Spirit of the Lord. Judg. 13:25; 14:6.

18. What exploit did Samson perform at the vineyards of Timnath?—He rent a young lion as he would a kid.

19. Did he tell his parents of this?—No.

20. Why did he go to Timnath? —To contract a marriage with a young Philistine woman.

21. Did his parents approve of this marriage?—They did not.

22. When he returned to Timnath for his bride what did he find on the way?—The dried carcass of the lion, with a swarm of bees and honey in it.

23. What riddle did he put forth at the marriage feast?—Out of the eater came forth meat, and out of the strong came forth sweetness.

24. What reward did Samson promise the Philistines if they solved the riddle?—Thirty sheets and thirty changes of raiment.

25. What gifts did he demand if they could not tell it?—The same as he offered them.

26. Could they solve the riddle? —They could not during the seven days of the feast.

27. What plan did they devise to find the answer?—They threatened to burn the bride and her father's house with fire if she did not entice it out of her husband.

28. Did she succeed?—She did.

29. What then happened?—She told the Philistines, and they answered Samson.

30. What did Samson say?—If ye had not plowed with my heifer ye had not found out my riddle.

31. What means did Samson take to pay his forfeit?—He slew thirty of the Philistines, and took their garments, and so paid the reward he had offered.

32. Was Samson angry with the Philistines for their conduct?—He was so angry that he went back to his father's house.

33. Did his wife go with him? —No.

34. How did Samson avenge himself on the Philistines when he found his wife was given to another?—He caught three hundred jackals, and tied them together in couples, tail to tail, with firebrands in the midst. These he set there on fire, and then turned the jackals loose among the wheat fields of the Philistines. Judg. 15:3-5.

35. What did the Philistines do when they discovered this?—They burned his wife and her father with fire. Judg. 15:6.

36. What did Samson then do to the Philistines?—He smote them hip and thigh with a great slaughter.

37. How did the men of Judah treat Samson?—They came to the rock Etam to find him and deliver him to the Philistines.

38. When Samson was brought to the Philistines what did he do? —He broke his bonds asunder, and seizing the new jawbone of an ass leaped upon the Philistines and killed a thousand of them before his fury was assuaged.

39. How did he obtain water to quench his thirst?—He prayed to God for help. God then smote a hollow place in the ridge, and water flowed out from it. Judg. 15:19.

40. How did Samson escape from the Philistines at Gaza?—He arose at midnight and took the doors of the gate of the city and the two posts, and carried them up to the top of a hill near Hebron. Judg. 16:1-3.

41. What at last procured Samson's ruin?—He fell in love with a Philistine woman of Sorek, named Delilah; and when she made him sleep on her lap she called for a man and caused him to shave off the locks of Samson's hair. After this was done she began to afflict him, and his strength went from him.

42. Did Samson's strength lie in his hair?—No.

43. In what?—In God. So long as he remained faithful to his vows as a Nazarite and did not have his

hair cut God was with him.

44. What was done to Samson?—His eyes were put out, and he was made to turn a millstone.

45. How did the Philistines celebrate their victory over Samson?—They made a great feast in the temple of their god Dagon, and offered sacrifices. Then they called for Samson to make sport for them.

46. What did Samson do to his enemies at this time?—He took hold of the two pillars upon which the house stood, one with his right hand and one with his left. Then he said, "Let me die with the Philistines;" and bowing himself he pulled the pillars out of their place, and the house fell upon all the lords and people of the Philistines, killing more than he had killed during his life. He also perished at the same time.

47. How long did Samson judge Israel?—Twenty years.

THE STORY OF MICAH, AND THE CLOSE OF THE JUDGES. (Judg. 17-21.)

1. Who was Micah?—A resident of Mount Ephraim.

2. When a man does "that which is right in his own eyes" what is he sure to do?—Wrong. Prov. 16: 25; Judg. 17:6.

3. What standard has God given us by which we may judge ourselves?—His holy word.

4. What proof do Micah and his mother give that by doing "that which was right in their own eyes" they did wrong?—They both worshiped God with idolatrous rites, though perhaps sincerely, and Micah committed theft. Judg. 17: 2, 3, 5.

5. Which commandments of God's law did Micah break?—The second and the eighth.

6. Who acted as priest for Micah?—One of his sons.

7. Did Micah seem to be satisfied with this arrangement?—No; for he afterward hired a Levite to become a priest for him.

8. Was it wrong to take a Levite for his priest?—The duties of the Levites were at the tabernacle in Shiloh; and none of them could be priests but those called by God.

9. Were Micah and his mother actual idolaters?—They certainly worshiped Jehovah; because Micah said, "Now I know that Jehovah will do me good, seeing I have a Levite for my priest."

10. How did the Danites enlarge their inheritance?—They captured Laish, naming the city Dan, after their father.

11. Where was Dan?—In the extreme north of Palestine.

12. How did the Danites treat Micah?—They persuaded his priest to go with them; they also took the religious symbols and sacred furniture of Micah.

13. What were these?—A carved and molten image, an ephod, and teraphim.

14. What did the Danites do with Micah's graven image?—They set it up as the center of their tribal worship.

15. In what respect did their worship differ from that introduced by King Jeroboam?—In none, perhaps, except that it was more limited.

16. Were the Danites excusable in introducing this mode of worship?—They were guilty of a flagrant violation of the first commandment.

17. Did God approve of this worship?—No.

18. How long was Micah's image the center of this worship?—Until the ark was captured by the Philistines. Judg. 18:31.

19. Have we the same law as the Danites had to be our guide?—The same law, and the teaching of the prophets of our Lord, and of his apostles besides.

20. To what is the word of God compared in Heb. 4:12?—To a "two-edged sword," so thoroughly does it pierce our hearts and expose our sin.

21. How shall we be judged at the last day?—According to our

59

deeds. Rom. 2:6.

22. Is the Scripture our appointed rule, and is it sufficient?—Yes; see 2 Tim. 3:16, 17.

23. What will be our punishment if we neglect it?—Everlasting destruction from the presence of the Lord, and from the glory of his power. 2 Thess. 1:9.

THE BENJAMITES' WICKEDNESS. (Judg. 19-22.)

1. Where did the Levite lodge who was returning with his concubine from Bethlehem?—At the house of an old man. Judg. 19:16-21.

2. What became of his concubine?—She was so badly abused by a crowd of wicked men that came to assault her husband that she died. Judg. 19:27.

3. What did her husband do after she was dead?—He took her body to his home, divided it into twelve parts, and sent them into all the coasts of Israel. The body thus divided was received with horror, and all that saw it said that never was such a deed done since the day when the children of Israel came out of Egypt; and they assembled before the Lord at Mizpeh, where the woman's husband related the whole story of his treatment. Judg. 19:29; 20:1-6.

4. Did the Israelites prepare to war with the Benjamites?—They did.

5. Of how many did the army of the Israelites consist?—Four hundred thousand.

6. Would the Benjamites surrender the men who had committed the wickedness?—They would not. Judg. 20:13.

7. How many men were in the army of Benjamin?—Twenty-six thousand.

8. What was remarkable with respect to seven hundred of them? —They were all left-handed; every one could sling stones at a hair and not miss. Judg. 20:17.

9. What was the result of the first battle?—Twenty-two thousand of the Israelites were slain.

10. How were the children of Israel affected with this defeat? —They wept before the Lord, and asked counsel of the Lord, who directed them to make another attack.

11. What was the result of the second battle?—Eighteen thousand Israelites perished in the battle.

12. Why were they thus defeated?—Probably because they went out to battle trusting in their own strength and not in the Almighty.

13. What did the Israelites then do?—They wept and fasted and offered burnt offerings and peace offerings before the Lord; and inquired again of the Lord, who now assured them of the victory.

14. What was the result of the third battle?—All the men of Benjamin were slain except six hundred.

15. How did the Israelites treat the people of Benjamin who were not in the army?—They smote them with the edge of the sword. Judg. 20:48.

16. What oath had the Israelites taken with respect to Benjamin?—That none of them would give his daughter to Benjamin for a wife.

17. How did they supply wives for four hundred of them?—They smote the inhabitants of Jabeshgilead, but spared four hundred young women for the Benjamites. These were brought to the camp in Shiloh; and then they sent to the rock Rimmon and concluded a peace with the Benjamites and gave them the captive maidens for wives.

18. How were the remaining two hundred supplied?—They allowed the Benjamites to capture the young maids that came out to dance at the grape vintage in Shiloh, when the feast of ingathering was celebrated.

NAOMI AND RUTH. (Ruth.)

1. Who was Elimelech?—A man of Beth-lehem-judah. Ruth 1:1, 2.

2. What was the name of his wife?—Naomi.

3. What were the names of his two sons?—Mahlon and Chilion.

4. To what country did they remove?—To the country of Moab.

5. Why did they remove?—Because of a famine in their own land.

6. At what time did they live? —In the days of the judges. Ruth 1:1.

7. Whom did the sons marry?— Orpah and Ruth, women of Moab. Ruth 1:4.

8. Did they prosper and have long life?—Both the father and the two sons soon died. Ruth 1:5.

9. What became of Naomi after the death of her husband and sons?—She returned to Judah. Ruth 1:6, 7.

10. What difference was there in the behavior of her daughters-in-law toward her?—Both were distressed at the idea of parting with her, and said they would go with her; but only Ruth went.

11. Did God accept this stranger who determined to forsake her people and her gods and trust in him?—He did, and showed her much favor.

12. And is God the same now as he was then?—Yes; he receives all who receive Christ.

13. What is the meaning of the name Naomi?—"Pleasant." Ruth 1:20, margin.

14. To what name did Naomi wish hers changed, and why?—To Mara, or "bitter," because of the sorrows she had suffered.

15. When did they return?—In the beginning of the barley harvest.

16. What rich and noble kinsman of her husband had Naomi in her native place?—Boaz. Ruth 2:1.

17. In whose field did Ruth happen to glean?—In the field of Boaz. Ruth 2:2.

18. What notice did Boaz take of Ruth?—He told her to glean his fields until the end of harvest, and gave orders for her refreshment and protection, and for a plentiful gleaning. Ruth. 2:4-17, 21.

19. What description can you give of Boaz, besides that he was rich and noble?—He was a kind-hearted and good man, who honored God. Ruth 2:8-12.

20. What effect did his kindness have on Naomi when she heard it?—She blessed God for his goodness, and told Ruth how to claim Boaz as her kinsman in the manner which the custom of the country allowed. Ruth 2:19, 20; 3:1-4.

21. Did Ruth do as her mother-in-law bade her?—She did. Ruth 2:5-7.

22. What did this prove?—That she knew the privileges of filial obedience.

23. Did Boaz answer the high expectation that Naomi had of him?—Yes; he behaved both well and kindly to his virtuous relative, and promised to do a kinsman's duty to her according to the law. Ruth 2:8-17.

24. Was he the nearest relative that Naomi had?—He was not. Ruth 2:12; 4:1.

25. On whom did the duty of kinsman or redeemer fall?—On the brother of the deceased husband. Deut. 25:5-10.

26. Might any other kinsman act as redeemer?—Yes, the next nearest kinsman might perform this duty.

27. Why was this custom established?—To perpetuate the name and inheritance of the deceased husband.

28. Was the law compulsory?— It was not; the nearest kinsman might refuse.

29. What was the penalty for refusal?—Contumelious treatment and a dishonored name. Deut. 25:5-10.

30. Did the nearest kinsman perform his duty to Naomi?—No; he declined doing it. Ruth 4:1-6.

31. What was the custom in such cases?—For the person who

gave up his right to hand his shoe as a token of such giving up to the person who took his place. Ruth 4:7.

32. Who stepped in and took his place?—Boaz. Ruth 4:9, 10.

33. Was marriage with a foreign woman sanctioned by the law?— Ruth had become a proselyte to the Hebrew faith, and the marriage was allowable. See Deut. 21:10-13.

34. How do we know that she was a proselyte?—She had already confessed to her mother-in-law, "Thy people shall be my people, and thy God my God." Ruth 1:16.

35. What blessing did the elders of Israel pronounce upon Ruth when she became the wife of Boaz?—They prayed that God would make her like Rachel and like Leah, which two did build the house of Israel.

36. What was the name of the son whom God gave to Ruth?— Obed. Ruth 4:17.

37. What were the names of his son and of his grandson?—Jesse and David.

38. What relation, then, was Ruth to David?—Great-grandmother.

39. Of what glorious Person was Ruth thus the ancestress?—Of Christ.

40. What is the meaning of the name Boaz?—"Strength" or "Swiftness."

ELI AND SAMUEL. (1 Sam. 1-3.)

1. Who was Eli?—The high priest. 1 Sam. 1:9.

2. By whom was the priesthood established?—By God himself.

3. Who was the first high priest? —Aaron.

4. Who ought to have succeeded him in the high priesthood?—His eldest son, Nadab. Lev. 10:1.

5. Which of Aaron's sons became high priest at his father's death?—Eleazar.

6. Why was not one of his elder brothers, Nadab or Abihu, ap-

pointed?—Both had perished because of their disobedience to God's law. Lev. 10:2.

7. From whom had Eli descended?—From Ithamar, Aaron's younger son.

8. Did his sons walk in the way of their father, Eli?—No; they were very wicked. 1 Sam. 2:12-17.

9. What sin brought upon Eli God's anger?—Only mildly reproving his wicked sons when he should have restrained them. 1 Sam. 2:23, 24; 3:13, 14.

10. Who was Elkanah?—An Ephrathite of Mount Ephraim, a Levite. 1 Sam. 1:1; 1 Chron. 6:23.

11. What were the names of his wives?—Hannah and Peninnah.

12. Which did he love the more? —Hannah. 1 Sam. 1:5.

13. What great trial had Hannah?—Not having any child. 1 Sam. 1:10, 11.

14. To whom did she tell her sorrow?—To God.

15. Where was the tabernacle for worship at this time?—In Shiloh.

16. What opinion did Eli form of Hannah?—That she was drunken. 1 Sam. 1:13.

17. When he found that he was mistaken what did he say?—See 1 Sam. 1:17.

18. Did this comfort Hannah's heart?—Her countenance was no more sad, and a son was born to her. 1 Sam. 1:18, 20.

19. What name did she give him?—Samuel.

20. What is the meaning of that name?—"Asked of God."

21. Why did she not go up with her husband to worship the next year?—She preferred waiting until her child was old enough to remain altogether in the house of the Lord to be his servant, according to her vow. 1 Sam. 1:11, 22.

22. By whose command used the children of Israel to go up to Shiloh to worship?—By God's command.

23. How many times a year

62

were all the men to appear before the Lord?—Three times. Exod. 23:17.

24. Which feast must this have been when the women met as well?—The passover, to which women sometimes went.

25. At what time of the year was the feast held?—About the end of March or beginning of April.

26. Did Hannah do with the child as she had promised?—She did. 1 Sam. 1:24-28.

27. How old was he when his mother dedicated him to the Lord?—He "was young," perhaps six years old. 1 Sam. 1:24, margin.

28. Why was it wrong of Eli's sons to take the part of the sacrifice they liked?—Their impiety consisted in taking it before any of it was offered to God, thus preferring themselves to God.

29. Which part had God appointed for the priest's use?—The breast and the right shoulder. Lev. 7:31-34.

30. What had God commanded relative to the fat of his sacrifices?—Read Lev. 3:14-17.

31. What condemnation did Eli's sons bring on themselves by eating the fat of the sacrifices?—That of being cut off from God's people. Lev. 7:25.

32. Did the Lord send any messenger to warn Eli of the sin his sons were committing?—He sent a prophet. 1 Sam. 2:27-36.

33. Is there any rule by which we may know if we are doing the will of God or not?—God's word. Psalm 119:105.

34. Did Eli regard this awful message?—Not sufficiently, as another denunciation was made to him some years afterward. 1 Sam. 2:25.

35. Who called the child Samuel when he had lain down to sleep?—The Lord.

36. How often was Samuel called?—Three times.

37. Whom did he suppose to have called him?—Eli.

38. What instructions did Eli give him?—To answer, if the call was repeated, "Speak, Lord, for thy servant heareth."

39. How old was Samuel when this occurred?—About twelve, but some think he was much older.

40. Had Eli instructed Samuel in the knowledge of God before this time?—Probably, but Samuel had no experience yet of God's special way of making himself and his word or will known to his prophets. 1 Sam. 3:7.

41. Are there any children now who, though often seen in God's house, yet know him not?—Doubtless there are many.

42. How early may children give their hearts to God?—Just as soon as they learn the difference between right and wrong.

43. When God called to Samuel the fourth time what did he answer?—Speak, for thy servant heareth. 1 Sam. 3:10.

44. What solemn message did th Lord give Samuel concerning Eli's house?—That he would punish it forever. 1 Sam. 3:11-14.

45. Did Samuel inform Eli?—He feared to tell Eli; but, being urged by the aged priest, he told him every whit.

46. How did Eli receive the message?—He answered, "It is the Lord; let him do what seemeth him good."

47. Did the Lord continue to manifest himself to Samuel rather than to Eli?—He did. 1 Sam. 3:19-21.

48. What did this show?—That God honors those who honor him. 1 Sam. 2:30.

THE TAKING OF THE ARK.
(1 Sam. 4-7.)

1. Who were Israel's greatest enemies at this time?—The Philistines.

2. What sinful act did Israel resort to when they found themselves smitten before the enemy?—They brought the ark from its place at Shiloh. 1 Sam. 4:3-5.

3. What effect did it have on the

Philistines?—They were afraid at first, but roused each other to a great effort. 1 Sam. 4:7-9.

4. Of what was this a proof?—That God was not with Israel, though the ark was.

5. What was the result of the battle?—The Israelites were defeated with a very great slaughter, thirty thousand of them being slain. 1 Sam. 4:10.

6. What was the fate of the ark and of those who carried it?—The ark was taken, and Eli's sons were slain. 1 Sam. 4:11.

7. How did Eli bear the tidings?—He fell backward off his seat, and his neck was broken. 1 Sam. 4:18.

8. How old was Eli at that time?—Ninety-eight years.

9. How long had he judged Israel?—Forty years.

10. What sorrowful event happened to the wife of Phinehas?—She died in childbirth. 1 Sam. 4:19-22.

11. What name did she give her son ere she died?—Ichabod.

12. What is the meaning of that name?—"Where is the glory?"

13. Why did she choose it?—Because the glory had departed from Israel, the ark being taken.

14. What did the Philistines do with the ark?—They set it in the house of Dagon at Ashdod beside their idol Dagon. 1 Sam. 5:1, 2.

15. How was Dagon represented?—It had the head and trunk of a human being, but all the rest of the body was a fish.

16. Why was the ark placed in the temple of Dagon?—It was customary in ancient times to dedicate spoils taken from the enemy to the gods.

17. What happened to their idol?—It fell on its face before the ark. 1 Sam. 5:3, 4.

18. Did this convince them of the sin of idolatry?—Not at all.

19. Whose office is it to open our minds to receive the truth?—That of the Holy Spirit.

20. Had they not full opportunity, living with the land of Israel, to know about the true God?—Yes.

21. After this overthrow of Dagon to what place was the ark taken?—To Gath.

22. Did it long remain there?—No; it was carried to Ekron.

23. What calamities did God's presence bring on his enemies?—A painful disease and a plague of mice, and deadly destruction besides. 1 Sam. 5:6, 9, 11, 12; 6:4, 5.

24. What did they resolve to do?—To send back the ark with a trespass offering. 1 Sam. 6:2, 3.

25. What test did they employ to ascertain if indeed the God of Israel had brought on them all these miseries?—They yoked to a new cart that carried the ark two cows, to see if they would go to the land of Israel without their calves. 1 Sam. 6:7-12.

26. In what did the trespass offering consist?—Five golden images of mice, and five golden figures representing the plague.

27. Who had power over the instincts of these kine in making them go opposite to their natural feelings?—God alone.

28. How was the ark received?—With joy and a sacrifice of thanksgiving to God. 1 Sam. 6:13-15.

29. Of what act of impiety were the men of Beth-shemesh guilty?—Of looking into the ark. 1 Sam. 6:19.

30. Why was this act of theirs inexcusable?—It was forbidden by the law. Num. 4:20.

31. Where was the ark taken?—It was taken to Kirjath-jearim. 1 Sam. 7:1.

32. Why was it not sent to Shiloh, where it had been before?—Shiloh had probably been destroyed by the Philistines.

33. How long did it remain there?—Twenty years, until the repentance of Israel. 1 Sam. 7:2.

34. Who afterward removed it, and where did it go?—David removed it to Mount Zion. 2 Sam.

6:2-17.

35. Did Israel repent of their sins?—They did at the call of Samuel. 1 Sam. 7:3-6.

36. To whom did they apply?—To Samuel, to pray for their delivery from the Philistines. 1 Sam. 7:8.

37. What did he do for them?—He offered a sacrifice and cried unto the Lord. 1 Sam. 7:9.

38. What proof did the Lord give that he accepted their sacrifice and heard their prayer?—He caused a great thunderstorm and a defeat of the Philistines. 1 Sam. 7:10.

39. Of what use could the offering of the lamb be to them?—It typified or referred to Jesus, "the Lamb of God, which taketh away the sin of the world." John 1:29.

40. Is Samuel mentioned among those who had faith in Him who was to come?—Yes, in Heb. 11:32.

41. What memorial did Samuel set up in remembrance of this delivery once?—A stone called Ebenezer, or "the stone of help." 1 Sam. 7:12.

42. What three characters did Samuel unite in his person?—Priest, prophet (or teacher), and judge.

43. When Samuel was old whom did he make judges over Israel?—His two sons. 1 Sam. 8:1.

44. How did his sons conduct themselves?—They turned aside after gain, took bribes and perverted judgment.

45. What did the elders of Israel ask of Samuel at Ramah?—A king.

46. Was Samuel pleased at their request?—He was not. 1 Sam. 8:6.

47. Did the Lord direct Samuel to accede to it?—He did.

48. What did Samuel tell the people would be the manner of their kings when established?—Read 1 Sam. 8:11-18.

49. What effect did this representation produce?—They still insisted on having a king

SAUL. (1 Sam. 9-31.)

1. Who was Saul?—The son of Kish. 1 Sam. 9.

2. Of what tribe was he?—Benjamin.

3. What was remarkable about his person?—He was very tall and handsome. 1 Sam. 9:2.

4. What brought him to Samuel?—He consulted Samuel about the lost asses of his father.

5. How did Samuel know that Saul was the man whom God had chosen?—The Lord told him the day before that he would come, and when he saw him the Lord said, "Behold the man whom I spoke to thee of! This same man shall reign over my people."

6. What power did God allow to rest upon him?—His Spirit, in his gifts, but not his graces. I Sam. 10:10.

7. Are there not some characters more difficult to understand than others?—There are, as the tares of the East resemble the wheat, and the sheep the goats.

8. What contradictions do there appear in Saul's character?—In many things he honored Samuel and honored God, but he was superstitious, proud, disobedient, and self-willed.

9. In what spirit did the Lord give them a king?—In anger: I gave thee a king in mine anger. Hosea 13:11.

10. What did Samuel do before they parted?—He took a vial of oil and poured it upon Saul's head, and kissed him, declaring that God had anointed him to be captain over his inheritance.

11. Where did the tribes assemble to receive their king?—At Mizpeh.

12. How was Saul chosen?—By lot.

13. Where did the people find him?—Saul had hidden himself among the stuff, and they ran and fetched him thence.

14. Who followed Saul?—A band of men whose hearts God had

65

touched. 1 Sam. 10:26.

15. How did God establish the kingdom in his hand?—By a victory over the Ammonites. 1 Sam. 11:11-15.

16. Did Saul follow up this victory?—He next attacked the Philistines. 1 Sam. 13.

17. Who was Jonathan?—Saul's son.

18. What marked difference was there between him and his father? —He was of a modest and affectionate disposition, and loved David.

19. Who obtained the victory recorded in 1 Sam. 13:3?—Jonathan.

20. Who reaped the honor of it? —Saul. 1 Sam. 13:3, 4.

21. Was it not unworthy of Saul to take the glory that did not belong to him?—It was.

22. How did Saul again show his mean spirit as recorded in this same chapter?—By retiring to Gilgal, leaving Jonathan and his men exposed to the enemy. 1 Sam. 13:2, 4.

23. What did Samuel say to Saul when he came?—He reproved him for offering a sacrifice to God without the high priest. 1 Sam. 13:13.

24. What proof does this chapter give us of the degraded state into which Israel had fallen?—The Philistines did not allow them arms, or even a smith to sharpen their tools. 1 Sam. 13:19, 20.

25. What glorious victory does 1 Sam. 14:4-23, 31 record?—Over the Philistines between Michmash and Aijalon.

26. Who was the brave warrior here?—Jonathan. 1 Sam. 14:4-14.

27. How did Saul nearly spoil the victory of that day?—By pledging his people to eat nothing all day until the battle was won. 1 Sam. 14:24.

28. Was not an oath a very sacred thing?—The Lord thy God will surely require it of thee. Deut. 23:21, 22.

29. What proof can you give of this in 2 Sam. 21:7?—King David spared Mephibosheth, the son of Jonathan the son of Saul, because of the Lord's oath that was between them.

30. Was not the slaughter of the Gibeonites another proof of Saul's cowardly disposition? Who were the Gibeonites?—It was cowardly of Saul to kill those who trusted to the Israelites' oath, and were not prepared to defend themselves. 2 Sam. 21:2. The Gibeonites were Amorites who had deceived the Israelites, but whom they had promised not to kill. Josh. 9.

31. What great touchstone has God given to try man by?—Not every one that saith unto me, Lord, Lord, shall enter into the kingdom of heaven; but he that doeth the will of my Father which is in heaven. Matt. 7:21.

32. What nation did the Lord send Saul to destroy?—The Amalekites.

33. What test of obedience did God require from Saul?—That in fighting with the Amalekites he should utterly destroy them, with their sheep and oxen. 1 Sam. 15:3.

34. How did he act?—He spared the best of them and brought King Agag a captive. 1 Sam. 15:9.

35. How did Samuel feel?—He was grieved. 1 Sam. 15:11.

36. How did Saul try to justify himself?—He said the people spared the best of them for a sacrifice to the Lord.

37. What did Samuel answer?— That to obey was better than sacrifice.

38. How did Samuel act?—He told Saul that he should be no longer king. 1 Sam. 15:23.

39. Did Saul at length acknowledge his sin?—He did. 1 Sam. 15:24.

40. What did he request of Samuel?—To pardon his sin and join with him in worshiping the Lord.

41. What did he do when Samuel refused?—He took hold of Sam-

uel's garment, and it was rent.

42. What did Samuel then say to Saul?—The Lord had rent his kingdom from him and given it to a better man.

43. Did Samuel finally consent to turn with Saul to worship the Lord?—He did. 1 Sam. 15:31.

44. What was done with Agag? —He was cut in pieces by Samuel before the Lord.

45. When did Saul next see Samuel?—When Saul prophesied before him in Ramah, whither Saul had gone to see him. 1 Sam. 19, 24.

46. Did Samuel mourn for Saul? —He did.

DAVID. (1 Sam. 16.)

1. For what did the Lord reprove Samuel?—Because he continued to mourn for Saul, whom the Lord had rejected. 1 Sam. 16:1.

2. Whither did the Lord send Samuel to anoint a king?—To Bethlehem.

3. Why did Samuel object to going?—He feared that if Saul heard it he would kill him.

4. What did the Lord direct him to do to avoid the danger?—To take a heifer, and say that he had come to offer a sacrifice to God.

5. Was this allowing a deception?—No; for all great enterprises should be begun with religious ceremonies and worship.

6. What prophecy was spoken of the tribe of Judah by Jacob? —Judah, thou art he whom thy brethren shall praise: thy hand shall be in the neck of thine enemies; thy father's children shall bow down before thee. Gen. 49:8.

7. Why did the Lord reject Saul from being king?—Because he had not obeyed his commands. 1 Sam. 15:11, 23.

8. Whom did he choose in his place?—David. 1 Sam. 16:1, 11-13.

9. Who was David?—The youngest son of Jesse, a Bethlehemite. 1 Sam. 16:11.

10. Why had the Lord chosen

Saul?—God was displeased with the Israelites on account of their asking for a king. 1 Sam. 9:2.

11. Why was David chosen?— He was chosen on account of his qualities of mind and heart. I Sam. 16:6, 7.

12. How was Samuel taught this?—By being told to reject Jesse's elder sons.

13. What occupation was David following at this time?—Keeping sheep. 1 Sam. 16:11.

14. What deplorable loss did Saul sustain when the Spirit of the Lord rested upon David?—The Spirit departed from himself. 1 Sam. 16:14.

15. What evil power took possession of Saul?—An evil spirit, by permission of God.

16. In what way did he obtain comfort?—By having some one play to him on the harp. 1 Sam. 16:16.

17. Who was selected as his minstrel?—David. I Sam. 16:18-23.

18. What did this prove?—The guiding providence of God.

19. As David was then a shepherd what psalm may we suppose he sang on his harp to the king? —Perhaps the twenty-third.

20. What effect did David's sweet harp have on the king?— He was soothed and refreshed.

DAVID AND GOLIATH.
(1 Sam. 17.)

1. Did David continue to live with Saul?—No; he returned to his father's sheep. 1 Sam. 17:15.

2. Did his intercourse with Saul's court unfit him for a shepherd's life?—By the grace of God it seems not to have done so.

3. Where were David's brothers at this time?—The three eldest went with Saul to battle. 1 Sam. 17:13.

4. What did Jesse desire David to do?—To take his brothers a present and see how they fared. 1 Sam. 17:17, 18.

5. Who were Israel's greatest

enemies at this time?—The Philistines.

6. Who was the champion of the army of the Philistines?—The giant Goliath. 1 Sam. 17:4-11.

7. What was his height?—Six cubits and a span (about ten feet).

8. What armor did he have?—Read 1 Sam. 17:5-7.

9. Where was the army at that time?—At Shochoh.

10. Where was the camp of the Israelites?—By the valley of Elah.

11. What challenge did Goliath make to the Israelites?—Give me a man, that we may fight together.

12. How long did he challenge and defy them?—Forty days.

13. Did anyone accept his challenge?—No.

14. What did David do when he got to the camp?—He asked who Goliath was and what was to be the reward for killing him. 1 Sam. 17:26.

15. What effect did David's questions have on his brothers?—Eliab thought him proud and presumptuous, and was angry with him. 1 Sam. 17:28.

16. How did David answer them?—Meekly and calmly. 1 Sam. 17:29.

17. What psalm did David probably write on this occasion?—The one hundred and thirty-first.

18. For what pleasing traits of character was David always remarkable?—Gentleness, patience, humility, and forbearance.

19. What was he called?—A man after God's own heart. Acts 13: 22.

20. What promise did Saul make to the man who would kill the giant?—That he would enrich him, and give him his daughter for a wife, and make his father's house free in Israel.

21. Did David gain the information that he sought?—He did. 1 Sam. 17:25-27.

22. What was the result?—David undertook to fight with the Philistine. 1 Sam. 17:32.

23. How did Saul wish to prepare David?—With Saul's own armor. 1 Sam. 17:38.

24. Did he use the armor?—No; because he was unaccustomed to it.

25. What preparation did David make?—He only took his staff and sling and five stones in a bag. 1 Sam. 17:40.

26. What was the result of the engagement?—The giant was killed by the first stone slung. 1 Sam. 17:49.

27. Was only the giant slain?—The Philistines fled, and many of them were slain.

28. What did David do with the head and armor of Goliath?—He brought the head to Saul and to Jerusalem, and put the armor in his tent.

29. How was it that David had such power?—Because he trusted in the Lord his God.

30. How old was David at that time?—He is supposed to have been about twenty-two or twenty-three years old.

31. Is his act of faith mentioned in Heb 11?—Yes; in verse 32.

DAVID AND JONATHAN.

(1 Sam. 17:55-58; 18:19, 20.)

1. What remarkable question did Saul ask Abner when David went to fight the giant?—Whose son David was. 1 Sam. 17:55.

2. Was Abner able to answer Saul's question?—He was not.

3. How did they ascertain who the young conqueror was?—Saul ascertained it from David's own mouth.

4. Which of Saul's sons standing by felt his soul knit to David?—Jonathan. 1 Sam. 18:1.

5. What touching proof did he give of his love?—He gave him his robe and some of his arms. Compare 1 Sam. 18:4 with 1 Sam. 13:22.

6. What joyful song did the women sing when they went to meet the conquerors after the battle?—Saul has slain his thousands.

68

and David his ten thousands. 1 Sam. 18:7.

7. What effect did this have on Saul?—It made him jealous and angry.

8. How did David behave himself?—Wisely. 1 Sam. 18:14.

9. Did Saul remember his promise to give his daughter in marriage to the man who should slay Goliath?—He gave her to another man. 1 Sam. 18:17-19.

10. What artful design did he form to get David slain?—He required him to kill one hundred Philistines as the price of his daughter Michal, hoping he would have been killed himself. 1 Sam. 18:25.

11. Did it succeed?—David slew two hundred, and was unhurt.

12. What was Saul obliged to do?—To give him his daughter Michal for his wife. 1 Sam. 18:27.

13. Did Saul's daughter love David?—Yes. 1 Sam. 18:20, 28.

14. How did she prove this?—By letting him down from a window, that he might escape her father's rage. 1 Sam. 19:12-17.

15. What excuse did Michal make to the messengers of Saul?—She said that David was sick, and showed to them the image in the bed.

16. What order did Saul make?—To bring David in the bed, that he might slay him.

17. Why was David obliged to flee?—Because he discovered that Saul designed to kill him. 1 Sam. 19:10.

18. Would Jonathan believe this?—No. 1 Sam. 19:4-7; 20:1, 2.

19. To whom did David first escape?—To Samuel, in Ramah. 1 Sam. 19:18.

20. What wonderful power did God exercise over the messengers sent to take David?—He caused them to prophesy like Samuel's prophets. 1 Sam. 19:20, 21.

21. How did Saul succeed when he went himself?—He also began to prophesy.

22. Did David venture into Saul's presence again?—He seems to have done so at Naioth in Ramah. 1 Sam. 19:22-24; 20:5.

23. How did Jonathan assure himself that his father desired David's death?—By what David said. 1 Sam. 20:3.

24. When he discovered it what course did he take?—He promised to tell David of Saul's designs. 1 Sam. 20:9.

25. How did Saul regard Jonathan?—His anger was kindled against him when they had sat down at a feast.

26. What did he do?—He cast a javelin at him.

27. How did Jonathan act?—He arose from the table in wrath, and the next morning had an interview with David.

28. What covenant did they make together?—That Jonathan should warn David and that David should be kind to Jonathan and his children. 1 Sam. 20:13-16.

29. Where did they each go afterward?—David to his former hiding place, and Jonathan to his father. 1 Sam. 20:42.

DAVID A FUGITIVE.
(1 Sam. 21-31.)

1. Whither did David flee?—To Nob, to Ahimelech the priest.

2. What did he obtain there?—Some bread.

3. Did he do this honorably?—No; he pretended he was on the king's business. 1 Sam. 21:2.

4. What made him tell a lie?—Want of food and fear that the priest would not give it him.

5. Did not this show a want of faith in the living God, who had hitherto so wonderfully preserved him?—It did.

6. Who of Saul's servants was at Nob at this time?—Doeg, the Edomite.

7. To what place did David proceed?—To Gath. 1 Sam. 21:10.

8. How did he act when he

69

found himself to be known?—He pretended to be mad, that he might escape being imprisoned. 1 Sam. 21:11-13.

9. What does this show us?— That even the best men often fall into weakness and sin through their forgetfulness of God.

10. Where did he go when he left Achish?—To the cave Adullam. 1 Sam. 22:1.

11. Who came to him there?— Everyone that was discontented or in debt or distress. 1 Sam. 22: 2.

12. How many came to David here?—About four hundred men.

13. What kind of care did he take of his father and his mother? —He got the king of Moab to receive and protect them. 1 Sam. 22:3, 4.

14. Why were they obliged to leave Bethlehem?—Because the garrison of the Philistines was there. 2 Sam. 23:14; 1 Chron. 11:15, 16.

15. Who warned David that he was not safe at Adullam?—The prophet Gad.

16. What did David then do?— He departed and came into the forest of Hareth.

17. Who informed Saul of what Ahimelech had done for David?— Doeg.

18. What did Saul do?—He sent for Ahimelech and all the priests at Nob and ruthlessly put them to death, and then sacked the city of Nob, slaughtering both men and women, children and babes, oxen, asses, and sheep, with the sword.

19. Did any of the priests escape?—Only Abiathar, the son of Ahimelech, who fled after David.

20. What warlike expedition did David undertake?—He went to Keilah, and rescued it from the Philistines. 1 Sam. 23:5.

21. When Saul heard it what did he resolve to do?—To besiege Keilah and take David prisoner. 1 Sam. 23:7, 8.

22. How many followers had David now?—Six hundred men.

23. When Saul came down to Keilah whither did David go?— To the wilderness of Ziph, where he remained in a mountain.

24. Who joined David here?— Jonathan. 1 Sam. 23:15, 16.

25. What did Jonathan say to David?—He told him not to fear, and that his father should not find him; that he should be king over Israel, and that Jonathan himself would be his friend forever. 1 Sam. 23:18.

26. How did the Lord deliver David when Saul had nearly taken him?—By causing the Philistines to invade the land.

27. Did Saul again go after David?—Yes; in the wilderness of Engedi. 1 Sam. 24:1, 2.

28. How did David behave when the Lord put Saul in his power?—He would not kill him nor allow his men to do so. 1 Sam. 24:4-7.

29. What effect did this have on Saul?—He wept and spoke kindly to David.—1 Sam. 24:8-22.

30. What was the result of their interview?—David promised Saul that he would not revenge himself on Saul's house after he became established on the throne.

31. Where did Saul and David go?—Saul went home, but David returned to his hold in the wilderness. 1 Sam. 24:22.

32. What honors were paid to Samuel when he died?—All the Israelites were gathered together to lament him, and they buried him in his own house at Ramah. 1 Sam. 25:1.

33. To what place did David now go?—To the wilderness of Paran.

34. What treatment did David at this time meet with from Nabal?—Nabal refused to give food to David and his men. 1 Sam. 25:1-13.

35. What was the name and what the character of his wife?— Her name was Abigail, and she was a woman of good understanding and of a beautiful counte-

nance.

36. What of Nabal?—He was churlish and evil in his doings. His n a m e —"Foolishness"—describes his character. 1 Sam. 25: 25.

37. How did Nabal's wife act? —She went to David with a supply of food. 1 Sam. 25:14-31.

38. What became of Nabal?— He died suddenly, after a drunken feast. 1 Sam. 25:37, 38.

39. What proof did Abigail give of the high honor in which she held David (though an exile) after her husband's death?—She became his wife. 1 Sam. 25:39-42.

40. Did Saul again seek after David?—Yes, in the wilderness of Ziph. 1 Sam. 26:1, 2.

41. How did David revenge himself?—By again sparing Saul's life. 1 Sam. 26:7-12.

42. With what heathen did David again join himself?—With Achish, king of Gath. 1 Sam. 27.

43. Was this right?—No; it was contrary to God's commandments to Moses and Joshua.

44. What difficulties did David bring upon himself by this alliance?—He was invited by Achish to join him in fighting against the Israelites. 1 Sam. 28:1, 2.

45. Where was David when the last decisive battle between Saul and the Philistines was fought? —At Ziklag.

46. To which side did David offer himself and his men?—To Achish. 1 Sam. 29:8.

47. Is it not likely he would have gone over to the side of Israel?—He probably would have done so or remained neutral.

48. How did God preserve him from so very dangerous a position? —By inducing the Philistine leaders to object to his being with them. 1 Sam. 29:4, 5.

49. What event happened to him and his men while they were absent from Ziklag?—The Amalekites burnt the city, and carried away the women and children captive. 1 Sam. 30:1, 2.

50. Did they recover their treasures?—Yes.

51. How?—They pursued and slew the Amalekites and recovered all, after David had laid his trouble before God, and obtained direction from him. 1 Sam. 30:6-20.

52. What did he do with the spoil that they won?—He divided it among all his men who had taken part in the pursuit or fight. 1 Sam. 30:21-25.

53. What tremendous battle was happening in Israel while David and his men were thus employed? —A battle with the Philistines in Mount Gilboa. 1 Sam. 31:1.

54. What was the result of this battle?—Saul and his sons were slain, and the Israelites forsook the cities and fled.

DAVID KING IN HEBRON.
(2 Sam. 1-4.)

1. Where was David when the news came to him of the death of Saul and Jonathan?—At Ziklag. 2 Sam. 1:1.

2. What effect did Saul's death have on David?—He mourned for him and wept. 2 Sam. 1:12.

3. How did Saul die?—By his own hand, after being wounded by the Philistines. 1 Sam. 31:3, 4.

4. What did David do to the young man who by his own confession had killed Saul?—He ordered one of his soldiers to kill him. 2 Sam. 1:14-16.

5. What touching record did David leave of his love to Saul and Jonathan?—A song of lamentation. 2 Sam. 1:17-27.

6. Did David at once go and possess the kingdom?—Yes; after seeking direction from God he went up to Hebron, and was there anointed king. 2 Sam. 1-4.

7. Which tribe first acknowledged David's claim?—Judah.

8. What act of unnecessary bloodshed took place at Gibeon? —A battle between the men of Judah and the men of Israel. 2 Sam. 2:8-17.

9. Which were victorious, Joab's men or Abner's?—Joab's.

10. What happened to Asahel, Joab's brother?—He was killed by Abner. 2 Sam. 2:18-23.

11. How long did the war continue between the houses of Saul and David?—About two years. 2 Sam. 2:10; 3:1.

12. What event turned the scale on David's side?—Abner's deserting Israel on account of a quarrel with Ish-bosheth and offering to make terms with David. 2 Sam. 3:7-20.

13. Did David receive Abner?—Yes; with hospitality and honor. 2 Sam. 6:20.

14. How did Joab like this?—He blamed David for it. 2 Sam. 3:24, 25.

15. What did Joab do?—He killed Abner in revenge for the death of Asahel. 2 Sam. 3:27.

16. What course did David take when he heard this?—He called upon all the people to mourn with him for Abner. 2 Sam. 3:31.

17. What traits of character does David's conduct display?—Tenderness of heart and readiness to forgive.

18. Did David approve of Joab's conduct?—No; as Abner was no longer a rebel, and as Joab had killed him deceitfully and revengefully in time of peace.

19. Why did he not punish him?—Because he had not the power. 2 Sam. 3:39.

20. Who was Zeruiah?—The mother of Abishai, Joab, and Asahel.

21. Of what acts of treachery were the servants of Ish-bosheth guilty?—They killed their master. 2 Sam. 4:2, 5-8.

22. Did not the death of Ish-bosheth clear the way to David's ascent to the throne of Israel?—It did, as no one else was seeking to be king.

23. Did David on this account reward the murderers?—So far from rewarding them for their treachery and infidelity he ordered them to be slain.

24. Did the kings of Israel have the sole power of life and death? —Yes; they were absolute monarchs.

DAVID AND THE ARK OF GOD.

(2 Sam. 5, 6; 1 Chron. 14-16.)

1. How old was David when all Israel came to anoint him king?—Thirty years. 2 Sam. 5:4.

2. What was David's first conquest?—The stronghold of Zion. 2 Sam. 2:5, 7.

3. Was the rest of Jerusalem already subjugated to David?—It was.

4. What foreigners still retained Zion?—The Jebusites.

5. Who first scaled the walls and entered the fortress?—Joab. 1 Chron. 11:6.

6. What captains of David's army were the chief of his mighty men?—Joab first; then Jashobeam, and next Eleazar. After them were Abishai and Benaiah.

7. How many captains were there?—Thirty. 1 Chron. 11:15, 25.

8 Were there others who were reckoned among David's valiant men?—Yes. 1 Chron. 11:26-47.

9. What gallant achievement was done by the first three?—When David was in the hold at Adullam he longed to drink of the water out of the well at Bethlehem, which was then held by the Philistines. These three broke through the Philistine host and drew water from the well and brought it to David. 1 Chron. 11:16-19.

10. What king made presents to David?—Hiram, king of Tyre. 2 Sam. 5:11.

11. Where was Tyre?—To the north of Canaan, on the borders of the Mediterranean Sea.

12. For what was Tyre remarkable?—For its manufacture of purple dresses and for its commerce.

13. Did the Philistines treat David as Hiram did?—No; they went to fight against him. 2 Sam. 5:18.

14. What did the Philistines

take with them to battle?—Images of their gods. 2 Sam. 5:21.

15. How was David guided?—By God, whose direction he had sought. 2 Sam. 5:19.

16. Which host conquered?—David's. 2 Sam. 5:20.

17. What became of the gods of the Philistines?—David burnt them. 2 Sam. 5:21.

18. What was David's next act?—To bring the ark up to Zion. 2 Sam. 6:2, 3.

19. What was there about Zion that make it of peculiar interest?—David pitched there a new tabernacle for the ark of the Lord.

20. Where was the ark at this time?—At Kirjath-jearim.

21. How long had it been there?—Twenty years. 1 Sam. 7:2.

22. How came the ark to be at that place?—Because God had not yet directed it to be removed thence.

23. Where was the old tabernacle at this time?—In Gibeon. 2 Chron. 1:3, 4.

24. In whose house had the ark been kept?—In the house of Abinadab in the hill. 1 Sam. 7:1.

25. In what way did they bring it?—In a new cart. 2 Sam. 6:3.

26. What happened to Uzzah?—He died by the hand of God for taking hold of the ark when it seemed about to fall. 2 Sam. 6:6, 7.

27. How did David feel?—He was displeased, and afraid to go farther. 2 Sam. 6:8-10.

28. What did he do with the ark then?—He placed it in the house of Obed-edom the Gittite. 2 Sam. 6:10.

29. How ought the ark to have been brought?—By hand, with staves. Num. 4:15.

30. How many months elapsed before David had courage to fetch the ark?—Three. 2 Sam. 6:11.

31. What induced him then to do it?—The blessing that rested upon those who had the charge of it. 2 Sam. 6:12.

32. How was it accomplished this time?—The Levites bore the ark with staves upon their shoulders. 1 Chron. 15:2, 15.

33. What ceremonies accompanied the bringing up of the ark?—Sacrifices and dancing and shouting and the blare of trumpets.

34. Did David take part in these rejoicings?—Girded with a linen ephod he danced before the Lord with all his might. 2 Sam. 6:14.

35. When the ark was set in its place what was done?—Burnt offerings and peace offerings were offered, and the people were feasted on bread and flesh and wine.

36. What reproof did Michal give to David?—She reproved him for behaving unseemly in dancing before the ark.

37. What answer did David make?—He said that he did it as a religious act, and not wantonly.

38. Was he satisfied with placing the ark in the new tabernacle?—No; he desired to build for the ark a house of cedar. 1 Sam. 17:1.

39. Did the Lord permit him to do it?—No.

40. How did the Lord make his will known to David?—By Nathan the prophet. 1 Sam. 7:3-15.

41. How did David feel?—Deeply humble and unworthy of God's promised blessings, and prayed to God to confirm his word. 1 Sam. 7:16-27.

42. In whom was David's house to be confirmed forever?—In Jesus Christ. Luke 1:68-70.

43. Was the claim of Jesus as "son of David" acknowledged when he was on earth?—Yes; when he rode into Jerusalem.

44. Where does Jesus call himself "the offspring of David?"—Matt. 22:42-45; Rev. 22:16.

45. Has he yet sat on David's throne?—Yes; after his ascension he sat down upon it. Acts 2:30; Rev. 3:21.

46. Is this throne an earthly one?—No; it is spiritual.

47. Where is it said the Lord

God shall give unto him the throne of his father David?—See Luke 1:32.

DAVID'S CONQUEST.
—HIS SIN.
(2 Sam. 8-12; 1 Chron. 18-20.)

1. What had God's promise been of the boundary of Israel's possession?—From the river of Egypt unto the river Euphrates.

2. What conquests did David make which fulfilled this?—Of the Philistines, Moabites, Ammonites, and Syrians. 2 Sam. 8:1, 2, 6, 12, 14; 10:19.

3. What splendid armor had the Syrians?—Golden shields. 2 Sam. 8:7.

4. What did David do with the presents that were given to him, and spoil that he took in battle?—He gave the gold and silver and brass for the ornament and service of the tabernacle. 2 Sam. 8:10, 11.

5. How did he arrange his kingdom?—He made Joab commander in chief, Jehoshaphat historian, Zadok and Ahimelech priests, and his own sons and others judges and officers. 2 Sam. 8:15-18.

6. Did he forget his lamented friend Jonathan in his prosperity?—No; he inquired after the family of Saul, and gave Saul's land and a place at his own table to Mephibosheth, son of Jonathan. 2 Sam. 9.

7. For what did David send messengers to Hanun, king of Ammon?—To comfort him concerning the death of his father, who had showed kindness to David. 2 Sam. 10:2.

8. How did Hanun treat them?—He shaved off one half of their beards and cut off their garments in the middle.

9. What was the consequence?—David could not brook the insult, and made war upon Hanun.

10. What was the issue of the first battle?—The Ammonites and hireling Syrians fled before Joab and his men.

11. Did the Syrians renew the war?—Yes. 2 Sam. 10:15.

12. What then did David do?—He passed over Jordan and defeated them with immense slaughter.

13. What was the result of the war?—The kings that were tributary to Hadarezer, king of the Syrians, made peace with David, and served him. 2 Sam. 10:19.

14. When was it customary for kings to go forth to battle?—"At the return of the year," or in spring.

15. Whom did David send to besiege Rabbah?—Joab. 2 Sam. 11:1.

16. Where was David?—At Jerusalem.

17. Of what sin was David guilty at this time?—He violated the seventh commandment.

18. With whom was this sin committed?—With Bath-sheba, the wife of Uriah the Hittite. 2 Sam. 11:3-5.

19. How did David endeavor to conceal his sin?—He sent for Uriah to come home.

20. Did Uriah do as David expected?—He returned to Jerusalem, but would not go down to his house. 2 Sam. 11:11.

21. How did David still hope to succeed?—He invited Uriah to a feast, where he made him drunk with wine.

22. Was David again disappointed?—Yes; Uriah remained overnight with David's servants, but went not down to his house. 2 Sam. 11:13.

23. Why did David send Uriah with a letter to Joab, telling him to put him in the front of the battle?—That he might be killed. 2 Sam. 11:15.

24. Why did David wish Uriah to die?—That Uriah might never learn of his sin and that he might get possession of his wife.

25. Was not this a very great sin?—Yes; it was adding murder to his other shocking sin.

26. Whom did the Lord send to

convince David of his sin?—Nathan, the prophet. 2 Sam. 12:1.

27. How did he do it?—By a parable.

28. Did the Lord pardon David? —Yes, and said he should not die. 2 Sam. 12:13.

29. Did he not say also that in his feelings as a father he would chastise him for it?—Yes; by the death of his child; and he was also punished by the murder of his son Amnon and by the rebellion of Absalom and Adonijah.

30. How did David feel?—It is believed that his deep sorrow for his sin is expressed in the fifty-first Psalm.

31. Did the Israelites conquer Rabbah?—Yes. 2 Sam. 12:26.

32. What message did Joab send to David?—That he should come and have the honor of completing the conquest of the city himself. 2 Sam. 12:27, 28.

33. Although David got the honor of conquering Rabbah, and had the crown placed on his head, do you think he felt happy in it when the brave Uriah had died under the walls?—No; he said his sin was ever before him. Psalm 51:3.

34. What became of the people of Rabbah?—They were reduced to slavery, and compelled to saw wood, make harrows, chop down trees, and manufacture bricks. 2 Sam. 12:31.

35. What signal proof did the Lord give to David of his full and free forgiveness?—By giving him another child. 2 Sam. 12:24.

36. What was the name of this child?—Solomon.

37. What is the meaning of the name?—"Peaceable."

38. What name did Nathan the prophet give to the child?—Jedidiah, "Beloved of the Lord." 2 Sam. 12:25.

39. Through whom must we obtain forgiveness of our sins?—Through Jesus Christ.

40. Is there any limit to God's forgiving grace?—No; he will abundantly pardon. Isa. 55:7.

41. What did Jesus say to the woman whom he forgave when on earth?—Neither do I condemn thee: go and sin no more. John 8:11.

DAVID AND ABSALOM.
(2 Sam. 13-22.)

1. Who was Absalom?—A son of David. 2 Sam. 13:1.

2. Why did he flee away to Geshur?—Because he had killed his half-brother Amnon for outraging his sister Tamar. 2 Sam. 13:28, 32, 37.

3. How long did he stay there? —Three years.

4. Who brought him back again? —Joab, who by a kind contrivance had gotten David's leave. 2 Sam. 14:23.

5. How did he repay his father's kindness?—By making a conspiracy against him. 2 Sam. 15.

6. What punishment had the Lord said should spring from David's own house?—The sword and other evils. 2 Sam. 12:10, 11.

7. Why?—Because of his taking Uriah's wife.

8. How did Absalom steal away the people's affections from David?—By artful speeches and promises and civilities. 2 Sam. 15:2-6.

9. When David heard of the conspiracy what did he do?—He fled from Jerusalem. 2 Sam. 15:13-16.

10. Who went with him?—All his household and six hundred men from Gath. 2 Sam. 15:16-18.

11. Who insulted and maltreated David as he fled from Jerusalem?—Shimei, one of the house of Saul.

12. Of what treachery was Ziba, the servant of Mephibosheth, guilty?—He pretended that his master was a traitor to David, and hoped to gain the throne. David thereupon gave Ziba his master's estates.

13. What directions did David give to Zadok and Abiathar the priests?—To return to Jerusalem, and to keep him informed by messengers of the progress of events.

14. What famous counselor followed Absalom?—Ahithophel. 2 Sam. 15:31.

15. Who managed by an artifice to set his counsel aside?—Hushai, David's friend. 2 Sam. 15:32-37; 17:1-14.

16. Whose advice did Absalom follow?—Hushai's. 2 Sam. 17:14.

17. What effect did this have on Ahithophel?—He hanged himself. 2 Sam. 17:23.

18. Why did Hushai give this advice?—That he might secure David's escape.

19. How did David receive word from the priests?—By their two sons, Jonathan and Ahimaaz.

20. What adventure did these young men have?—They were hidden from Absalom by a woman in a well. 2 Sam. 17:22.

21. Who slew Absalom?—Joab.

22. How was it done?—As Absalom hung from an oak tree by his head Joab thrust him through with a dart. 2 Sam. 18:9-15.

23. What command had David given about Absalom to his captains?—That they should deal gently with him for his sake. 2 Sam. 18:5.

24. Did Joab seem to care for this?—Not at all. 2 Sam. 18:11, 14.

25. How did David feel, and what did he say, when Absalom was slain?—He was deeply distressed, and said, "Would God I had died for thee, O Absalom, my son, my son!" 2 Sam. 18:33; 19: 1-4.

26. Of what sin was Absalom guilty?—Rebellion against his father and against his king.

27. Describe Absalom's person. —He was the handsomest man in the country, and was remarkable for his long, flowing hair. 2 Sam. 14:25, 26.

28. What kindness was shown to David on his return?—Barzillai, who had supplied him with necessary stores at Mahanaim, came down to meet him and conduct him over Jordan.

29. How did the king reward him?—He made Chimham, his son, a member of his royal household. 2 Sam. 19:38.

30. How did Shimei act as the king was returning?—He craved the king's pardon, which David granted.

31. How did the king act toward Mephibosheth?—He learned that Ziba had deceived him, and restored to Mephibosheth his share of his paternal revenues.

32. Was peace at once again restored to Israel?—It was. 2 Sam. 19:9, 14.

33. Whom did David appoint captain of his host instead of Joab? —Amasa. 2 Sam. 19:13.

34. Why did he wish to supplant Joab?—Because of Joab's disobedience to orders, probably.

35. How did Joab act on hearing this?—He treacherously killed Amasa. 2 Sam. 20:9, 10.

36. What relation was Amasa to David?—Nephew, as son of his sister Abigail.

37. Did David again spare Joab from punishment?—Yes; he continued to be commander in chief. 2 Sam. 20:23.

38. What insurrection was made against David?—A Benjamite named Sheba made an insurrection, which was speedily put down. 2 Sam. 20.

39. Who quelled the insurrection?—Joab.

40. What was a famine in Israel a sign of?—National guilt. Deut. 28.

41. What were David's feelings when a famine of three years visited Israel?—Doubtless he felt compassion for his suffering people. 2 Sam. 21.

42. Of whom did he inquire?— Of the Lord. 2 Sam. 21:1.

43. What was the Lord's reply? —That the famine was in consequence of the guilt incurred by the nation when Saul and his people slew the Gibeonites. 2 Sam. 21:1, 2.

44. What expiation did the Gib-

eonites require?—The death of seven of Saul's sons. 2 Sam. 21:6.

45. What touching proof of a mother's love did Rizpah give?— She watched the bodies of her sons night and day, to prevent their being torn by birds or beasts. 2 Sam. 21:10.

46. What did David do to the remains of Saul and his sons?—He brought them to the burial place of Kish, the father of Saul, and there interred them. 2 Sam. 21: 12-14.

47. What old enemies of David's again showed themselves?—The Philistines. 2 Sam. 21:15.

48. What proof have we of David's declining strength and of the faithful love of his followers?—He was faint in battle, and Abishai preserved his life, and his people said he should no longer go out with them to battle. 2 Sam. 21: 15-17.

49. What is the twenty-second chapter of 2 Sam. about?—It is David's psalm of thanksgiving for deliverance from his enemies.

DAVID'S TRANSGRESSION.
(2 Sam. 24.)

1. By whom was David tempted to number Israel?—Satan. 1 Chron. 21:1.

2. What is Satan called in 1 Peter 5:8?—A roaring lion, walking about, seeking whom he may devour.

3. Did David order Joab to number the people?—Yes. 2 Sam 24:2.

4. Did Joab approve of this?— He did not.

5. How long was Joab in the work?—Nine months and twenty days.

6. How many men of war did Israel and Judah contain?—In Israel eight hundred thousand men, and in Judah five hundred thousand.

7. What was David's sin in ordering this census?—It was a sin of pride—a "presumptuous sin."

8. Did David's heart smite him

after he had done it?—Yes; he said he had sinned greatly, and done very foolishly. See 2 Sam. 24:10.

9. What was God's promise to Abraham as to the number of Israel?—That it should be very great, like the number of the stars.

10. Whom did the Lord commission to reprove David?—The prophet Gad. 2 Sam. 24:11.

11. What did he offer him?—The choice of one of three punishments.

12. Which did David choose, and why?—Famine or pestilence, rather than war; the immediate hand of God, rather than the hand of man.

13. At what spot did the destroying angel stop?—The threshing-floor of Araunah. 2 Sam. 24: 16.

14. What event had occurred on that hill about eight hundred years before?—The offering up of Isaac (in the opinion of some).

15. Of what was that circumstance a type?—Of the sacrifice of Christ as the atonement for sin.

16. How did David know that the Lord had accepted his offering?—By the plague being stayed. 2 Sam. 24:25.

17. What did David purchase of Araunah?—The threshing-floor where he saw the angel.

18. Why?—Because the prophet Gad instructed him to rear there an altar to God.

19. How much did he pay for it?—Fifty shekels of silver.

20. What did David do there?— He built an altar and offered burnt offerings and peace offerings. 2 Sam. 24:25.

21. Why did he not go up to the tabernacle at Gibeon?—Because he was afraid of meeting the angel again at the place of God's special presence. 1 Chron. 21:29, 30.

DAVID'S OLD AGE AND DEATH. (1 Kings 1:2; 1 Chron. 22-29.)

1. Did not Adonijah, David's son, attempt to be king?—Yes. 1 Kings 1:5.

2. What principal men were in his interest?—Joab and Abiathar.

3. When Adonijah made a feast whom did he invite?—He called Joab and Abiathar, and all the sons of the king except Solomon.

4. What advice did Nathan give to Bath-sheba?—To go in to David and claim the throne for Solomon.

5. What did Bath-sheba do?—She followed Nathan's advice.

6. Who had David declared should be his successor?—He had promised Bath-sheba that Solomon should be king.

7. What directions did the king give?—For Zadok and Nathan to cause Solomon to ride on the king's mule to Gihon, and there to anoint him king, and blow with the trumpets, and say, "God save King Solomon."

8. What did the people do when Solomon was anointed?—They piped with pipes and rejoiced with great joy. 1 Kings 1:40.

9. What effect had the news upon Adonijah and his guests?—They were alarmed, and Adonijah went and caught hold on the horns of the altar.

10. What message did Solomon send to Adonijah?—If he shall show himself worthy not a hair of him shall fall to the earth; but if wickedness shall be found in him he shall die. 1 Kings 1:52.

11. What did Solomon say to him when he came before him?—Go to thine house.

12. What charge did David give to Solomon before he died?—To be strong and show himself a man, to keep the charge of the Lord, to walk in his ways, and to observe the commandments written in the law of Moses.

13. What materials did he provide for the future building of the temple?—Hewn stone, gold, silver, iron, brass, and cedar. 1 Chron. 22:2-5, 14-16.

14. What direction did David give to Solomon concerning the temple?—To build it, as David himself had desired to do. 1 Chron. 22:6-16.

15. What other arrangements did David make?—He divided the priests and Levites and other officers into orders and fixed their duties. 1 Chron. 23:23-27.

16. Who showed David the pattern of the future temple?—God himself, by his Spirit. 1 Chron. 28:12, 19.

17. Did anyone besides David contribute toward the future glory of the temple?—The chiefs and the people. 1 Chron. 29:6-9.

18. What charge did David give to Solomon concerning Joab and Shimei?—That they should receive the punishment due to their guilt. 1 Kings 2:5, 6, 8, 9.

19. What were the last words of David?—Now bless the Lord your God. 1 Chron. 29:20.

20. How old was David when he died?—Seventy years.

21. How many years had he reigned?—In Hebron he reigned over Judah seven years and six months; and in Jerusalem he reigned thirty and three years over all Israel and Judah. 2 Sam. 5:4, 5.

22. In what respect was David a man after God's own heart?—In the general character of his life, and in his firm adherence to the worship of Jehovah and the law.

SOLOMON. (1 Kings 1-11; 1 Chron. 22-29; 2 Chron. 1-9.)

1. What request did Adonijah make of Bath-sheba?—To ask Solomon that Abishag, the Shunammite, should be given to him for a wife.

2. How did Solomon show his respect for his mother when she appeared before him?—He placed a seat for her on the right of his throne.

3. What did Solomon say concerning Adonijah's request?—Why dost thou ask for Abishag only?

Ask for him the kingdom also; for he is my elder brother; even for him and for Abiathar the priest, and for Joab.

4. What became of Adonijah? —Solomon had him executed at once as guilty of plotting against the government.

5. What did Solomon do to Abiathar?—He spared his life, but banished him.

6. What prediction was fulfilled by this?—The one spoken to Eli concerning his house in Shiloh. 1 Sam. 2:13-35.

7. What did Joab do when he heard of these things?—He fled to the altar that was in the tabernacle. 1 Kings 2:28.

8. What was his fate?—He was slain at the altar.

9. Did the altar secure a murderer against punishment?—No. Exod. 21:14.

10. Who became captain of the host instead of Joab?—Benaiah.

11. What was the decision of Solomon regarding Shimei?—That he was to build a house in Jerusalem and not to leave the city under penalty of death. To this Shimei agreed. I Kings 2:38.

12. Why did Shimei violate this agreement?—Two of his slaves escaped to Gath, and Shimei left Jerusalem to recapture them.

13. What was the consequence? —He broke his contract, and was put to death. 1 Kings 2:46.

14. For what did Solomon go to Gibeon?—To offer sacrifices. 1 Kings 3:4.

15. How many did he offer?—A thousand burnt offerings.

16. Did he offer sacrifices elsewhere?—Yes; he offered sacrifices and burned incense in high places.

17. What did God say to Solomon in a dream?—Ask what I shall give thee. 1 Kings 3:5.

18. What was Solomon's choice? —An understanding heart to be able to judge his people.

19. Did the Lord grant his request?—Yes. See 1 Kings 3:13, 14.

20. When Solomon awaked what did he do?—He came to Jerusalem and offered up burnt offerings and peace offerings and made a feast to all his servants.

21. What foreign alliance did Solomon make?—He made affinity with Pharaoh, king of Egypt, and took Pharaoh's daughter to wife.

22. Was this marriage forbidden by the law?—Yes. Exod. 34:16; Deut. 7:3, 4.

23. Did Solomon contract other foreign marriages?—Yes. See 1 Kings 11:1, 2.

24. How numerous was Solomon's harem?—He had seven hundred wives, princesses, and three hundred concubines. 1 Kings 11: 3.

25. What judgment did Solomon render in the case of two mothers claiming the same child?—He ordered the living child to be cut in two, and each mother to take half, when the real mother besought the king to let the false mother take the child herself.

26. What effect did this decision have upon Israel?—They feared the king, because they saw in him great wisdom to do judgment. 1 Kings 3:28.

27. How many officers had Solomon to provide food for his household?—Twelve. 1 Kings 4:7.

28. Was the reign of Solomon prosperous?—It was. 1 Kings 4: 20.

29. How extensive was his kingdom?—From the Euphrates to the land of the Philistines and the border of Egypt.

30. What were the daily provisions for his court?—Thirty measures of fine flour, sixty measures meal, ten fat oxen, and a hundred sheep, besides supplies of wild game. 1 Kings 4:22, 23.

31. How many horses and horsemen did Solomon have?—Forty thousand stalls of horses for chariots, and twelve thousand horsemen, besides dromedaries.

32. What was done for fodder? —The officers provided barley and

straw, every man according to his charge.

33. For what was Solomon famous?—For his wisdom.

34. How many proverbs and songs did he speak?—Three thousand proverbs and over a thousand songs. 1 Kings 4:32.

35. Was Solomon's wisdom confined to these?—No.

36. Are any of Solomon's proverbs still extant?—Only a few which are attributed to him.

37. Are any of his songs in existence?—The Song of Songs and two psalms (the seventy-second and the one hundred and twenty-seventh—if, indeed, Solomon wrote the latter).

38. Did the fame of Solomon's wisdom bring him many visitors? —Yes. 1 Kings 4:34; 2 Chron. 9:23.

39. Who was king of Tyre at this time?—Hiram. 1 Kings 5:1.

40. Whom did he send to Solomon?—Some of his courtiers.

41. For what purpose?—To do him honor.

42. Why?—Because Hiram was ever a lover of David.

43. What did Solomon determine to build unto the Lord?—A house of worship, or temple.

44. What kind of a temple did Solomon propose to build?—The house which I build is great; for great is our God above all gods. 1 Chron. 2:5.

45. Was this the character that David had intended for it?—It "must be exceeding magnifical, of fame and of glory throughout all countries." 1 Chron. 22:5.

46. What preparations had David made for the temple?—A hundred thousand talents of gold, and a thousand thousand talents of silver, and of iron and brass without weight; also cedar trees in abundance. Besides he had masons to hew wrought stones for the purpose. Other things were also collected. 1 Chron. 22:14; 29:2, 3.

47. Why did not David build it?—The word of the Lord came to him, saying: Thou shalt not build a house unto my name, because thou hast shed much blood upon the earth in my sight. I Chron. 22:8.

48. But did God approve of David's design?—He did, though he committed the carrying out of the plan to another. 2 Sam. 7:13.

49. What did Solomon desire Hiram to do?—To command that cedar and fir and algum trees be hewed out of Lebanon by the servants of Hiram, assisted by his own servants.

50. What answer did Hiram make to this proposition?—He wrote to Solomon, saying: I will do all thy desire concerning timber of cedar and concerning timber of fir. I Kings 5:8.

51. What arrangements were made for transporting the timber? —The timber was brought in floats from Tyre to Joppa, and thence carried to Jerusalem.

52. What payments did Solomon make yearly to Hiram?— Twenty thousand measures of beaten wheat, twenty thousand measures of barley, twenty thousand baths of wine, and twenty thousand baths of oil. 2 Chron. 2:10.

53. How many workmen had Solomon in Lebanon?—Thirty thousand men in all; ten thousand a month by courses. Besides, he had seventy thousand that carried burdens, and eighty thousand hewers in the mountains.

54. Who were thus employed as workmen by Solomon?—The strangers that were in the land of Israel, who were found to be one hundred and fifty-three thousand and six hundred.

55. How many overseers of the workmen were there?—Thirty-three hundred (1 Kings 5:16), or thirty-six hundred. 2 Chron. 2:18.

THE BUILDING OF THE TEMPLE. (1 Kings 6, 7; 2 Chron. 3, 4, 5.)

1. When did Solomon begin to build the temple?—In the four hun-

dred and eightieth year after the children of Israel were come out of Egypt. 1 Kings 6:1.

2. In what year of Solomon's reign was this?—In the fourth year. 2 Chron. 3:2.

3. On what day was the work commenced?—The second day of the second month.

4. What were the dimensions of the temple?—The length was sixty cubits, and breadth twenty cubits, and the height thirty cubits. The cubit may be reckoned at twenty-one or twenty-two inches.

5. How large was the porch?—Twenty cubits wide and ten deep.

6. What addition did Solomon build to the temple?—Against the wall of the house he built chambers.

7. How many stories high were these chambers?—Three. 1 Kings 6:6.

8. Were they all the same size?—The lowest were five cubits wide, the middle six, and the highest seven. 1 Kings 6:6.

9. How may we account for this difference?—Because of the varying thickness of the wall.

10. How high were the chambers?—Five cubits.

11. Where was the stairway for them?—In the middle chamber. 1 Kings 6:8.

12. What were these chambers intended for?—Probably for the use of the priests and for storage purposes.

13. Of what was the temple constructed?—Of hewed stone. 1 Kings 6:7.

14. Where was the stone hewed?—In the quarries, before it was brought to the building. 1 Kings 5:1.

15. Was any noise of hewing stone heard at the temple itself?—No. 1 Kings 6:7.

16. What encouragement did Solomon receive while he was building the temple?—The conditional pledge of God's presence with Israel. 1 Kings 6:12, 13.

17. How was the temple divided?—Into two parts.

18. How large were these two sections?—The inner part was twenty cubits long, and the outer part forty cubits.

19. How was the temple covered?—With beams and boards of cedar. 1 Kings 6:9.

20. Of what were the sides, floors, and ceiling of the temple constructed?—The walls and ceiling were covered with boards of cedar, and the floor with planks of fir. 1 Kings 6:15.

21. How were these boards decorated?—They were overlaid with pure gold; but the cedar of the house within was carved with knops and open flowers and with carved figures of cherubim and palm trees.

22. How was the most holy place separated from the outer room?—By a veil of blue and purple and crimson and fine linen, with cherubim embroidered on it. 2 Chron. 3:14, 16; 1 Kings 6:31.

23. What other decorations were made for the oracle?—Two cherubim of olive wood, covered entirely with gold, two outstretched wings extending to the sides of the temple, and two extending toward the center, until they touched each other. 1 Kings 6:23-28.

24. Of what and how were the temple doors constructed?—They were of fir, and were double folding doors, hung on posts of olive wood. All were richly carved. 1 Kings 6:33, 34.

25. Of what was the altar of incense made?—Of cedar wood, overlaid with gold. 1 Kings 6:20.

26. What was the use of the windows in the temple?—Probably for ventilation and not for light. For light, lamps were used.

27. How long was the temple in building?—Seven years and six months. 1 Kings 6:37, 38.

28. Where was the temple built?—On Mount Moriah.

29. How was this place prepared for the temple?—It was graded and

leveled, and terraced on the east side of the hill.

THE TEMPLE FURNITURE.

1. What furniture was made for the temple?—A great altar of brass; a molten sea containing three thousand baths (about 16,000 gallons), set upon twelve oxen of metal; ten lavers, each containing forty baths (210 gallons); ten lampstands of gold; an altar for incense; ten tables for the showbread; a hundred basins of gold; tongs of the same metal; shovels, snuffers, spoons, flesh hooks, pots or bowls, and censers. 2 Chron. 4.

2. What skilled workman was employed to make the castings of these utensils?—Hiram, the son of a Tyrian by a woman of the tribe of Dan. 2 Chron. 2:14; 1 Kings 7:14.

3. Where were the castings made?—In the plain of Jordan, or Zarthan. 1 Kings 7:46; 2 Chron. 4:17.

4. What were the lavers and sea of brass intended for?—The sea was for the priests to wash in, but the lavers were for the washing of such things as were offered for the burnt offerings. 2 Chron. 4:6.

5. Where were the lampstands placed?—In the first room of the temple. Here also stood the incense altar and the tables of show-bread.

6. Where did the great brass altar and the lavers and sea of brass stand?—In the court of the priests, outside of and in front of the temple, on the east.

7. How large was the court surrounding the temple?—Josephus quotes an author who wrote just after the time of Alexander the Great, who said the sacred inclosure was five hundred feet one way by two hundred cubits the other. It thus probably included the court of the women.

8. What ornaments were added to the porch of the temple?—Two immense pillars, highly decorated with fancy work in brass, which were erected before the entrance on either side. These Solomon named Jachin and Boaz.

DEDICATION OF THE TEMPLE. (1 Kings 8; 2 Chron. 5-7.)

1. When the temple was completed what was done?—Solomon brought in all the things which his father David had dedicated, and which he had constructed for the temple service. 1 Kings 7:51.

2. What was done with the ark? —It was set down beneath the cherubim in the most holy place. 1 Kings 8:4.

3. Who were present to witness this ceremony?—The heads of the tribes of Israel. 2 Chron. 5:2.

4. What was contained in the ark?—The two tables of stone which Moses put there at Horeb (1 Kings 8:9), and probably Aaron's rod that budded, and the pot of manna (Heb. 9:4). It may also have contained the book of the Mosaic law. Deut. 31:26; 2 Kings 22:8.

5. What religious ceremonies accompanied its removal?—Sacrifices were offered; the priests sounded with trumpets, and they all lifted up their voices in song, accompanied with the music of cymbals, psalteries, harps, and trumpets. 2 Chron. 5:12, 13.

6. How did God manifest his divine presence?—The glory of God filled the temple. 1 Kings 8:10, 11.

7. What did Solomon then do?— He offered the temple to the God of Israel as a house to dwell in, a settled place for him to abide in forever. 1 Kings 8:13.

8. What more did Solomon do? —He blessed the whole congregation of Israel and announced that Jerusalem was now the abiding place of the ark, to which the tribes were to come for their solemn feasts and to worship. 2 Chron. 6:4-11.

9. Where did Solomon stand? —On a brazen platform five cubits

square and three high, which was set before the altar in the midst of the court.

10. Was prayer offered?—Yes. 2 Chron. 6:14-42.

11. What took place at the end of the praying?—Fire came down from heaven and consumed the burnt offering and the sacrifices. 2 Chron. 7:1.

12. What festivities followed the dedication?—Sacrifices were offered by both the king and the people. Solomon himself offering twenty-two thousand oxen and a hundred and twenty thousand sheep. 2 Chron. 7:7.

13. How long did this feast continue?—Seven days, the religious festivities having taken seven days. 1 Kings 8:65.

14. How many took part in it? —Practically the whole nation. 2 Chron. 7:8.

OTHER WORKS OF SOLOMON.

(1 Kings 9; 2 Chron. 8.)

1. For what did the Lord appear to Solomon the second time?—To assure him that his prayer was heard, and that he had accepted the house which had been built for him, and to renew his covenant with him. 1 Kings 9:1-9.

2. What other structure did Solomon rear?—A royal palace for himself in Jerusalem, the house of the forest of Lebanon, and also a house for Pharaoh's daughter. 1 Kings 7:1-12.

3. Were these palaces in building while the erection of the temple was going on?—Probably they were.

4. What payment did Solomon make to Hiram, king of Tyre, for the materials obtained from him?— He ceded to him twenty cities in the land of Galilee. 1 Kings 9: 11, 14.

5. Was Hiram pleased with this cession?—He was not.

6. Did Solomon construct other works?—He built besides store cities, Millo, and the wall of Jeru-

salem; Hazor, Megiddo, Beth-horon the upper and Beth-horon the nether, Baalath and Tadmor in the wilderness. 1 Kings 9:15-17; 2 Chron. 8:2-6.

7. What present did Pharaoh make to his daughter, Solomon's wife?—Gezer; but Solomon had to rebuild it. 1 Kings 9:16, 17.

8. Whom did Solomon employ in these works?—The strangers left in Israel who were under tribute to the king.

9. Were any Israelites thus employed?—Only as officers over the people that wrought in the work.

10. How many?—Five hundred and fifty. 1 Kings 9:23.

11. Where did Solomon make a navy of ships?—In Ezion-geber, beside Eloth on the shore of the Red Sea, in the land of Edom.

12. What did Solomon do for mariners?—Hiram sent shipmen that had knowledge of the sea, to go with the servants of Solomon. 1 Kings 9:27.

13. What voyage did they make? —They went to Ophir, whence they brought gold, four hundred and twenty talents. 1 Kings 9:28.

14. Where was Ophir?—Probably in Arabia.

15. What amount of gold came to Solomon in one year?—Six hundred and sixty-six talents, besides that which traders and merchants brought. 2 Chron. 9:13.

16. Did Solomon receive any gold in addition to this?—The kings of Arabia and governors of the country brought both gold and silver.

17. What sumptuous furniture did he make for his palace?—He made two hundred targets of beaten gold, each worth six hundred shekels ($6,540), and three hundred shields of gold, each worth three hundred shekels ($3,270). These were put in the house of the forest of Lebanon. Then he made a great throne of ivory, overlaying it with pure gold. The ascent to the throne was six steps, and on each step, on each end, was the figure

of a lion. The footstool was gold, and the steps were fastened to the throne by stays on each side of the seat.

18. What kind of tableware did Solomon have?—All his drinking vessels were of gold, and all the vessels of the house of the forest of Lebanon were of pure gold. 2 Chron. 9:20.

19. What other voyages besides that to Ophir did Solomon's ships make?—They went to Tarshish; and once every three years they came bringing gold and silver and ivory, apes and peacocks.

20. Where was Tarshish?—This name is indefinite. Here it probably designates a port of Arabia, or some point on the Persian Gulf, in or near to Ophir. 2 Chron. 9:21.

21. Besides this supply of merchandise what else did the ships bring?—Precious stones and almug timber. 1 Kings 10:11.

22. What kind of timber was this?—It is supposed to be sandalwood.

23. What queen came to visit Solomon?—The queen of Sheba. 1 Kings 10:1.

24. Where was Sheba?—Probably in Arabia Felix or Yemen. Some think it was Abyssinia. Matt. 12:42.

25. Did she come in state?—She came with a very great train, with camels that bore spices and very much gold and precious stones.

26. Why did she come?—To prove Solomon's wisdom with hard questions.

27. Was she satisfied?—Solomon told her all her questions. 1 Kings 10:3.

28. What effect did Solomon's wisdom and magnificence have on the queen?—There was no spirit left in her. and she said that the report which she had heard in her own country was true, but that the half had not been told her. 1 Kings 10:5-7.

29. What did she do?—She gave the king a hundred and twenty talents of gold, and of spices very great store, and precious stones.

30. What return did Solomon make?—He gave unto the queen all her desire, whatsoever she asked, besides what he gave her of his royal bounty.

31. How did Solomon keep up his royal magnificence?—By imposing heavy taxes upon his people. 2 Chron. 10:4.

32. Was there anything in the world equal to it?—Solomon in all his glory was not arrayed like one of these lilies. Matt. 6:28, 29.

SOLOMON'S IDOLATRY.
(1 Kings 11.)

1. From what nations did Solomon select the women of his harem?—From the Egyptians, Moabites, Ammonites, Edomites, Zidonians, and Hittites. 1 Kings 11:1.

2. Did any of these become proselytes to the true faith?—Probably not.

3. What influence did they have over Solomon?—They turned away his heart.

4. What did Solomon do for them?—He built a high place for Chemosh and for Molech.

5. But did he not worship Jehovah?—He did for some years, keeping all the feasts and offering the required sacrifices. 2 Chron. 8:13.

6. Did he become himself an idolater?—Yes. 1 Kings 11:5, 6.

7. When was this?—When he was old.

8. What did the Lord say to Solomon?—That he would rend the kingdom from him and give it to one of his servants; but for the sake of David it should not be rent from him until the days of his son; nevertheless he would give his son one tribe to reign over. 1 Kings 11:9-13.

9. What adversaries did the Lord stir up against Solomon?—Hadad the Edomite, Rezon the Syrian, and Jeroboam the son of Nebat.

10. Who was Hadad?—He was

of the royal family in Edom. After Solomon came to the throne he became an adversry of Israel, and probably refused to pay tribute. 1 Kings 11:14-22.

11. Who was Rezon?—The son of Eliadah, who fled from his lord, Hadadezer, king of Zobah; he was an adversary of Israel all the days of Solomon. 1 Kings 11:23-25.

12. Who was Jeroboam?—He was a man of valor, and Solomon, seeing that he was industrious, made him ruler over the whole house of Joseph. He superintended some of Solomon's public works.

13. How did Jeroboam become Solomon's adversary?—See 1 Kings 11:29, 39.

14. What did Solomon try to do to Jeroboam?—He sought to kill him. 1 Kings 11:40.

15. How did Jeroboam escape? —He arose and fled to Egypt, and was there until the death of Solomon.

16. How long did Solomon reign?—Forty years. 1 Sam. 11:42.

17. Was his reign prosperous? —For a number of years, but at the time of his death Israel was ready to revolt.

18. Was God's promise of a long life fulfilled in Solomon's case?— He was probably only about sixty years old at the time of his death.

19. Did he repent of his idolatry and his evildoings?—We have no evidence that he did.

20. Can the reign of Solomon be regarded as a type of Christ's? —In nothing except that it was peaceable and extended. See Psalm 72.

21. What is the chief lesson to be derived from his life?—That in God's favor is life and in keeping his commandments there is great reward. All things else are empty and unsatisfying.

REHOBOAM.

(1 Kings 12; 2 Chron. 10-12.)
1. Who succeeded Solomon as king?—Rehoboam, his son. 1 Kings 11:43.

2. Where did the Israelites assemble to make Rehoboam king? —At Schechem.

3. What request did they make of him?—They asked that the grievous service of his father should be made lighter.

4. What did they agree to do if this were done?—To serve him. 1 Kings 12:4.

5. How soon did Rehoboam promise an answer?—In three days' time.

6. With whom did he first consult?—With his father's counselors.

7. What advice did they give? —To accede to the request of the people.

8. Did he follow their advice?— He forsook their counsel and laid the matter before young men.

9. What did the young men advise?—To say that instead of relieving them he would add to their burdens.

10. Did he do this?—He answered as the young men advised.

11. What was the consequence? —The people revolted.

12. Who was the leader of the revolt?—Jeroboam.

13. How many tribes joined in the revolt?—Ten.

14. What tribe was left to Rehoboam?—The tribe of Judah; the tribe of Benjamin and many of the Levites joined with Judah.

15. What did Rehoboam first do?—He sent Adoram to collect the revenue.

16. How did the people receive him?—They stoned him so that he died, and Rehoboam fled to Jerusalem. 1 Kings 12:18.

17. Did Rehoboam quell the insurrection?—He intended to fight the insurgents, but was prevented from attacking them by the prophet Shemaiah, who brought a message to him from the Lord.

THE KINGDOM OF ISRAEL ESTABLISHED.

1. What was the northern kingdom called?—Israel.

2. Where did King Jeroboam establish his capital?—At Shechem, in Mount Ephraim.

3. What plan did Jeroboam devise to keep the Israelites from going up to Jerusalem to worship?—He made two calves of gold and told the people: These are the gods which brought you up out of Egypt.

4. What further did he do?—He built a temple and made priests of the lowest of the people. 1 Kings 12:31.

5. What feast did Jeroboam ordain?—A feast similar to the passover, on the fifteenth day of the eighth month.

6. Did Jeroboam act as a priest himself?—He offered upon the altar and burned incense.

7. Where was this altar?—At Beth-el.

8. What did the man of God from Judah cry against it?—That a king of Judah should hereafter slay upon it the idolatrous priests of the Israelites and pollute it by burning dead men's bones upon it. 1 Kings 13:2.

9. What sign did he give that this would come to pass?—Behold, the altar shall be rent, and the ashes that are upon it shall be poured out. 1 Kings 13:3.

10. How did the king act when he heard these things?—He attempted to seize the prophet and called upon others to lay hold upon him, but the king's hand became palsied.

11. Was the altar rent?—It was, and the ashes upon it poured out.

12. What did the king ask the man of God to do for him?—To entreat the Lord that his hand might be restored to him again.

13. Was the withered hand restored?—It was.

14. What invitation did the king then give to the prophet?—To go home with him and refresh himself and receive a reward.

15. Was the invitation accepted? —No.

16. Why?—Because it had been charged him by the word of the Lord that he should eat no bread nor drink water in that place, nor return by the way that he came.

17. What did the old prophet of Beth-el do when he heard of these things?—He rode after the man of God to bring him back. 1 Kings 13:13.

18. When he overtook him what did he ask?—He asked whether he was the man of God that had come to Beth-el, and when he learned that he was he desired him to return home with him.

19. What was the answer?—The same as had been made to the king.

20. What did the old prophet then say?—That he was himself a man of God and that an angel had spoken to him by the word of the Lord, saying: Bring him back with thee into thine house, that he may eat bread and drink water.

21. Did he speak the truth?— No.

22. What did the man of God then do?—He went back to Beth-el.

23. What word came to him from the Lord while he sat at the table?—That because of his disobedience a lion should slay him.

24. What became of him?—He was slain as predicted.

25. Where was the body of the man of God buried?—In the old prophet's tomb.

26. What did he say to his sons after he had buried it?—To lay him, when he died, beside the man of God in the same sepulcher.

27. What effect had these things on Jeroboam?—He returned not from his evil way.

28. Who of Jeroboam's family after this fell sick?—His son Abijah. 1 Kings 14:1.

29. What did Jeroboam direct his wife to do?—To disguise herself and go to Shiloh to the prophet Ahijah and inquire what would become of the child.

30. What did Ahijah say to her

as she entered the door?—Come in, thou wife of Jeroboam; why feignest thou thyself to be another? for I am sent to thee with heavy tidings. 1 Sam. 14:6.

31. How did he know her?—The Lord had told him.

32. What message did he have for her from the Lord?—That God would bring evil upon the house of Jeroboam by utterly exterminating it, and upon Israel, because of their iniquities; and that the child of Jeroboam should die, and be the only one of Jeroboam that should come to the grave.

33. When was this prophecy of Ahijah fulfilled?—As soon as Jeroboam's wife reached the threshold of the door in Tirzah, where the child lay sick, it died.

34. How long did Jeroboam reign?—Twenty-two years.

35. How is Jeroboam frequently referred to in Bible history?—As "Jeroboam, the son of Nebat, who made Israel to sin."

36. Who succeeded him?—Nadab his son.

37. How long did he reign?—Two years. 1 Kings 15:25.

38. Did he restore the true religion to Israel?—No; for he walked in the way of his father, and in his sin wherewith he made Israel to sin.

39. What was his end?—He was slain by Baasha, the son of Ahijah, of the house of Issachar.

40. Did Baasha fulfill the prediction of the prophet Ahijah in destroying the house of Jeroboam? —He smote all the house of Jeroboam. 1 Kings 15:29.

41. How long did Baasha reign over Israel?—Twenty-four years.

42. What was the character of his reign?—He did evil in the sight of the Lord, as did Jeroboam.

43. What severe sentence was pronounced against him?—Behold I will take away the posterity of Baasha and the posterity of his house; him that dieth of Baasha in the city shall the dogs eat, and him that dieth of his in the fields

shall the fowls of the air eat. 1 Kings 16:3, 4.

44. Who reigned after Baasha? —His son Elah. 1 Kings 16:8.

45. For how long?—Two years.

46. What misfortune befell him? —He was slain.

47. In what disgraceful state was Elah when he was slain?— He was drunk. 1 Kings 16:9.

48. By whom was he slain?—By his servant Zimri.

ZIMRI AND OMRI, KINGS OF ISRAEL. (1 Kings 16-22.)

1. Who was Zimri?—One of the captains of Elah.

2. What vengeance did he execute on the wicked family of Baasha?—He killed Elah, the successor of Baaha.

3. How long did Zimri reign?— About seven days. 1 Kings 16: 15-19.

4. What was his end?—He burnt himself in his house when surrounded by his enemies.

5. Who reigned over Israel next? —Omri. 1 Kings 16:16.

6. Who was he, and how long did he reign?—He was commander of the army, and reigned twelve years. 1 Kings 16:23.

7. What city did he found and make the capital of Israel?—Samaria. 1 Kings 16:24.

8. How did he acquire possession of this place?—By purchase.

THE KINGDOM OF JUDAH

1. How long did Rehoboam reign over Judah?—Seventeen years.

2. What was his age when his reign began?—Forty-one years.

3. What was his mother's name? —Naamah.

4. Of what nation was she?—Of the Ammonites.

5. What was the character of the people in his reign?—For three years they walked in the way of David and Solomon; but afterward they did evil in the sight of the Lord, and they provoked him to jealousy. 1 Kings 14:22.

6. Did the king and his people again return to the Lord?—When the king humbled himself the wrath of the Lord turned from him. 2 Chron. 12:12.

7. What king assaulted Jerusalem and levied tribute on Rehoboam?—Shishak, king of Egypt.

8. What treasures did he take? —The treasures of the house of the Lord and of the king's house, and all the shields of gold which Solomon had made. 1 Kings 14:26.

9. How did Rehoboam replace the shields?—He made brazen shields to take their place.

10. For what purpose were they used?—In the royal processions, when the king went into the house of the Lord.

11. What public works did Rehoboam undertake?—He built fifteen cities for defense in Judah and Benjamin, and fortified the strongholds, and put officers in them, with store of victuals, oil, and wine. 2 Chron. 11:5-12.

12. Did many of the Israelites from the other tribes come to Jerusalem?—The priests and Levites that were in all Israel; and, out of all the tribes, such as set in their hearts to seek the Lord God of Israel came to Jerusalem. 2 Chron. 11:13, 16.

13. How many wives and concubines did Rehoboam have?—Eighteen wives and sixty concubines.

14. Who was his favorite wife? —Maachah or Michaiah, the daughter of Uriel of Gibeah, and granddaughter of Absalom. 2 Chron. 11:21; 13:2.

15. How many children did he have by her?—Four.

16. Who succeeded Rehoboam as king?—Abijah, his son by his favorite wife.

17. What disposition had Rehoboam made of his sons?—He disposed of them throughout all the countries of Judah and Benjamin, unto every fenced city, and he gave them victuals in abundance. Only he made Abijah the chief among them. 2 Chron. 11:22, 23.

18. How long had Jeroboam been on the throne of Israel when Abijah began to reign over Judah? —Seventeen years and over. 2 Chron. 13:1.

19. What war did he have?—A war with Jeroboam.

20. What was the result of this war?—God delivered the children of Israel into their hand, not less than five hundred thousand of Israel being slain. 2 Chron. 13:17.

21. Why was this victory so easily gained?—Because the children of Judah relied upon the Lord God of their fathers.

22. What cities did Abijah capture from Jeroboam?—He took Beth-el, Jeshanah, and Ephrain with their towns. 2 Chron. 13:19.

23. Did Jeroboam recover from the effects of this defeat?—He did not. He died two or three years later.

24. How long did Abijah reign? —Three years.

25. Did he walk in the ways of God?—The ordinances of the Lord's house were observed and the daily sacrifices to Jehovah were offered (2 Chron. 13:11), but he walked in all the sins of his father. 1 Kings 15:3.

26. How many wives did Abijah marry?—Fourteen.

27. What was the number of his children?—He had twenty-two sons and sixteen daughters.

28. Who succeeded him on the throne?—Asa, his son. 2 Chron. 14:1.

29. What was Asa's character in God's estimation?—He did what was good and right.

30. What proof did he give of his heart being right with God when he first came to the throne? —He destroyed many idols and their temples.

31. What did he do for the true religion?—He commanded Judah to seek and serve the Lord God of their fathers.

32. Was his early reign prosperous?—Yes, his land was at

peace.

33. What public works did he engage in?—He built fenced cities in Judah.

34. How were they constructed? —With walls and towers, gates and bars.

35. What was the size of his army?—He had five hundred and eighty thousand men. 2 Chron. 14:8.

36. How did he behave when the vast army from Ethiopia came up against him?—He prayed to God and fought in his name.

37. What was the result?—The Ethiopians fled, and Asa and his people pursued them to Gerar and brought away much spoil.

38. Is God the same as he was then?—The same now and forever.

39. Does he hear and answer prayer now as he did then?—Yes, as everyone, whether old or young, can testify who really prays.

40. What encouragement did the Lord give Asa by the mouth of Azariah the prophet?—That God would be with him as long as he was with God, or obedient to him. 2 Chron. 15:1-7.

41. What further reforms did Asa effect?—He destroyed all the idols in Judah and Benjamin, sacrificed of the spoil which they brought, seven hundred oxen and seven thousand sheep unto the Lord, and entered into a covenant with him to seek him with all their heart and with all their soul. He also removed Maachah the queen-mother from being queen, and cut down her idol that she had erected.

42. Did this happy state of things continue to the end of Asa's reign?—It continued to the thirty-fifth year of his reign, when he sent to the king of Syria for help against Israel. 2 Chron. 16: 1-4.

43. Did the Lord suffer this to go unnoticed?—No; he sent Hanani to reprove him.

44. What did the prophet say to Asa?—He reminded him of God's readiness to help his people, and told him that henceforth he should have wars.

45. How did Asa receive the reproof?—He was enraged and put the prophet in prison.

46. What disease affected Asa? —A disease of the feet—perhaps the gout.

47. How long did he reign?— Over forty years.

48. Where was he buried?—In his own sepulcher in the city of David.

AHAB, KING OF ISRAEL.
(1 Kings 16.)

1. What was the name of Omri's son?—Ahab.

2. How was Ahab distinguished above the kings that went before him?—In wickedness. 1 Kings 16: 30.

3. Who was his wife?—Jezebel, daughter of the king of Zidon. 1 Kings 16:31.

4. What new idol worship did she introduce?—The worship of Baal.

5. What is recorded of Jericho in Ahab's reign?—That it was rebuilt by Hiel. 1 Kings 16:34.

6. What did Joshua say of the rebuilding of Jericho?—Cursed be the man before the Lord that riseth up and buildeth this city Jericho: he shall lay the foundation thereof in his firstborn, and in his youngest son shall he set up the gates of it. Josh. 6:26

7. Can God's word ever fall to the ground?—No; all must come to pass.

8. Did Jericho afterward become an important place?—Yes; as a commercial town.

ELIJAH DURING FAMINE.
(1 Kings 17.)

1. Who was Elijah?—A prophet of Gilead.

2. Where was Gilead?—On the east of Jordan.

3. What was Elijah comsioned to tell Ahab?—That there should be neither dew nor rain.

4. Why did God send a famine on the land?—Because the Israelites had disobeyed his commandments. Deut. 28:15-18.

5. Where did God promise to provide for Elijah, and how?—By the brook Cherith, and by means of ravens.

6. When the brook dried up where did the Lord command Elijah to go?—To Zarephath (1 Kings 17:9), where a widow would sustain him.

7. Where was Zarephath?—Between Tyre and Sidon, but nearer to the latter.

8. In what sorrowful employment did Elijah find the woman engaged?—In gathering sticks to dress her last meal.

9. What provisions did she have in the house?—A handful of meal and a little oil.

10. What did the prophet say to her?—He told her not to fear, for that neither the meal nor the oil should fail until the Lord should send rain on the earth.

11. Did she believe the prophet?—Yes.

12. What calamity befell her?—Her son fell sick and died.

13. What miracle did Elijah perform on the widow's son?—He restored him to life.

14. What did she say when her son was restored?—Now by this I know that thou art a man of God, and that the word of the Lord in thy mouth is truth.

ELIJAH ON CARMEL.
(1 Kings 18.)

1. Was Israel at this time idolaters or worshipers of the true God?—Worshipers of Baal.

2. Were all worshipers of Baal? No; seven thousand of them were not.

3. Who was Obadiah?—Governor or steward of Ahab's house.

4. What kind act had he performed when Jezebel, the wicked queen, slew the Lord's prophets?—He had hid and fed them.

5. How many years had the famine lasted when Elijah stood before Ahab?—Above two years. 1 Kings 18:1.

6. What did Ahab accuse Elijah of doing?—Of being the cause of Israel's trouble.

7. What was Elijah's answer?—I have not troubled Israel; but thou, and thy father's house.

8. What did he request Ahab to do?—To assemble all the priests of Baal, and the people of Israel and the prophets of the groves which ate at Jezebel's table at Mount Carmel.

9. Did Ahab comply?—He did, except that he could not induce the prophets of the groves to come.

10. What did Elijah say to the people when they were gathered together?—See 1 Kings 18:21-25.

11. Did the people assent to his proposition?—They said, It is well spoken.

12. What did Elijah do?—He built an altar of twelve stones and digged a trench about it, and having prepared the wood, laid the slain bullock upon the wood, in readiness to be consumed as a whole burnt offering.

13. Did the prophets of Baal do likewise?—They prepared their altar and wood, and laid their offering upon it.

14. How did they then proceed?—They cried unto Baal to hear them.

15. Was it of any use for Baal's priests to cry to him?—None at all.

16. How did Elijah mock them?—By telling them to cry aloud, as their god might be talking, or hunting, or traveling, or asleep. 1 Kings 18:27.

17. Did he give them time enough to make a fair trial?—Yes; from morning till evening. 1 Kings 18:26, 29.

18. When Baal did not respond what did the priests do?—They leaped upon the altar, cutting their flesh, and acting in a frenzy.

19. Did their god vouchsafe any answer?—No.

20. About what time in the day

was it when Elijah built his altar to the true God?—About evening. 1 Kings. 18:29, 30.

21. Of what use was the trench he had made round the altar?—That the water which he directed to be poured over the slain bullock, the wood, and the stones, might not escape.

22. Why did he drench the sacrifice with water?—To show the power of the fire.

23. How was the power of God manifested?—By the fire burning the sacrifice, the wood, the stones the dust, and the water.

24. What effect did it have on the people?—They acknowledged that Jehovah was the true God. 1 Kings 18:39.

25. What became of Baal's priests?—They were slain.

26. Did Ahab consent to this slaughter?—He did not interfere.

27. What did Elijah venture to promise Ahab even before there was any appearance of it?—Abundance of rain.

28. On what did Elijah's faith rest?—On the promise of God. 1 Kings 18:1.

29. What is faith?—Faith is the assurance of things hoped for, a conviction of things not seen. Heb. 11:1. (Rev. Translation—Am. Com.)

30. How many times did Elijah ask ere the promised blessing appeared?—Seven times.

31. What should this teach us? —Always to pray and not to faint. Luke 18:1-7.

32. How was the Lord's power again manifested on Elijah, although he had had a day of such extraordinary energy?—In enabling him to run before Ahab's chariot.

33. Was Elijah like one of us, or was he a supernatural being?— He was a man subject to like passions as we are. James 5:17, 18.

34. Was there a plentiful rain? —There was a great rain. 1 Kings 18:45.

35. Is God as much the hearer and answerer of prayer now as he was then?—He is always the same.

36. Did Ahab tell Jezebel what Elijah had done?—Yes. 1 Kings 19:1.

37. How was Jezebel affected at the news?—She became furiously angry, and sent word to Elijah that she intended to take his life within twenty-four hours. 1 Kings 19:2.

38. Why did she not execute her threat at once?—She may have been afraid, and only wanted to get rid of Elijah.

ELIJAH IN THE DESERT.
(1 Kings 19.)

1. To what place did Elijah flee for fear of Jezebel?—To Beersheba. 1 Kings 19:3.

2. What proof did he give that he was "a man subject to like passions as we are?"—In his weakness he requested that he might die. 1 Kings 19:4.

3. What kind care did the Lord take of him there?—An angel brought him bread and water.

4. Was he more than once invited to eat?—Yes; twice. 1 Kings 19:7.

5. For how long did that food sustain him?—Forty days and forty nights.

6. When he was revived, to what place did he go?—To Mount Horeb.

7. Is it the Lord's will that his servants should be idle?—No; he has work for everyone to do.

8. What did the Lord say to Elijah?—What doest thou here, Elijah?

9. Is this a proof that God does not wish his people to live the life of a hermit?—It is.

10. Can any former work excuse them from future service?—Not while the means are in their power.

11. What is God's way of speaking to his people?—By his providences, his word, and through the Spirit's whisper to the heart.

12. Can any supposed mystery in the dealings of God be an excuse for neglect of duty?—No.

13. What further work did the Lord give Elijah to do?—To anoint two men to be kings and one to be a prophet. 1 Kings 19:15, 16.

14. What two kings were these? —Jehu to be king over Israel, and Hazael over Syria.

15. Who was the prophet?—Elisha.

16. How many were left in Israel who had not bowed the knee to Baal?—Seven thousand.

17. Where did Elijah find Elisha?—In the fields plowing, with a company of other men.

18. What did Elijah then do?— He cast his mantle on him.

19. What effect did the casting of Elijah's mantle on Elisha have? —It made him leave his work and his home for God's service.

20. Did Elisha wait till Elijah was taken up, or did he follow him at once?—He followed him at once.

21. What does the Lord say in Prov. 8:17 to encourage young people to follow him?—Those that seek me early shall find me.

AHAB'S PUBLIC AND PRIVATE CHARACTER.
(1 Kings 20 and 21.)

1. What was Ahab's character in the sight of God?—He did more to provoke him than all the kings of Israel before him. 1 Kings 16:33.

2. Had God at this time given up Israel?—No; he still warned them by his prophets.

3. Were there other prophets at this time in Israel besides Elijah?—Yes, both false and true.

4. Who were Israel's greatest enemies at this time?—The Syrians.

5. What was the capital city of Syria?—Damascus.

6. Who was king of Syria at this time?—Ben-hadad.

7. What did he propose to do to Israel?—To destroy Samaria. 1 Kings 20:10.

8. What message did he send to Ahab?—That Ahab's gold and silver, his wives and children, must be given to him for tribute.

9. What answer did Ahab return?—That he and all that he had should be tributary to Ben-hadad.

10. What further claim did Ben-hadad make?—That not only the king, but also the treasures of the city, should be given to him.

11. Did Ahab agree to this demand?—He did not.

12. What did Ben-hadad then do?—He swore by his gods that he would wipe out the city of Samaria completely.

13. Was Ahab frightened at this threat?—He calmly sent word to Ben-hadad: Let not him that girdeth on his harness boast himself as he that putteth it off.

14. Who came to Ahab to encourage him?—A prophet of the Lord.

15. What did he say?—That God would give the army of the Syrians into his hands.

16. What was the result of the war which followed?—The Syrians were defeated.

17. Was the war renewed?— Yes.

18. When?—The next year.

19. What change did Ben-hadad make in his mode of attack?—He attacked the Israelites in the plain and appointed captains acquainted with tactics to lead his army instead of his confederate kings.

20. Did his plan succeed?—No.

21. What was the issue of the battle?—A hundred thousand footmen of the Syrian army were slain, twenty-seven thousand perished by the falling of walls in Aphek.

22. What compact was made between Ahab and Ben-hadad?—Ben-hadad restored to Ahab the cities which his father took from the Israelites and allowed him to establish an emporium in Damascus for trade.

23. Was the Lord pleased with Ahab for sparing Ben-hadad?—No; he reproved him.

24. Who was Naboth?—The owner of a vineyard near Ahab's palace in Jezreel. 1 Kings 21.

25. What did Ahab covet that belonged to Naboth?—Naboth's vineyard.

26. Did Naboth accept Ahab's offer?—No.

27. Why did he not let Ahab have his vineyard?—Because he was forbidden by the law to part with what had come to him from his fathers. Lev. 25:23, 24.

28. How was Ahab affected by Naboth's refusal?—He acted pettishly.

29. What wicked act did Jezebel stir Ahab up to do?—To kill Naboth and take his vineyard.

30. Did God suffer this to go unpunished?—No.

31. Who was sent to Ahab?—Elijah.

32. How did Ahab salute him? —As his enemy. 1 Kings 21:20.

33. What fearful prediction did he utter?—That God would destroy Ahab's family, and that the dogs should eat the flesh of Jezebel and lick his own blood.

34. How did Ahab receive the tidings?—He humbled himself before God.

35. What proof is there in this place of the truth of Jonah 4:2?—God delayed the punishment.

JEHOSHAPHAT. (2 Chron. 17; 1 Kings 22.)

1. Who succeeded Asa on the throne of Judah?—Jehoshaphat, his son. 2 Chron. 17:1.

2. What character did he bear? —He sought the God of his father and walked in his commandments.

3. Was Jehoshaphat's a prosperous reign?—Yes; he was long without war, and became a very great king, and had riches and honor in abundance.

4. How large was his army?— besides the forces which he placed in the fortress cities of Judah he had eleven hundred and sixty thousand men, all well officered. 2 Chron. 17:14-19.

5. For what purpose did Jehoshaphat send his princes and Levites throughout Judah?—To teach the people in the law of the Lord.

6. How extensive was this teaching?—They went about throughout all the cities of Judah.

7. Were any nations tributary to Jehoshaphat?—Some of the Philistines and Arabians were subject to him.

8. How did he strengthen Judah for defense?—He built castles and cities of store.

9. What was the great error of Jehoshaphat's life?—His making an alliance with Ahab.

10. Was Ahab glad to make the compact?—Yes; he made a feast for Jehoshaphat and his servants.

11. Who were the enemies that still fought against Israel?—The Syrians.

12. What place had they taken?—Ramoth-gilead.

13. Where was it?—In the tribe of Gad, on the east of Jordan.

14. What did Jehoshaphat require before he would go up to fight?—That the will of God should be known.

15. What did all Ahab's prophets say?—That he might go, and God would be with him. 2 Chron. 18:5.

16. Was the king of Judah satisfied?—No.

17. Whom did he wish to consult?—Micaiah.

18. Why did not Ahab like Micaiah?—Because he always prophesied evil unto him.

19. Was it not very foolish of Ahab to be satisfied with lies?—Very.

20. When are we like Ahab in this?—When we take counsel of selfishness.

21. What is the only sure test of truth?—God's word.

22. What did Jehoshaphat's love of truth prove him to be?—A true servant of God.

23. What imagery did Micaiah use?—Of God upon his throne, and the host of heaven around him, and of an evil spirit going forth to entice Ahab to his fall.

24. Is there in Scripture any

93

other imagery describing the unseen world?—In Job 1 and Isa. 6, etc.

25. How did Ahab reward the faithful prophet?—He put him in prison.

26. What did Ahab do to make his prediction false?—He disguised himself.

27. What narrow escape had Jehoshaphat in the battle?—The Syrians surrounded him.

28. How was he delivered?—God moved them to leave him.

29. Can any circumstances be too difficult for the Lord to overrule?—None.

30. How was Ahab killed?—By an arrow shot at random.

31. Was Elijah's prediction in 1 Kings 21:19 fulfilled?—It was partly fulfilled when the dogs licked up Ahab's blood in his chariot.

32. Was it of any use that Ahab disguised himself in the battle?—None at all.

33. Can we hide ourselves from God?—We cannot.

34. What during his life did Ahab build?—Some cities, an ivory house, and a sepulcher.

35. Have these works rendered his name honorable?—No.

36. What alone is true honor?—That which comes from God.

ELIJAH AND THE LIVING GOD. (2 Kings 1 and 2.)

1. Which of Ahab's sons succeeded his father?—Ahaziah. 1 Kings 22:40.

2. What character did he bear? —He was wicked and idolatrous. 1 Kings 22:52, 53.

3. What accident befell him?— He fell from an upper room. 2 Kings 1:2.

4. What means did he take for his recovery?—He sent to an idol god. 2 Kings 1:2.

5. What testimony did Elijah bear to this impiety when he learned of it?—He said that he should not recover.

6. What course did Ahaziah take?—He sent three separate bands of fifty soldiers, with their captains to take Elijah.

7. What befell his messengers? —Two companies were consumed by fire from heaven.

8. Did the third company meet with the same fate?—It was spared in answer to their leader's prayer.

9. What did Elijah then do?— He went with the last body of messengers to visit the king.

10. Was Elijah induced to alter his denunciation against the king when he saw him?—No.

11. How long did Ahaziah reign? —Two years. 1 Kings 22:51.

12. Who reigned in Israel after Ahaziah?—His brother, Jehoram, because he had no son. 2 Kings 1:17; 3:1.

13. What peculiar testimony did Elijah bear all through life?— Against idolatry and for the honor of God.

14. Was not Elijah privileged to manifest this in his departure from this world?—God's glory was shown in the miracle he wrought and in his translation to heaven.

15. How did that event take place?—In a whirlwind, by a chariot and horses of fire. 2 Kings 2:11.

16. Who was permitted to witness it?—Elisha.

17. What favor did Elijah grant Elisha as he was parting from him?—To ask what he should do for him.

18. What did Elisha request?—A double portion of Elijah's spirit.

19. How often in Elijah's history is his mantle mentioned?— Three times. 1 Kings 19:13, 19, and 2 Kings 2:8.

20. How did Elisha use it?—To divide the waters of Jordan.

21. How many times before this had Jordan been miraculously divided?—Twice—when Israel entered Canaan, and when Elijah crossed before his death.

22. How did the other prophets recognize the superiority of Elisha?—By the spirit of Elijah resting upon him. 2 Kings 2:15.

94

23. How did they manifest their unbelief?—By proposing to send men to search for Elijah.

24. Did Elisha yield?—He did, at last.

25. What proof did Elisha at once give that he, like Elijah, was the prophet of the living God?—By healing the unwholesome water at Jericho.

26. What proof of Israel's impiety did the young men of Bethel give?—They mocked Elisha.

27. What did they mean by "Go up?"—Go up to heaven, like Elijah.

28. How were they punished?—They were killed by bears.

WAR WITH THE MOABITES AND AMMONITES. (2 Kings 3; 2 Chron. 19, 20.)

1. Did the Lord suffer the evil confederacy which Jehoshaphat had made with Ahab to go unnoticed?—No.

2. Whom did the Lord send to warn the king?—Hanani the seer.

3. How did the Lord show his displeasure when Jehoshaphat joined affinity with Ahaziah, Ahab's son, in sending ships to go to Tarshish?—The ships were wrecked. 1 Kings 22:48.

4. When Ahaziah afterward wished his servants to go with Jehoshaphat's what was his conduct?—He refused. 1 Kings 22:49.

5. Was Jehoram (son of Ahab) a better man than either his brother Ahaziah or his father?—He was better in putting away the image of Baal; but in other respects he was very wicked. 2 Kings 3:2, 3.

6. Did Jehoshaphat consent to go to battle with him?—He did. 2 Kings 3:7.

7. Whom did they go to fight?—Mesha, the king of the Moabites.

8. What other king went with them?—The king of Edom. 2 Kings 3:9.

9. What tribute had Mesha been paying to the king of Israel?—A hundred thousand lambs and a hundred thousand rams with the wool.

10. When he rebelled, what did Jehoram do?—He took a census of all Israel.

11. Of what were the armies of the allied kings in want?—They lacked water. 2 Kings 3:9.

12. To get water what did they do?—They made a compass of seven days' march.

13. What effect did this long march have upon Jehoram?—He was frightened, and said: Alas, that the Lord hath called these three kings together to deliver them into the hand of Moab.

14. What did Jehoshaphat reply?—He inquired whether there was not there a prophet of the Lord, so that they might inquire of the Lord by him. 2 Kings 3:11.

15. What prophet was named to them?—Elisha.

16. Then what was done?—Jehoram and Jehoshaphat and the king of Edom went down to him.

17. What signal honor did the prophet Elisha put upon Jehoshaphat?—He told Jehoram that he would not have noticed him but for Jehoshaphat's sake. 2 Kings 8:14.

18. Why was Elisha interviewed?—To know from him whether the Moabites would be defeated or not.

19. How did the Lord appear for them?—He deceived the Moabites, by the miraculous appearance of reddened water, with the belief that the armies of the three kings had destroyed one another. 2 Kings 3:16, 20-23.

20. What frightful sacrifice did the king of Moab offer to propitiate his gods?—His eldest son as a burnt offering. 2 Kings 3:27.

21. How did the king of Moab soon after try to revenge this defeat?—By making war against Jehoshaphat. 2 Chron. 20:1.

22. What kings joined with him?—The Ammonites and others.

23. How did Jehoshaphat feel?

—He was afraid. 2 Chron. 20:3.

24. What did he do?—He proclaimed a fast and prayed to God before the people.

25. Who was Jahaziel?—A Levite.

26. What gracious message did the Lord send by him?—That he would destroy their enemies without a battle.

27. Did Jehoshaphat and his people believe the message?—Yes, and united together in praising God.

28. Does not God always honor faith in himself?—He does.

29. Did Jehoshaphat and his people wait till after the victory before they began to praise, or did they begin before the fight?—As soon as his promise was given.

30. Did this prove their faith in God's word?—It did.

31. What spoils did they gain? —Abundance of riches and jewels. 2 Chron. 20:25.

32. What effect did this great conquest have on the nations around?—They troubled Jehoshaphat no more. 2 Chron. 20:29, 30.

33. With whom is Jehoshaphat compared as to goodness?—With Asa his father.

34. What great abomination did he, notwithstanding all his excellence, leave in the land?—The high places of the heathen gods.

35. Which of his sons did Jehoshaphat make king during his own life?—Jehoram.

36. How long did Jehoram enjoy this honor before his father's death?—About a year. Compare 2 Kings 1:17 with 2 Kings 3:1; 8:16; and 2 Chron. 20:31.

37. How old was Jehoshaphat when he died, and how long had he reigned?—Sixty years old, having reigned twenty-five.

ELISHA'S MIRACLES—THE WATERS OF JERICHO.
(2 Kings 2.)

1. Which was the last city Elijah and Elisha visited ere Elijah ascended to heaven?—Jericho. 2 Kings 2:4.

2. Where did Elijah ascend?— Beyond Jordan, opposite to Jericho.

3. By whom was Jericho chiefly inhabited at this time?—By students in the schools of the prophets.

4. Did Elisha return there?— Yes. 2 Kings 2:18.

5. How long did he stay there? —Only a short time. 2 Kings 2:23, 25.

6. What did the men of the city say to Elisha?—They said the situation was pleasant, but the land was barren and the water naught.

7. What did they hope would be done?—That Elisha would sweeten the water.

8. Was Elisha permitted to do this?—Yes.

9. How?—By casting a little salt into it, accompanied by the healing power of God.

10. Are the waters of Jericho still sweet?—Modern travelers speak of the excellence of the water that flows from the spring near Jericho.

11. Of what was salt a type in Scripture?—Of divine grace in the heart and life. Matt. 5:13.

12. What peculiar quality has salt besides its being savory?—Of preserving things from corruption.

13. Were the children of Israel commanded to use salt with their sacrifices?—Yes. Lev. 2:13.

THE WIDOW'S OIL. (2 Kings 4:1-7.)

1. Who cried to Elisha?—The widow of one of the sons of the prophets.

2. Why did she cry to him?— Because he was the chief of the prophets.

3. What was her trouble?—A creditor had taken her two sons for bondmen for the debt.

4. What plea had she to offer? —That her husband had been a servant of God.

5. What did he command her to do?—To borrow empty vessels and

fill them from her pot of oil.

6. When did the oil stop running?—When there were no more vessels to fill.

7. Where was Shunem?—In the tribe of Issachar.

8. How was Elisha entertained by a rich woman there?—She and her husband set apart a room for his use whenever he came that way. 2 Kings 4:8-10.

9. What kind gift did the Lord bestow upon her for Elisha's sake? —A child when she had none.

10. What happened to this child?—He died by a sunstroke.

11. Where was Elisha at the time?—At Mount Carmel. 2 Kings 4:25.

12. How did the mother act when her son was dead?—She set off quickly to Elisha.

13. What was her reply when the servant of Elisha inquired after the welfare of her household?—It is well. II Kings 4:26.

14. Why did she thus answer?— Her answer was evasive, as she had business with the prophet alone.

15. What means did Elisha at first use to recover the child?— His servant laid Elisha's staff upon the child. 2 Kings 4:31.

16. Why did Elisha do this?— His motive is not revealed.

17. Did the Lord permit it to be effectual?—No.

18. Was the mother satisfied with the prophet's indifference?— She was not.

19. What did she then do?— She clung to the prophet until he agreed to accompany her.

20. What did Elisha do?—Elisha accompanied her home, he prayed, and then stretched himself upon the child, and he revived.

21. Can God work without means?—He can.

22. How does the Lord usually act?—By means.

23. What did the restoration of this child prove Elisha to be?—A true prophet and servant of God.

24. How did the Saviour treat the Syrophenician woman that cried unto him?—At first with seeming indifference, but at the end with abundant mercies. Matt. 15:22-28.

25. What compliment did he pay this woman?—O woman, great is thy faith!

26. Is our faith as great as the woman's?—Lord, increase our faith!

THE MEAL AND THE CORN.
(2 Kings 4:38-44.)

1. What miracle did Elisha first perform at Gilgal?—He cast meal into some poisoned pottage and made it nourishing.

2. What is the wild gourd thought to have been?—The fruit of the colocynth vine, a species of wild cucumber.

3. What are its effects when eaten?—They are poisonous.

4. Is it of use in pharmacy?— Yes.

5. What immunity from poison did the Saviour promise his disciples?—They shall take up serpents, and if they drink any deadly thing it shall not hurt them. Mark 16:18.

6. Was this promise ever fulfilled, and when?—When the viper fastened itself on Paul's hand. Acts 28:5.

7. What gift did Elisha receive at Gilgal?—Twenty loaves of barley, and full ears of corn in the husks. 2 Kings 4:42.

8. How did Elisha dispose of this present?—He ordered it to be given to the people to eat.

9. How many were there to eat of it?—A hundred men.

10. What did Elisha's servant say?—What, shall I set this before so many men?

11. Did Elisha withdraw the order?—No; he said again: Give to the people that they may eat; for thus saith the Lord, They shall eat and leave thereof.

12. Was the order obeyed, and with what result?—He set it before them and they did eat, and left thereof.

13. Of what miracles of the Lord does this remind you?—His feeding the multitudes in the wilderness. Mark 6:35-43; 8:1-8.

14. Had the miracles of Elisha the effect of winning Israel back from their fearful idolatry?—No.

15. What was the Lord's merciful design in sending Elisha with such signs and wonders to his people?—To bring them back to himself, and save them from the punishment due to their guilt.

16. Did the miracles of the Lord Jesus convince the children of Israel in his day that he was "God manifest in the flesh?"—No; they would not believe.

17. Should not this check the feeling that may arise in our hearts that if we had seen the miracle we should certainly have believed?—Yes.

NAAMAN. (2 Kings 5.)

1. With what disease was Naaman afflicted?—Leprosy.

2. Who was he?—Commander of the army of the king of Syria.

3. How did he hear that the prophet Elisha could probably heal him?—Through a little captive Hebrew maid that waited on his wife.

4. What did the little maid say?—She wished he was with Elisha, as he would cure him. 2 Kings 5:3.

5. What made the young slave girl say this?—She had probably been well trained in the true faith.

6. What did the king of Syria do when her words were reported at court?—He sent Naaman with a letter to the king of Israel, asking the king to recover him of his leprosy.

7. What did the king of Israel say and do when he received this letter?—He rent his clothes and said: Am I God, to kill and to make alive, that this man sendeth unto me to recover a man of his leprosy? Wherefore consider, I pray you, and see how he seeketh a quarrel against me.

8. When Elisha heard of the king's distress, what did he do?—He sent word to the king, saying: Let him come to me, and he shall know that there is a prophet in Israel.

9. Did Naaman come to the prophet?—Yes.

10. Did Elisha receive him in his house or come out to see him?—No.

11. How did he receive him?—He sent a message to him to wash in Jordan. 2 Kings 5:10.

12. What had Naaman expected?—That Elisha would come to him and in a solemn manner call upon God to heal him.

13. Was he induced to try the remedy?—Yes; his pride and anger yielded to the wise advice of those about him.

14. What was the result?—He was perfectly cured.

15. After the cure was effected how did Naaman show his gratitude?—He came back to the prophet and insisted on his accepting a reward.

16. Would Elisha receive it?—No.

17. What acknowledgment did he make concerning the true God?—Now I know that there is no God in all the earth, but in Israel.

18. What favor did he ask of Elisha?—To be permitted to carry away two mules' burden of earth.

19. For what purpose?—To erect an altar upon which to offer burnt offerings and other sacrifices to the Lord.

20. In what thing did he ask to be pardoned?—That he had worshiped in the temple of his god Rimmon, and had bowed himself down before his heathen idols. 2 Kings 5:18.

21. How was he dismissed?—In peace.

22. Did Elisha accept of Naaman's gifts?—He would accept

nothing.

GEHAZI. (2 Kings 5:20-27.)

1. What did Gehazi do when Naaman was gone?—He ran after him and took somewhat of him.

2. How did he proceed in the matter?—He pretended that the prophet had just then been visited by two young men, and needed for them a talent of silver and two changes of raiment.

3. Did Naaman give what he asked for?—He gave him two talents of silver and the two changes of garments.

4. What was the sin of Gehazi in this matter?—Covetousness.

5. Did Gehazi's sin find him out?—Yes.

6. What judgment did the prophet denounce against him?— That the leprosy of Naaman should cleave to him and to his seed forever. 2 Kings 5:27.

7. Was Gehazi dismissed from Elisha's service?—He was.

8. What was he compelled from this day and forward to do?—To live apart. Lev. 13:45, 46.

SUNDRY MIRACLES OF ELISHA. (2 Kings 6—8:1-6.)

1. What miracle did Elisha perform when the sons of the prophets were cutting timber by Jordan?—He made an iron ax head to swim. 2 Kings 6:6.

2. For what purpose was this timber cut?—To enlarge their habitation.

3. Through whom did the king of Israel learn the stratagems of the king of Syria?—Elisha informed him.

4. How did Elisha get the information?—From God. 2 Kings 6:9.

5. How was the king of Syria affected by this?—He was troubled and suspected his servants.

6. What was he told?—That none of his servants were treacherous, but that Elisha the prophet in Samaria told the king of Israel all the words that he spoke in his chamber.

7. What means did he use to prevent it?—He sent a host of men to take the prophet.

8. Who was king of Israel at this time?—Jehoram. 2 Kings 3:1.

9. How did Elisha's servant feel when he saw the host of Syrians? —He was greatly afraid.

10. Why was not Elisha equally frightened?—Because he had confidence in God.

11. How was the servant of Elisha reassured?—His eyes were opened so that he could see the mountain full of horses and chariots of fire round about Elisha.

12. What and how many were these chariots?—The chariots of God are twenty thousand, even thousands of angels. Psalm 68:17.

13. Where was Elisha at this time?—At Dothan.

14. What did Elisha tell them when they came to him?—This is not the way, neither is this the city: follow me, and I will bring you to the man whom ye seek. 2 Kings 6:19.

15. To what city did he lead them?—To Samaria.

16. By what means did Elisha lead this host from Dothan to Samaria?—By smiting them with blindness.

17. Were there eyes then opened?—They were.

18. What did the king of Israel ask Elisha when he saw them?— Shall I smite them?

19. Did Elisha permit this?—No.

20. What did he direct the king to do?—To set bread and water before them, so that they might eat and drink and return to their master.

21. How then did the king entertain them?—He prepared provision for them, and afterward he sent them away.

22. What effect did this treatment have on the Syrians?—They came no more.

23. Did this teach the king of Israel to depend upon God's fa-

99

vor for help?—No.

THE FAMINE IN SAMARIA.
(2 Kings 6:24—33; 7.)

1. What was the cause of the great famine in Samaria?—The straitness of the siege which Benhadad, king of Syria, levied against it.

2. What complaint did a woman make to the king of Israel as he was passing on the wall?—That she and another woman had agreed together to cook their two sons, and that after she had performed her part of the contract the other woman had hid her son.

3. What effect had this upon the king?—He was greatly shocked and rent his clothes.

4. What resolution did he make? —To put Elisha to death, as being either the cause of the famine or unwilling to remove it.

5. What did he thereupon do? —He sent a man from before him to behead the prophet.

6. How did Elisha receive the king's messenger?—He ordered him to be shut out.

7. Did Jehoram himself follow the executioner?—He did, probably to countermand his order.

8. How did Elisha receive the king?—He called upon him to hear the word of the Lord.

9. What word of the Lord did Elisha deliver to the king?—That on the next day there should be great plenty of food in Samaria. 2 Kings 7:1.

10. Who accompanied the king? —One of his lords.

11. What unbelieving speech did he make?—That unless God were to make windows in heaven the promise could not be fulfilled.

12. What reply did Elisha make to him?—That he should see it, but should not eat thereof.

13. How was the wondrous change of events brought about? —By making the Syrians fancy they heard the noise of a great host, God caused them to fly for their lives, and leave all their provisions behind.

14. What did certain lepers outside the gate of Samaria do?— They went into the Syrian camp in the twilight to give themselves up, and found it deserted.

15. What did the lepers do when they saw that the Syrians had fled?—They obtained food, gold, silver, raiment, and other things, which they carried off and hid.

16. Did they bring the news to the city?—They called the porter and told him all they had seen.

17. Was this word brought to the king?—Yes.

18. What did the king do?—He rose in the night and sent messengers with two chariot horses to go and learn the facts.

19. What word did the messengers bring back?—That the army of the Syrians had hurriedly passed over the Jordan, abandoning everything they could not carry along the way.

20. How did the people of Samaria act when they heard these things?—They spoiled the tents of the Syrians.

21. What became of the unbelieving lord?—He was trampled to death by the throng of people at the city gate.

THE SHUNAMMITE'S LAND RESTORED. (2 Kings 8:1-6.)

1. What led the Shunammite woman, whose son Elisha had restored to life, to go into the land of the Philistines?—A seven years' famine which Elisha foretold.

2. When the famine was over did she return?—Yes.

3. What petition did she make to the king?—That her house and her land be restored unto her.

4. Who happened to be with the king when the woman came to him?—Gehazi.

5. What was he doing?—Telling the king of the great things Elisha had done.

6. Did he tell the story of the Shunammite woman and her son?

—He did.

7. Was the king satisfied that the woman's claim was just?—Yes.

8. What did he direct should be done?—That her land should be restored, and all the profits of it from the time she had left it.

HAZAEL BECOMES KING OF SYRIA. (2 Kings 8:7-15.)

1. To what city did Elisha go? —To Damascus.

2. Did the king of Damascus hear that he was there?—Yes.

3. What was the king's condition?—He was sick.

4. What did he do?—He sent Hazael to inquire whether he should recover.

5. How did Hazael go to the prophet?—He took as a present forty camels' burden of the good things of Damascus.

6. Did he accomplish the king's mission?—Yes.

7. What was the prophet's reply to Hazael?—He said, "Go, say unto him, Thou mayest certainly recover: howbeit the Lord hath showed me that he shall surely die;" and then, gazing long and steadfastly into Hazael's face, he burst into tears.

8. When Hazael inquired why he wept what answer was returned?—Because I know the evil that thou wilt do unto the children of Israel: their strongholds wilt thou set on fire, and their young men wilt thou slay with the sword, and wilt dash their children and rip up their women with child.

9. Was not Hazael greatly shocked when he heard this?— No; on the contrary, he replied in mock humility: What, is thy servant a dog, that he should do these great things?

10. What did Elisha tell him?— That the Lord had showed him he should be king of Syria.

11. What means did Hazael use to become king?—He smothered the king to death, and, seizing the throne, reigned in his stead.

JEHU. (2 Kings 9 and 10.)

1. Whom had the Lord already appointed king of Israel?— Jehu. 1 Kings 19:16.

2. Who anointed him?—A young prophet sent by Elisha. 2 Kings 9:1-6.

3. Who was with Jehu when the young prophet came?—The captains of the host.

4. When they learned that Jehu was anointed king what did they do?—They put their garments under him and blew with trumpets, crying, "Jehu is king!"

5. Who was Jehu, and where was he at this time?—A captain in the army, at Ramoth-gilead.

6. Where was Jehoram, king of Israel, at this time?—At Jezreel. 2 Kings 9:15.

7. Who was visiting Jehoram? —Ahaziah, king of Judah. 2 Kings 9:16.

8. Was Jehu long is executing God's vengeance?—No; he set about it instantly.

9. What was Jehu's first move? —To seize the capital city where Jehoram was.

10. When he approached it what did the watchman tell the king?—I see a company.

11. What did Jehoram do?—He sent horsemen to inquire whether this advance meant peace.

12. How did Jehu treat the messengers so sent?—He made them go to the rear.

13. When Jehoram and Ahaziah rode out in their chariots to meet him what did the king say?—Is it peace, Jehu?

14. What was Jehu's answer?— What peace, so long as the whoredoms of thy mother Jezebel and her witchcrafts are so many?

15. When Jehoram discovered the attitude of Jehu what did he do?—He turned and fled.

16. What did Jehu do to Jehoram?—He drew a bow with his full strength and smote him that

101

he died.

17. What did Jehu do with his body?—He commanded Bidkar his captain to cast it into the field of Naboth.

18. What became of Ahaziah? —He was smitten in his chariot, and fled to Megiddo, where he died.

19. What was done to Jezebel? —At the command of Jehu her servants flung her from an upper window, and the horses of Jehu trod her under their feet.

20. What became of her body? —It was devoured by dogs.

21. What prophecy was thus fulfilled?—The prophecy of Elijah. 1 Kings 21:23.

22. What was done to the seventy sons of Ahab in Samaria? —They were put to death, at Jehu's command, by the lords of Samaria.

23. What did Jehu do to the whole house of Ahab?—He slew them until he left none remaining.

24. What did he do to the brethren of Ahaziah, king of Judah?—They were captured and slain.

25. Why were Ahaziah and his brethren included in this general slaughter?—Ahaziah was the son-in-law of Ahab, and Jehu did not want to leave any who might avenge the death of Ahab's family and his connections.

26. How long had Ahaziah been king when he was put to death? —One year.

27. How did Jehu get the prophets and worshipers of Baal in his power?—He proclaimed a solemn assembly for Baal, and gathered all the worshipers of Baal at the temple of the god, where they were all clad in vestments to distinguish them. Then they went in to offer sacrifices and burnt offerings.

28. What was done with them? —They were all slain with the sword.

29. What did Jehu do to the images and house of Baal?—He burned the images and broke down the house.

30. Did he forsake the worship of the golden calves that Jeroboam introduced?—No.

31. What promise did the Lord make to him?—That his children should sit upon the throne of Israel unto the fourth generation.

32. From whom had the Israelites trouble in his reign?—From Hazael, king of Syria.

33. How long did Jehu reign, and by whom was he succeeded? —He reigned twenty-eight years, and was succeeded by Jehoahaz.

JEHU'S DYNASTY—ELISHA'S DEATH. (2 Kings 13-15:1-12.)

1. What character did Jehoahaz bear?—He was a wicked man. 2 Kings 13:2.

2. How did the Lord punish Israel?—By delivering them into the hands of the king of Syria.

3. What effect did this have upon the king?—He prayed to God for relief, and was heard, but idolatry still continued in the land.

4. How long did he reign?— Seventeen years.

5. Who succeeded him?—Joash his son.

6. Was he a better king?—No.

7. What sorrowful event happened in this reign?—The death of Elisha.

8. When Joash heard of the prophet's illness what did he do? —He went to see him, and wept over him.

9. What did Elisha direct the king to do?—To open the window and shoot an arrow with his bow eastward.

10. Of what was this a sign?— Of the king's smiting the Syrians in Aphek.

11. What further did the prophet direct the king to do?—To smite with his arrows on the ground.

12. How often did the king smite?—Thrice.

13. Why was Elisha displeased? —Because he had not smitten the ground five or six times.

14. Of what was this act symbolical?—Of three victories the king would gain over the Syrians, which would not be sufficient to break their power.

15. What miraculous event took place in connection with Elisha's remains?—A dead man revived when his body touched them.

16. Where was Moab situated? —On the southeast of the Dead Sea.

17. Where was Elisha's grave, supposing he was buried in the inheritance of his fathers?—At Abel-meholah in Simeon, where his father lived.

18. Was Elisha's prophecy fulfilled in the days of Joash?—Joash defeated the Syrians thrice, as Elisha had said.

19. How came Israel and Judah to go to war in this reign?—Because the king of Judah challenged the king of Israel to do so. 2 Kings 14:8.

20. What message did Joash send to Amaziah?—He proudly replied that he would crush him as a wild beast does a thistle.

21. On which side did victory turn?—On Israel's side.

22. How long did Joash reign? —Sixteen years. 2 Kings 13:10.

23. Who succeeded Joash on the throne of Israel?—Jeroboam his son. 2 Kings 14:16.

24. How many years did he reign?—Forty-one. 2 Kings 14:23.

25. What was his moral character?—He did evil in the sight of the Lord.

26. What kind of king and warrior was he?—He was successful in war, and recovered some border lands which Israel had lost.

27. How came it that Jeroboam was so victorious?—Because of God's pity and promise. 2 Kings 14:25-27.

28. How many prophets besides Jonah prophesied in this reign?— Four: Isaiah, Hosea, Joel, and Amos.

29. Who succeeded Jeroboam II?—Zachariah, his son.

30. Was his a long or snort reign?—Only six months. 2 Kings 15:8.

31. How did he come to his death?—He was killed by Shallum. 2 Kings 15:10.

32. What promise had the Lord given Jehu?—That his sons should be kings of Israel for four generations.

33. How was this fulfilled?—In the succession of Jehoahaz, Joash, Jeroboam, and Zachariah.

JORAM (OR JEHORAM), KING OF JUDAH.
(2 Chron. 21.)

1. Whose son was Joram (Jehoram), king of Judah?—Son of Jehoshaphat. 2 Chron. 21:1.

2. Which of Israel's kings reigned at the same time?— Ahaziah, and afterward Jehoram. 2 Kings 1:17, 18.

3. Whose daughter was Joram's wife?—Ahab's. 2 Chron. 21:6.

4. What effect did this unholy alliance have on the king?—It led him into the sins of Ahab's house. 2 Chron. 21:6.

5. How many years did Joram reign jointly with his father?— About two. 2 Kings 8:16.

6. What was the first wicked thing he did after his father was dead and he reigned alone?—He killed his brothers. 2 Chron. 21: 4.

7. What kingdom revolted from under the sway of Judah in this reign?—Edom, and the city of Libnah.

8. What written message came to him from Elijah the prophet? —Of a great plague or affliction for his family and people, and a mortal disease for himself.

9. By what death did he die? —By a long and painful illness.

10. How long had he reigned? —Eight years.

11. Who succeeded him?—Aha-

ziah, his son.

12. By what three names is this king called?—Ahaziah, Jehoahaz, and Azariah. 2 Chron. 21:17.

13. By which is he more generally called?—Ahaziah. 2 Kings 9.

14. Which of Joram's sons was he?—The youngest.

15. Why did not Joram's eldest son reign?—Because he had been killed with his brothers.

16. What did this prove?—That Elijah's message had ,come true.

17. To what untimely end did this king of Judah come?—He was killed, with Joram, by order of Jehu.

18. How did it happen?—He had gone to visit Joram. 2 Kings 8:29; 2 Chron. 22:7.

19. What was the name of Ahaziah's mother?—Athaliah.

20. Who was Athaliah?—The daughter of Ahab and Jezebel.

21. What was her character?—She was ambitious, cruel, vindictive, and idolatrous.

ATHALIAH, THE QUEEN-MOTHER. (2 Kings 11.)

1. Who usurped the government of Judah after Ahaziah's death?—Athaliah, the king's mother.

2. What did she do to secure her position?—She destroyed all the seed royal.

3. Did any of the late king's family escape destruction?—Only one, his son Joash, an infant.

4. How did he escape?—His aunt, the sister of Ahaziah, secreted him.

5. How long was he concealed, and where?—Six years, in the chambers of the house of the Lord.

6. By what means was Joash acknowledged heir of the throne? —The priest Jehoiada sent and fetched the rulers over hundreds, with the captains of the guards, and brought them into the house of the Lord, and made a covenant with them, and took an oath of them, and showed them the king's son.

7. After this oath of allegiance what did Jehoiada do?—He stationed the troops around the temple, and brought forth the king's son, and put the crown on his head, and anointed him king.

8. How old was Joash at that time?—Seven years.

9. Did the people accept him as king?—Yes.

10. What did Athaliah do when she heard the noise?—She rent her clothes and cried, "Treason, treason."

11. Did she regain control of the kingdom?—No; Jehoiada ordered her to be put forth without the ranges; and there she was slain.

12. What was the first thing done after Joash became king?—Jehoiada made a covenant between the Lord and the king and the people, that they should be the Lord's people.

13. What effect did this covenant have upon the people?—They immediately went into the house of Baal and broke it down, and broke his images into pieces, and slew Mattan, the priest of Baal, before the altars. Then Jehoiada appointed officers over the house of the Lord.

14. Where did Joash after this reside?—In the king's house. 2 Chron. 23:20.

JOASH, KING OF JUDAH. (1 Kings 12; 2 Chron. 24.)

1. How long did Joash continue to do well?—During the life of Jehoiada the priest—about twenty-eight years.

2. What good service did he do the temple of God during Jehoiada's life?—He repaired and refitted it. 2 Chron. 24:4-14.

3. How was the money raised for this purpose?—Jehoiada the priest took a chest and bored a hole in the lid of it, and set it beside the altar; and the priests put into it all the money that was brought into the house of the

Lord.

4. How old was Jehoiada when he died?—One hundred and thirty years. 2 Chron. 24:15.

5. What honor did they show his remains?—They buried him among the kings.

6. How did Joash behave after his death?—He worshiped idols.

7. By whom was he seduced into idolatry?—By the princes of Judah.

8. Did the people forsake God and serve groves and idols?—They did.

9. Whom did the Lord send to warn them of their sins?—Prophets who testified against them.

10. What was the effect of their testimony?—The people would not give ear.

11. What prophet was moved by the Spirit of God to reprove them again?—Zechariah, the son of Jehoiada.

12. What did Joash cause to be done to him?—To be stoned to death.

13. What did Zechariah say in dying?—The Lord look upon it, and require it.

14. Is his death alluded to in the New Testament?—He is probably alluded to by Christ, in Matt. 23:35, though some ancient commentators think the father of John the Baptist is alluded to here.

15. How did the Lord punish Judah for their idolatry?—By the Syrian army, which came to Jerusalem and Judah, and destroyed all the princes of the people, and sent all the spoil of them to Damascus.

16. How did he punish Joash personally?—By great diseases.

17. In what way did he die?—He was killed by his own servants.

18. How long did he reign?—Forty years. 2 Chron. 24:1.

19. Who succeeded him?—Amaziah, his son.

AMAZIAH. (2 Kings 14; 2 Chron. 25.)

1. How old was Amaziah when he began to reign?—Twenty-five years.

2. What did he do to the murderers of his father?—He had them put to death.

3. What army did he gather?—Three hundred thousand choice warriors from Judah and Benjamin, and hired a hundred thousand men out of Israel for a hundred talents of silver.

4. When he was ready to go forth with this great army what prophetic word came to him?—O king, let not the army of Israel go with thee; for the Lord is not with Israel. For if thou wilt go, do so: be strong for the battle: God shall make thee fall before the enemy, for God hath power to help and to cast down.

5. Did he persist in retaining them in his service?—No.

6. What did he do?—He dismissed the army of Israel.

7. When he regretted having paid the hundred talents of silver what did the man of God tell him?—That God was able to give him much more than this.

8. How did the army of Israel behave when they were sent away?—They returned home in great anger, and fell upon the cities of Judah from Samaria to Beth-horon, and smote three thousand men of them and took much spoil.

9. Against whom did Amaziah make war?—The Edomites.

10. What was the result?—He smote of them in the valley of salt ten thousand, captured Seir by war, and took ten thousand prisoners, whom he put to death by casting them down from the tops of the rocks. 2 Chron. 25:11, 12.

11. Into what idolatry did Amaziah fall?—He worshiped the gods of the children of Seir. 2 Chron. 25:14.

12. How did God reprove him for this?—He sent a prophet to him, who said: Why hast thou sought after the gods of the peo-

105

ple, which could not deliver their own people out of thine hand?

13. Did the king repent?—No; and he even threatened the prophet with personal violence.

14. What means did Amaziah use to punish the army of the Israelites for falling upon his cities?—He challenged their king to fight.

15. Did their king accept the challenge?—No; he advised Amaziah to stay at home, lest he should be hurt.

16. Did Amaziah heed this counsel?—He did not, but led his armies against the king of Israel.

17. What was the issue of this campaign?—Judah was put to the worse before Israel.

18. What became of Amaziah?—Joash, the king of Israel, took him prisoner and brought him to Jerusalem.

19. How long did he reign?—Twenty-nine years.

20. How did he die?—A conspiracy was formed against him in Jerusalem, and he fled to Lachish; but the conspirators sent after him and slew him there. 2 Chron. 25:27.

21. Who succeeded him?—Uzziah, his son.

THE LAST KINGS OF ISRAEL. (2 Kings 15-17.)

1. Who slew Zachariah, the last of Jehu's dynasty?—Shallum. 2 Kings 15:10.

2. How long did he reign?—A month.

3. Who destroyed him?—Menahem.

4. How long did Menahem reign?—Ten years. 2 Kings 15:17.

5. What kind of a king was he?—A wicked one.

6. Who fought against him?—Pul, king of Assyria.

7. What tribute was Menahem compelled to pay?—A thousand talents of silver.

8. How did he collect this amount?—He exacted it of Israel, even of all the mighty men of wealth, of each man fifty shekels of silver.

9. Who succeeded Menahem?—Pekahiah, his son.

10. How long did Pekahiah reign?—Two years.

11. Who slew him?—Pekah, one of his captains.

12. How long did Pekah reign?—Twenty years.

13. What happened in his reign?—Tiglath-pileser, king of Assyria, came against Israel and took several districts, including Gilead and Galilee and all Naphtali, and carried off the inhabitants captive to Assyria.

14. Who was the last king of Israel?—Hoshea.

15. How did he come to the throne?—He made a conspiracy against Pekah, and slew him, and seized the government.

16. How long did he reign?—Nine years. 2 Kings 17:1.

17. Which of the kings of Assyria came against him?—Shalmanezer.

18. Did Israel conquer, or the Assyrians?—The Assyrians.

19. What did the king of Assyria do when he overcame the Israelites?—He carried them off as captives.

20. Had Israel been forewarned of such a fate?—Yes. See Deut. 28:36.

21. To what places was Israel carried captive?—To places in Media and Mesopotamia.

22. Were the Israelites ever restored to their native land?—No; at least not as a body.

23. What are they called in history?—The Lost Tribes of Israel.

24. Who are now thought to be the descendants of these lost tribes?—Various opinions are held concerning them. They are probably too widely scattered to be identified.

25. Who were brought in to fill the depopulated cities?—People from Babylon and the regions around it. 2 Kings 17:24.

26. What was the result?—A

mixture of the worship of God and of idols. 2 Kings 17:33.

UZZIAH. (2 Kings 15; 2 Chron. 26.)

1. Who succeeded Amaziah as king of Judah?—Azariah, otherwise named Uzziah.

2. How old was he when he began to reign?—Sixteen years.

3. Was his reign prosperous?—It was.

4. How?—He subdued the Philistines and planted garrisons among them. He also conquered the Arabians in Gur-baal, and the Mehunim, and compelled the Ammonites to pay tribute. He repaired the wall of Jerusalem, and built towers at the broken gates and in the desert, and digged wells for his cattle in the low country and plains, and employed husbandmen and vinedressers in the mountains and in Carmel.

5. What king was reigning in Israel at this time?—Jeroboam II.

6. How many prophets prophesied in the reign of Uzziah?—Five: Isaiah, Hosea, Joel, Amos, and Jonah.

7. What is said of Uzziah in 2 Chron. 26:5?—That while he sought the Lord he prospered.

8. How was this manifested in the early part of his reign?—By his great success in war. 2 Chron. 26:6-15.

9. What was the size of his army?—Three hundred and seven thousand and five hundred fighting men, and twenty-six hundred officers.

10. How were they armed?—With shields and spears, helmets and habergeons, and bows and slings.

11. What defenses were there on the towers?—Engines to shoot arrows and great stones.

12. By whose influence was he kept in the right way?—By the influence of Zechariah, a man of God.

13. What effect did prosperity have on him?—It lifted up his heart.

14. What does it mean by his heart being lifted up?—That he was proud and presumptuous.

15. What does the Lord say about pride in the Scripture?—That it "goeth before destruction." Prov. 16:18.

16. To what act of impiety did Uzziah's pride prompt him?—To burn incense like a priest.

17. How was it punished?—By his being smitten with leprosy.

18. What effect did his punishment have on him?—It made him go and live alone.

19. Of what was leprosy a type?—Of sin.

20. How many instances are recorded in Scripture of persons being punished by leprosy?—Three; those of Miriam, Gehazi, and Uzziah.

21. Did any of these persons recover?—Only Miriam.

22. What great deprivations did Uzziah suffer in consequence of this malady?—He was cut off from the house of the Lord, from the honors of a king, and from all human society.

23. How had Uzziah occupied himself?—In war, in building cities and towers, in digging wells, and in keeping much cattle; also in cultivating fruitful fields.

24. How long did he reign?—Fifty-two years.

25. Who shared the government with him when he was laid aside, and succeeded him on the throne of Judah?—Jotham, his son.

JOTHAM. (2 Kings 15:32-38; 2 Chron. 27.)

1. How old was Jotham when he began to reign?—Twenty-five years. 2 Chron. 27:1.

2. How is his character described?—He did that which was right in the sight of the Lord.

3. What is the secret of his prosperity?—He prepared (or established) his ways before God.

4. Were his subjects equally faithful?—They did corruptly.

5. What public works did he construct?—The high gate of the house of the Lord, and much of the wall of Ophel; also he built cities in the mountains of Judah, and castles and towers in the forest.

6. What war did he carry on?—With the Ammonites.

7. With what success?—He prevailed against them, and compelled them to pay tribute.

8. What was the tribute?—A hundred talents of silver, ten thousand measures of wheat, and ten thousand measures of barley for three consecutive years.

9. How long did he reign?—Sixteen years.

10. Who followed Jotham?—Ahaz, his son.

AHAZ. (2 Kings 16; 2 Chron. 28.)

1. How old was Ahaz when he began to reign?—Twenty years.

2. How did Ahaz differ from his father?—He did not right in the sight of the Lord.

3. In whose ways did he walk?—In those of the kings of Israel.

4. Who was king of Israel at this time?—Pekah.

5. What idol worship did Ahaz introduce?—That of Baal and of the gods of Syria. 2 Chron. 28:2, 23.

6. What cruel heathen practice did he exercise on his son?—He burnt him in sacrifice. 2 Chron. 28:3.

7. What enemies came against Judah as a punishment for their sins?—Pekah, and Rezin king of Syria.

8. Whom did Ahaz engage to help him against them?—Tiglath-pileser, king of Assyria.

9. What payment did Ahaz make him for his help?—He gave him the treasures of his house, of his princes, and of the temple.

10. How did he show his fealty to the king of Assyria?—He went to Damascus to meet him.

11. What directions did he send from thence to Urijah the priest?—To make an altar similar to one he saw in Damascus.

12. How soon was the altar completed?—By the time the king returned.

13. Did Ahaz offer sacrifices upon it?—Yes.

14. What was done with the altar of the Lord?—It was placed on the north side of the new altar.

15. How many in Judah did Pekah and the Israelites slay?—A hundred and twenty thousand men.

16. Were any carried off captive?—Yes. Two hundred thousand men, women, sons, and daughters, with much spoil.

17. When the captives were brought to Samaria what did the prophet Oded say?—He counseled the Israelites to set the captives free, for the fierce wrath of the Lord was upon them.

18. What was done with the captives?—They were left by their captors before the princes and all the congregation, who fed and clothed them, and transported them all to Jericho, where they were delivered to their brethren.

19. What other calamities befell Judah?—The Edomites assaulted the realm and carried off many captives, and the Philistines recovered some of their cities and villages.

20. Which of the prophets prophesied in his reign?—Isaiah, Hosea, and Micah.

21. How does Isaiah describe the state of Israel and Judah at this time?—Ah sinful nation, a people laden with iniquity, a seed of evildoers, children that are corrupters: they have forsaken the Lord, they have provoked the Holy One of Israel unto anger, they are gone away backward. Isa. 1:4.

22. How are the daughters of Judah described?—The daughters of Zion are haughty. Isa. 3:16.

23. What encouragement did the Lord give to Ahaz by the prophet Isaiah?—Take heed, and be quiet; fear not, neither be fainthearted for the two tails of these smoking firebrands, for the fierce anger of Rezin with Syria, and of the son of Remaliah. Isa. 7:4.

24. When Ahaz declared he would not ask a sign of God was that from reverence or disregard? —From disregard.

25. How did his seeking aid from the king of Assyria against his foes, and not from the Lord, decide this?—It showed he was determined to take his own course.

26. What was the consequence of his seeking to the Assyrians? —Embarrassment instead of support. 2 Chron. 28:20.

27. How long did he reign?— Sixteen years.

28. Where was he buried?—In Jerusalem; but not in the sepulcher of the kings.

HEZEKIAH, KING OF JUDAH.
(2 Chron. 29-32.)

1. Who reigned after Ahaz?— Hezekiah, his son.

2. How old was Hezekiah when he began to reign?—Twenty-five years.

3. Into what state of neglect had the temple fallen?—Into even a filthy state. 2 Chron. 29:5.

4. Did Hezekiah fear the Lord and serve him?—Yes.

5. What did he do to set up the worship of God again?—He called upon the priests and Levites to assist.

6. Did the priests, Levites, and people respond to the call?—Yes; very heartily. 2 Chron. 29:12-19.

7. When the temple and its vessels were cleansed and sanctified what was done?—The king and rulers of the city brought sacrifices, and the priests offered them on the altar in behalf of the sanctuary and the kingdom and Judah.

8. What worship was offered?— The king and congregation bowed themselves before the Lord, the singers sang, the trumpeters sounded, and the musicians played on the cymbals, the psalteries, and the harps.

9. What sacrifices did the people bring?—For burnt offerings, seventy bullocks, a hundred rams, and two hundred lambs; and for peace offerings and other offerings six hundred oxen and three thousand sheep, besides drink offerings.

10. Were the priests able to prepare all these sacrifices for offering?—They were not; for they were too few.

11. How did they manage?— They called on the Levites to assist them.

12. For how long?—Until a sufficient number of priests had sanctified themselves to perform the labor.

13. How did the king and people feel when the work of the temple was again set in order?— They rejoiced that God had prepared the people.

14. Was Hezekiah's reformation confined to Judah, or did he desire to extend it to all Israel? —He invited all Israel and Judah to join in a solemn passover.

15. In what state was the kingdom of Israel at this time?—In a sad and idolatrous state, under the reign of Hoshea. 2 Kings 17.

16. How were Hezekiah's messengers received?—They were laughed at and mocked. 2 Chron. 30:10.

17. Were there any who responded to his appeal?—Numbers came from Asher, Manasseh, Ephraim, Issachar, and Zebulun.

18. What prayer did Hezekiah offer for these?—That the good Lord would pardon everyone who had prepared his heart to seek him.

19. Did the Lord accept it?— He did. 2 Chron. 30:20.

20. How long did the people keep the feast?—They kept the holy feast two weeks.

21. How long had it been since there had been such a passover as this?—Three hundred years.

22. What effect did this joy in the Lord have on the people with regard to the idols of the land?—They destroyed them all. 2 Chron. 31.

23. What was the next proof the people gave that their hearts were right with God?—The abundance of their offerings. 2 Chron. 31:5-7.

24. How can we show our love for God's service?—By giving to it our money and our time.

25. What did Hezekiah do with the surplus of the offerings? —He had them stored up in the chambers of the Lord's house for the use of the priests and the Levites.

26. How was it ascertained who were entitled to the tithes thus accumulated?—From the genealogies of the house of Aaron and of the Levites. 2 Chron. 31:16-19.

27. Was the treasure that Ahaz paid to Tiglath-pileser a tempting bait to Assyria?—It undoubtedly was.

28. How was Hezekiah made to feel this?—Sennacherib, the succeeding king, was tempted to attack him.

29. Where was Sennacherib at this time?—At Lachish.

30. How did he try to bribe Sennacherib to depart from him? —By acknowledging himself his vassal, and offering tribute.

31. How much tribute money did the king assess?—Three hundred talents of silver and thirty talents of gold.

32. From what sources did Hezekiah get this?—From the house of the Lord, the treasury of the kingdom, and the doors and pillars of the temple.

33. Did this induce the king to depart from him?—No; it only whetted his appetite for more.

34. What did Sennacherib do? —He sent three of his generals, the chief of whom was Rabshakeh, with a very great army, against Jerusalem.

35. What did Hezekiah do when the Assyrians came against him?—He fortified Jerusalem and cut off the water from the enemy's camp.

36. On whom did he depend for succor?—On God alone. 2 Chron. 32:8.

37. How did the people feel when Hezekiah cheered them?— They rested on his words.

38. What did Rabshakeh do to shake their confidence in God?— He boasted of his master's victories in other lands.

39. Did he succeed?—No; the people held their peace. 2 Kings 18:36.

40. Who was the exalted prophet of Israel at this time?— Isaiah.

41. To whom did Hezekiah send, and what did he himself do?—He sent to Isaiah, and went into the temple for prayer to God. 2 Kings 19:1, 2.

42. How did the Lord appear for his people at this time?—He promised them the departure and death of Sennacherib. 2 Kings 19:6, 7.

43. Did Sennacherib address Hezekiah by a herald, as before, or send a letter to him?—He sent a letter.

44. What did Hezekiah do with the letter?—He spread it before the Lord in prayer.

45. Where should we go when in trouble?—Direct to God.

46. Is God now the hearer and answerer of prayer, as he was then?—He is.

47. What was Hezekiah's prayer?—That God would save them for his own glory. 2 Kings 19:15-19.

48. By whom did the Lord answer his prayer?—Isaiah.

49. What assurance did Isaiah

110

give to Hezekiah?—That Sennacherib should hear a rumor, and return to his own land, where he should fall by the sword. Isa. 37:7.

50. How was this wonderful deliverance effected?—2 Kings 19:35.

51. What was God's angel of destruction?—Probably the deadly sirocco of the desert; the blast that the prophet had foretold.

52. How many of the Assyrians perished?—One hundred and eighty-five thousand men. Isa. 37:36.

53. What was Sennacherib's miserable end?—He was killed by his own sons. Isa. 37:38.

54. What mighty city was the capital of the Assyrian empire?—Nineveh.

55. Are there any proofs in the present day of this Assyrian king's conquests and final defeat?—The ruins of Nineveh disclose them.

56. What is next recorded of Hezekiah?—That he was "sick unto death." 2 Kings 20:1.

57. Did he die of this illness?—No.

58. How was he restored to health?—In answer to prayer. 2 Kings 20:3-7.

59. Was there any part of Hezekiah's history that was discreditable to him?—Yes. 2 Kings 20:13.

60. Of what sin was he guilty?—Of pride. "A proud heart is sin." Prov. 21:4.

61. How does the Lord estimate pride of heart?—Prov. 16:5; Psalm 101:52.

62. What fearful prediction was Isaiah commissioned to take to him?—2 Kings 20:17, 18.

63. How did Hezekiah receive the reproof?—He humbly submitted to the will of God.

64. What did this prove him to be?—A true son of God.

65. What benefits did Hezekiah confer on Jerusalem?—He made a pool and a conduit, and brought water into the city.

66. How much of Hezekiah's history is written in the Book of Isaiah?—Nearly the whole.

67. How long did he reign?—Twenty-nine years. 2 Kings 18:2.

68. Where did they bury him?—In the chief sepulcher of the kings.

MANASSEH AND AMON, KINGS OF JUDAH.
(2 Chron. 33.)

1. Whose son was Manasseh?—Hezekiah's.

2. Was he a good king like his father?—No.

3. Why?—Because he restored idolatry and witchcraft, set up idols and altars in the temple itself, and dedicated his sons by fire to the false gods.

4. How was he punished by the Lord for this?—He was carried captive to Babylon.

5. What effect did captivity have on him?—It brought him, by the grace of God, to penitence and prayer.

6. Did the Lord hear and answer his prayer?—Yes; he restored him to his kingdom.

7. How did Manasseh act on his return to his kingdom?—He put away idolatry throughout all Judah, and repaired the waste places of the kingdom.

8. Was this reformation complete?—Not quite; for the people worshiped God irregularly.

9. What encouragement does his history give to us?—That if we confess and forsake our sins God will abundantly pardon.

10. Is God as compassionate now as he was then?—Yes; as thousands of true penitents can thankfully declare.

11. How old was Manasseh when he began to reign?—Twelve years.

12. How long did he reign?—Fifty-five years.

13. Who succeeded him?—Amon, his son.

111

14. Did he continue the reformation his father had made?—No.

15. How did he act?—He did evil in the sight of the Lord, and trespassed more and more.

16. How long did Amon reign?—Two years.

17. What was his melancholy end?—His servants conspired against him and slew him.

18. What did the people do to the conspirators?—They put them all to death.

19. Who was made king instead of Amon?—Josiah his son.

JOSIAH, KING OF JUDAH.
(2 Chron. 34, 35; 2 Kings 22, 23.)

1. How old was Josiah when he ascended the throne of Judah?—Eight years.

2. What character did he bear?—He did that which was right in the sight of the Lord.

3. How soon did he begin to manifest his piety?—At the age of fifteen. 2 Chron. 34:3.

4. What was the first reformation he affected?—The destruction of idol worship.

5. What wonderful discovery was made in cleansing the temple?—A book of the law.

6. What did this prove?—That it had been neglected and despised.

7. What effect did the reading of God's word have on the young king?—He was shocked and alarmed by the national guilt and danger.

8. To whom did he send to inquire the will of God concerning his people?—To Huldah, the prophetess.

9. Did God alter the word that had gone forth out of his mouth?—No. 2 Chron. 24:24, 25.

10. How did he comfort Josiah notwithstanding?—By promising that his judgments should not take place during Josiah's life.

11. What effect did this message have on Josiah?—He caused the book of the law to be publicly read, and induced the people to renew their covenant with God.

12. How does 2 Chron. 35:3 show us that the ark had been taken out of the temple?—By relating Josiah's order that it should be put in again.

13. Where had the ark been?—The Levites, who remained faithful to the Lord, had probably removed and secreted it when Manasseh desecrated the temple by placing an idol therein.

14. What multiplied idolatries does 2 Kings 23 show had gained footing in Judah at this time?—The worship of Baal and the abominations of Sidon, Moab, and Ammon.

15. How did Josiah deal with them all?—He destroyed the idols and defiled their altars.

16. What prophecy concerning an altar at Beth-el did he fulfill?—1 Kings 13:1, 2.

17. How?—By burning the bones on the altar and polluting it.

18. What further did he do in Samaria?—He destroyed the temples of idol worship and slew the priests of the high places there on the altars.

19. After these reformations were effected what did Josiah do?—He commanded all the people to keep the passover.

20. How was it kept?—2 Kings 23:22.

21. In what year of Josiah's reign was this passover held?—In the eighteenth year.

22. Could all Josiah's goodness turn away God's wrath from Judah?—No. 2 Kings 24:3, 4.

23. What was Josiah's end?—He was killed in battle.

24. How did this come about?—He had attacked the king of Egypt as he was going against the king of Assyria.

25. Was this the only failure recorded of this good and pious king?—It was.

112

26. Must not their transgressions have reached a fearful height, seeing even Josiah's reformation could not purge the land?—They must, indeed.

27. How was the news of his death received by his people?—With deep and universal mourning.

28. Which famous prophet is named as mourning for him?—Jeremiah. 2 Chron. 35:25.

29. How long did he reign?—Thirty-one years.

THE LAST KINGS OF JUDAH.
(2 Kings 23:31-37; 24, 25.)

1. By whom was Josiah succeeded?—By his son Jehoahaz.

2. How old was he when he began to reign?—Twenty-three years.

3. How long did he reign?—Three months.

4. What was his character?—He did that which was evil in the sight of the Lord.

5. What became of him?—Pharaoh-nechoh, king of Egypt, put him in fetters at Riblah in the land of Hamath, and carried him off a prisoner to Egypt, where he died.

6. What tribute did Pharaoh impose on the land?—A hundred talents of silver and a talent of gold.

7. Who was placed on the throne instead of Jehoahaz?—His brother Eliakim.

8. What name did Pharaoh give him?—Jehoiakim.

9. How did he raise the tribute money?—By taxation.

10. Did he remain tributary to Egypt?—No.

11. Why?—Because Nebuchadnezzar, king of Babylon, had taken from the king of Egypt all the territory lying between the river of Egypt and the Euphrates.

12. How long was Jehoiakim a vassal of Nebuchadnezzar?—Three years.

13. Why not longer?—Because he then turned and rebelled against him.

14. What was the issue of his rebellion?—Nebuchadnezzar came up against him and bound him in fetters to carry him to Babylon, and also seized and carried off all the vessels of the house of the Lord, and put them in his temple at Babylon. 2 Chron. 36:6, 7.

15. What was Jehoiakim's age when he began to reign?—Twenty-five years.

16. How long did he reign?—Eleven years.

17. What was his character?—He did that which was evil in the sight of the Lord. 2 Kings 23:37.

18. Who reigned instead of Jehoiakim?—Jehoiachin, his son.

19. How old was he at that time?—Eighteen years. 2 Kings 24:8.

20. How long did he reign?—Three months and ten days.

21. What became of him?—He was carried captive to Babylon. 2 Kings 24:12-16.

22. Whom did Nebuchadnezzar appoint king instead of Jehoiachin?—Mattaniah, an uncle of Jehoiachin.

23. What name did he give him?—Zedekiah.

24. What was his age at that time?—Twenty-one years.

25. How long did he reign undisturbed?—Nine years.

26. What did he then do?—He rebelled against Nebuchadnezzar.

27. What did Nebuchadnezzar do?—He was carried into captivity to Riblah by Nebuchadnezzar. 2 Kings 25:8-21.

28. Were any of the inhabitants of Judah left?—A few were left to be vinedressers and husbandmen. 2 Kings 35:12.

29. Who was made their governor?—Gedaliah.

30. What kindness was showed to Jehoiachin?—See Jer. 52:32-34.

31. What prophecies were thus

113

fulfilled?—Those of Moses (Deut. 28:36), of Jeremiah (Jer. 25:8-11), of Zechariah (Zech. 11:6), and of other prophets.

32. How long did the captivity continue?—Seventy years. 2 Chron. 36:20, 21; Jer. 25:12; Dan. 9:2.

THE RETURN FROM CAPTIVITY. (Ezra.)

1. Who gave permission to the Jews to return to their own land? —Cyrus.

2. Who was Cyrus?—The king of Persia, the conqueror of Babylon.

3. What was the proclamation he made?—See Ezra 1:1, 2.

4. What vessels of the Lord's house did Cyrus return to the Jews?—Ezra 1:9-11.

5. Who was the leader of the Jews that returned?—Zerubbabel.

6. Did those who stayed behind give liberally to those who went?—They did. Ezra 1:6.

7. How many at first returned? —42,360, besides 7,337 servants and maids, including 200 singing men and singing women.

8. What substance did they bring with them?—736 horses, 245 mules, 435 camels, 6,720 asses; besides much gold and silver and costly array.

9. How much did they give to rebuild the temple?—61,000 drams of gold, 5,000 pounds of silver, and 100 priests' garments.

10. Where did they establish themselves?—The priests and the Levites and others whose service was connected with the temple dwelt in their cities, and all Israel in their cities. Ezra 2:70.

11. After they became settled what was their first concern?— To reestablish the worship of God.

12. In what way?—They rebuilt the altar and offered upon it burnt offerings every morning and evening, commencing with the feast of tabernacles on the first day of the seventh month.

13. When did they lay the foundations of the temple?—In the second year of their coming, in the second month.

14. Who set this work forward? —Zerubbabel, and Jeshua the high priest, and the other priests and Levites.

15. What ceremonies accompanied the beginning of the work? —The music and the singing of the priests and Levites.

16. What materials were secured for the building?—Cedar trees from Lebanon, for which they paid to them of Tyre meat and drink and oil.

17. Did the work go on uninterruptedly?—No.

18. Who opposed it?—The adversaries of Judah and Benjamin.

19. What did they do?—They hired counselors against them at court.

20. How did these counselors act?—They tried to frustrate the purpose of Cyrus, etc. See Ezra 4:5-7.

21. With what effect?—The work was stopped by command of Artaxerxes until further orders. Ezra 4:21.

22. How long did it cease?— Until the second year of Darius, king of Persia. Ezra 4:24.

23. Which Darius was this?— He is supposed to be Darius the son of Hystaspes.

24. Who was the Artaxerxes named as having put a stop to the work?—Smerdis.

25. And who was Ahasuerus? —Cambyses.

26. What was the origin of the rancor between the Jews and the Samaritans?—The Samaritans desired to unite with the Jews in building the temple, but Zerubbabel would not allow it on account of their heathen alliances.

27. Who were the chief counselors of the Jews?—The prophets Haggai and Zechariah.

28. By whom was the work set forward again?—By Zerubbabel and Jeshua, the high priest. Ezra 5:2.

29. Who gave them authority? —Darius. Ezra 6:1-12.

30. What did he do to promote the work?—He restored the previous decree of Cyrus.

31. How soon did they finish the work?—On the third day of the month Adar, in the sixth year of the reign of Darius. Ezra 6:15.

32. How was the new temple dedicated?—With the sacrifice of bullocks, rams, and lambs; for a sin offering for all Israel, twelve he-goats were sacrificed.

33. Was the old order of the priesthood restored?—Yes, so far as possible.

34. Who was Ezra?—A ready scribe in the law of Moses, and a priest.

35. What commission did he receive from Artaxerxes?—See Ezra 7:11-26.

36. What immunity was granted to the priests, Levites, singers, porters, and other ministrants of the temple?—Exemption from taxation.

37. What was Ezra further directed to do?—To appoint magistrates and judges to judge the people, according to the law of God.

38. What penalty might be imposed upon those guilty of violating the law of God or of the king?—Death, or banishment, or confiscation of goods, or imprisonment.

39. What did Ezra and the people with him do at the river Ahava?—They proclaimed and kept a fast, to seek of God a safe journey.

40. On what day did they set out for Jerusalem?—On the twelfth day of the first month. Ezra 8:31.

41. How long were they in making the journey?—Nearly four months. Ezra 7:9.

42. What state of affairs at Jerusalem did Ezra find?—He found that the people had intermarried with the Gentile nations, and that the princes and rulers among them had been the chief offenders.

43. What did he do?—He prostrated himself in an agony of prayer to God, confessing and weeping and rending his clothes before the house of God.

44. What effect did this have on the people?—They also wept sore, and one of the sons of Elam proposed to make a covenant with God and put away all their strange wives and their offspring.

45. Did the people present agree to do this?—Yes.

46. How was the matter concluded?—Those who were guilty of the trespass were dealt with by the elders and the judges according to the law, and the priests who had trespassed gave their hands that they would put away their foreign wives. They then offered a ram of the flock for a trespass offering.

47. Did the children of Israel henceforth become zealous for the law?—They did. Rom. 10:2.

NEHEMIAH.

1. Who was Nehemiah?—The son of Hachaliah, of the tribe of Judah, but born in Babylon. There he became the cupbearer of King Artaxerxes Longimanus.

2. What account did Hanani give Nehemiah of the state of the Jews in Judah and Jerusalem? —He said they were in great affliction and reproach on account of their unprotected situation.

3. What effect did the news have upon him?—He sat down and wept, and mourned certain days, and fasted and prayed before the God of heaven.

4. What notice did the king take of him?—He asked why his countenance was sad, seeing that he was not sick. Neh. 2:2.

5. What was Nehemiah's reply?—He said he was sad because the city of his fathers and the places where they were buried

were lying waste and the gates were burned with fire.

6. What request did Nehemiah make?—That the king would send him to Judah, that he might rebuild the city.

7. Did the king grant his request?—Yes, with leave of absence for a definite time.

8. Who besides the king favored Nehemiah?—The king's favorite queen. Neh. 2:6.

9. In what year of the king's reign was this request granted? —In the twentieth.

10. What authority did the king give to Nehemiah?—He gave him a letter to Asaph, the keeper of the king's forest, to furnish him with timber for the gates of the palace and the walls of the city, and for the house he should enter into.

11. What was Nehemiah's first act when he came to Jerusalem? —To go over the whole city by night, to see the extent of the ruins.

12. Why did he go at night? —To escape the observation of enemies.

13. After this, what did Nehemiah do?—He called the nobles and priests and rulers of the city and told them all the words that the king had spoken to him, and said: Come, let us build up the wall of Jerusalem, that we be no more a reproach.

14. What was the result of this conference?—The people replied, "Let us rise up and build;" so they strengthened each other's hands for the work.

15. How did the Jews' enemies feel when they understood Nehemiah's errand?—They were much displeased. Neh. 2:10, 19; 4:1, 7.

16. Who assisted Nehemiah in repairing the wall?—The high priest, the priests, and many of the rulers, merchants, and others. Neh. 3.

17. Were they all regular masons and builders?—No; some were goldsmiths (ver. 32) and

apothecaries (ver. 8).

18. Who are spoken of in Neh. 3:12?—The daughters of a ruler, as giving their help.

19. Should not this teach us that in the Lord's work all can assist?—Yes, and that all should feel glad and honored to do so.

20. When the enemies of the Jews saw the wall of Jerusalem progressing, what did they wish to do?—To stop the work. Neh. 4:11.

21. What reproachful thing did they say of the work?—If a fox go up, he shall even break down their stone wall. Neh. 4:3.

22. Did they succeed in hindering the work?—No.

23. How did Nehemiah meet the danger?—By prayer and faith, and by being armed and watchful. Neh. 4:9-23.

24. What great zeal and self-denial does Neh. 4:23 record?— Their not putting off their clothes at night.

25. What great abuse did Nehemiah set himself to rectify?— The requiring of usury. Neh. 5.

26. Were the people willing to do as he said?—Yes, and did it at once. Neh. 5:12, 13.

27. What example did Nehemiah himself set them?—He declined receiving his own allowance, to spare the poor.

28. What wicked device did Sanballat and his companions next try to put the good Nehemiah in fear?—They invited him to a meeting in order to get him into their hands, and they sent him a false prophet to induce him to leave his work. Neh. 6.

29. Did they succeed?—No.

30. On whom did Nehemiah depend?—Upon God. Neh. 6:9.

31. How long was the wall building?—Fifty-two days. Neh. 6:15.

32. What hindered the completion of the work?—The king issued an order to stop the work, and Nehemiah was compelled to return to Persia. Ezra 4:7-23.

33. Where was the court of Persia at this time?—At Shushan, or Susa, one of the capitals of the empire. Neh. 1:1.

34. In what other chief cities did the kings of Persia hold their court?—In Ecbatana (or Achmetha, Ezra 6:2), Babylon (Ezra 1:11), and Persepolis (mentioned only by name in the Apocryphal writings—2 Macc. 9:2).

35. How did matters progress while Nehemiah was gone?—Nothing more was done.

36. When did Nehemiah return to Jerusalem?—In the thirty-second year of Artaxerxes. Neh. 13:6.

37. How long had he been away?—Twelve years.

38. Whom did Nehemiah appoint to the charge of Jerusalem?—He gave his brother Hanani, and Hananiah the ruler of the palace, charge over Jerusalem. Neh. 7:2.

39. What did God put into the heart of Nehemiah to do after this?—To make a register of the families that returned from Babylon. Neh. 7:5.

40. Why was the preservation of the genealogies of the children of Israel so important?—To show the fulfillment in Christ of the promise to Abraham, that in his seed should all the nations of the earth be blessed (Gen. 22:18), and of the promise to David that God would raise up a king to sit forever on his throne. Acts 2:29, 30; Luke 1:30-33.

41. What further arrangement was completed by the seventh month?—The settling of the Israelites in their cities. Neh. 7:73.

42. What special feast was to be kept in that month?—The feast of tabernacles. Neh. 8:14-18.

43. Of what was it a memorial?—Of the sojourn in the wilderness, when the Israelites dwelt in tents (Lev. 23:43). It was also a harvest feast of thanksgiving (Lev. 23:34-43).

44. Who read the law to Israel at this solemn feast?—Ezra himself.

45. Does not Neh. 8:8 show that their seventy years' residence in a foreign land had made them forget their mother tongue, Hebrew?—Yes, as distinct reading and explanation were required.

46. What effect did the reading of the law have on the people?—They wept, from mingled feelings of sorrow and of joy. Neh. 8:9.

47. How did Ezra encourage the people?—He said the joy of the Lord was their strength. Neh. 8:10.

48. Did Ezra have any assistance in reading the law?—Yes; from the priests and the Levites.

49. How did Ezra and Nehemiah dismiss the people?—They told them to go to their homes, and eat the fat and drink the sweet, and send portions to those for whom nothing was prepared.

50. How was the feast of tabernacles kept?—In reading the book of the law from day to day, with a solemn assembly on the eighth day.

51. What followed these days of feasting?—A solemn fast, with reading of the law and confession of sin.

52. What further arrangements were made?—The entering into a covenant with God for obedience to his law and as to the offerings for his service, and the selecting the inhabitants of the city and country.

53. How was the wall dedicated?—With music and thanksgiving and great joy. Neh. 12:27-43.

54. How long did this reformation last?—During the days of Zerubbabel and Nehemiah. Neh. 12:47.

55. What evils had Nehemiah discovered?—Abuse and neglect of the house of God, Sabbath-breaking, and heathen marriages.

56. How did he correct them?—He cleansed the temple and

117

made new treasurers of its funds, and closed the city gates against Sabbath traffic, and put an end to marriage of heathen wives.

57. How did Nehemiah regulate the priesthood?—By their genealogies. Neh. 12:1-21.

58. Were the Levites enrolled in the same manner?—They were. Neh. 12:22-26.

59. When was this enrollment made?—When Darius (Codomannus) was king. Neh. 12:22.

60. Had not the Sabbath day been the great token of the covenant between the Lord and Israel?—It had. Exod. 31:13, 17; Isa. 58:13, 14; Ezek. 20:12-20.

61. Will God suffer his laws to be trampled on without punishment?—No.

62. What command did the Lord give about marrying heathen wives?—See Deut. 7:2-4.

63. Did Nehemiah vigorously root out this evil?—He did. Neh. 13:25, 28, 30.

64. Where is Nehemiah supposed to have ended his days?—In Persia.

65. What is the character of Nehemiah?—A man with scarcely a single fault. He was a patriot; a reformer; a single hearted, unselfish ruler; sagacious and courageous, humble, liberal, and devout.

66. What means did Ezra and Nehemiah use for instructing the people?—They established synagogues where the people met to hear the law read and explained, and these in later Jewish times became very numerous. Ezra also collected all the sacred writings then in existence, and arranged them for reading. A copy of all the sacred books was placed in every synagogue so far as practicable, and the Jews became extremely zealous in keeping the covenant and the law of God. They never again lapsed into idolatry. Schools were founded, and in process of time every Jewish youth was taught to read

and write.

ESTHER.

1 Who was Ahasuerus?—He is generally thought to be the same as Xerxes.

2. How extensive was his empire?—He reigned from India to Ethiopia, over a hundred and twenty-seven provinces.

3. Where was his palace?—In Shushan, or Susa.

4. What did he do in the third year of his reign?—He made a feast to all his satraps and courtiers.

5. How long did this feast continue?—For six months.

6. When the feast was concluded what did the king do?—He made a feast to the people of his capital seven days in the court of his garden.

7. Did the queen also entertain?—She made a feast for the women in the royal apartments.

8. Who was the queen at that time?—Vashti.

9. Why was she deposed from being queen?—Because the king, when his heart was inflamed with wine, sent for her that he might show her beauty to his guests, and she (very properly) refused to come.

10. What did the king's courtiers advise?—That the king issue a royal commandment, "That Vashti come no more before King Ahasuerus; and let the king give her royal estate unto another."

11. Why did they advise thus?—Lest other women throughout the realm should disobey their husbands, when they should hear that the queen did so without punishment.

12. How did the king select a new queen?—He had gathered into his harem all the fair young virgins in his several provinces, and placed in the custody of his chamberlain, so that the one which pleased him the most might become queen.

13. Whom did he select?—A

118

young Jewish maid named Hadassah, or Esther.

14. Who was she?—A descendant of Kish, a Benjamite, one of the captives whom Nebuchadnezzar had carried away; she was brought up by her cousin Mordecai at Susa.

15. What service did Mordecai render to the king?—He discovered that two of the king's chamberlains had formed a plot against the king's life, and he told Esther the queen. She informed her husband, who executed the two traitors.

16. Who was Haman?—The son of Hammedatha, a descendant of Agag, an Amalekite.

17. When was he promoted by the king?—Probably not until after his disastrous expedition against Greece and his return to Persia.

18. Why was Haman angered at Mordecai?—Because Mordecai, as he sat at the king's gate, would not pay him the reverence which he thought was due to him.

19. What revenge did Haman determine on?—To destroy the whole nation of the Jews, including Mordecai.

20. What representation did he make to the king concerning them?—That they were a pestilent people dispersed throughout all the provinces of the kingdom, against the king's profit, having their own laws and not keeping the king's laws.

21. What did Haman propose to the king?—That the king make a law that they be destroyed.

22. Did the king agree to this proposal?—He did, and gave Haman full authority to act in the matter.

23. How did Haman proceed?—He wrote a decree in the king's name and sealed it with the king's seal, and sent it by messenger into all the provinces to destroy all Jews, both young and old, on the thirteenth day of the twelfth month, and to take the spoil of them for a prey.

24. What effect did this decree have upon the city of Shushan?—It was perplexed.

25. When Mordecai learned what was done what did he do? —He rent his clothes, put on sackcloth and ashes, went out into the midst of the city and cried with a loud and bitter cry.

26. How did the Jews feel when the decree was published?—In every province there was great mourning and fasting.

27. What did Queen Esther do when her maids and chamberlains told her about Mordecai's conduct?—She sent clean raiment to Mordecai, for she was much grieved.

28. When Mordecai refused it, what did she next do?—She sent to know the reason of his affliction; and Mordecai told the messenger every whit, and gave him a copy of the decree to show it to Esther, and to charge her to go in unto the king to make supplication unto him, and make request before him for her people.

29. Did Esther undertake to do this?—She agreed to do so if the Jews in Shushan would first fast for her three days and nights, while she and her maidens did the same.

30. When Esther went in unto the king how did he receive her? —With favor.

31. What did the king say?— What wilt thou, Queen Esther, and what is thy request? It shall be given thee, even to the half of the kingdom.

32. What petition did she make? —"Let the king and Haman come this day to the banquet which I have prepared for him;" and the king and Haman came to the banquet.

33. What did the king say to Esther at the banquet?—The same as before.

34. What answer did she return?—She invited the king and Haman to a banquet on the next day, when she would prefer her

request.

35. How did Haman feel when thus honored?—He was exceedingly puffed up, and went home and told his wife and his friends of the glory of his riches and the multitude of his children, and how the king had advanced him; and that the queen had invited him alone of all the king's courtiers to the banquet she had prepared; "but all this availeth me nothing," he said, "so long as I see Mordecai the Jew sitting at the king's gate."

36. What did his wife and friends advise?—That he erect a gallows, and speak to the king that Mordecai might be hanged thereon.

37. What reason had they to think the king would grant his request?—From his well-known indifference to the lives of his subjects.

38. What honor did the king confer on Mordecai?—The honor that Haman had proposed, and which he expected would be conferred on himself.

39. What request did the queen make at the banquet which followed?—She said: If I have found favor in thy sight, O king, and if it please the king, let my life be given me at my petition, and my people at my request; for we are sold, I and my people to be destroyed, to be slain, and to perish. But if we had been sold for bondmen and bondwomen I had held my tongue, although the enemy could not countervail the king's damage.

40. What was the king's reply?—He asked: Who is this enemy, and where is he that durst presume in his heart to do this thing?

41. Who was named as this enemy by the queen?—Haman.

42. What did the king do?—He rose from the banquet in great wrath and ordered that Haman should be hung on the gallows; then his wrath was appeased.

43. Had the king up to this time known the nationality of Esther?—No; for Mordecai had charged her not to show her people or her kindred.

44. What additional honors did he confer on Mordecai?—He gave him the signet ring which he had taken from Haman, thus making him his vizier.

45. How did the king grant Esther's request?—He said to Esther and to Mordecai: Write ye for the Jews, as it liketh you, in the king's name, and seal it with the king's ring.

46. What did the king and the vizier write?—That the king granted to the Jews to destroy, to slay, and to cause to perish all the power of the people and province that would assault them, upon one day in all the provinces of King Ahasuerus, namely, the thirteenth day of the twelfth month.

47. How was this order of the king published?—By messengers that rode upon mules and camels.

48. When the decree became known what effect had it?—The Jews had light and gladness, and joy and honor; and many of the people of the land became Jews, for the fear of the Jews fell upon them.

49. What had determined Haman to fix upon the thirteenth day of the twelfth month for the execution of his order?—He used divination to find a favorable day, according to his superstitious notions, and the day turned up by the lot which he cast was the one fixed upon.

50. In what month did Haman cast the lot?—In the first month, and this gave both the Jews and their enemies ample time to prepare for the intended spoliation and slaughter.

51. When the appointed day arrived what was done?—The enemies of the Jews were slain.

52. How many of them perished?—Seventy-five thousand in the provinces, and eight hundred, including the ten sons of Haman

in Shushan, the capital.

53. Why did not the king annul his first decree when Esther presented her first petition?—Because, by a foolish custom, the laws of the Medes and Persians might not be changed. Dan. 6: 12, 15.

54. What feast was instituted by Esther in commemoration of this event?—The feast of Purim, to be kept on the fourteenth and fifteenth days of the twelfth month annually.

55. Why was the feast called Purim?—Because Haman had cast Pur, that is, the lot, to destroy the Jews.

56. Has this feast been observed ever since then?—It has been, and is now celebrated every year.

57. Who wrote the book of Esther?—Mordecai is supposed to be the author, or Ezra.

58. What is there remarkable about it?—The name of God does not once occur in it, and yet it is regarded as canonical.

59. What is supposed to be the reason of this omission?—Some of the ancient Jewish teachers accounted for this omission by saying that it was a transcript, under divine inspiration, from the chronicles of the Medes and Persians, and that being meant to be read by the heathen, the sacred name was intentionally omitted.

JOB.

1. Who was Job?—A very rich man in the land of Uz, toward the north of Arabia, or south of Bashan. Job 1:3.

2. How was Job afflicted?—By the loss of all his property and servants, by the death of his children, and by a severe bodily disease brought on him by Satan.

3. When is he supposed to have lived?—Between the times of Abraham and of Moses.

4. Why?—From the age to which he lived, which was about two hundred years; from the very

early customs alluded to in the book, as the worship of the sun, moon, and stars, the use of engraving for writing, and the reckoning of riches by cattle. Job 21: 26-28; 19:23, 24; 1:3.

5. When was the Book of Job written?—It belongs to the Solomonic period of Hebrew literature, and was written probably between his age and Hezekiah's.

6. To what class of writings is it referred?—To what may be called the "wisdom literature" of the Hebrews.

7. What other writings are included in this class?—Proverbs, Ecclesiastes, and some of the Apocryphal books.

8. What is the intention of the book?—To discuss the problem of human life, and to present a theodicy, or "a vindication of the ways of God to man."

9. Who are the characters introduced into the drama?—The principal characters are Job and his three friends, Eliphaz the Temanite, Bildad the Shuhite, Zophar the Naamathite, then Elihu the Buzite, and lastly the Lord.

10. Of what did the three friends first named try to convince Job?—That his sufferings were inflicted upon him by God in punishment for his sins.

11. What reply did Job make to this?—He vindicated himself against the aspersions of his friends.

12. How did Elihu reprove both parties?—He reproved the three friends because they had accused Job wrongfully and had not proved their charge, and Job because he was self-righteous, and had not vindicated the Almighty in his dealings with him.

13. Does the Almighty reply to Job's argument?—He does not, but shows that he is almighty in power and infinite in wisdom, and leaves Job and his friends to make the proper inference for themselves as to his dealings with men.

14. What effect did the words of the Lord have on Job?—He humbled himself before God, and confessed his faults.

15. What did the Lord say to Job's three friends?—That his wrath was kindled against them because they had not spoken of him the right thing as his servant Job had done.

16. What did he direct them to do?—To bring sacrifices to Job, in order that he might offer them up in their behalf, and pray for them.

17. What was the result?—As Job prayed for his friends in the offering of these sacrifices his prayers were accepted, his own "captivity" was turned, and he was restored to soundness and prosperity.

18. How long after this did Job live?—One hundred and forty years.

THE PSALMS.

1. What is a psalm?—A sacred lyrical ode, intended to be accompanied in the singing with musical instruments.

2. Who wrote the earliest psalm found in the Bible?—Moses, after the passage of the Red Sea.

3. How many psalms are found in the Book of Psalms?—One hundred and fifty.

4. What division is made of these psalms?—They are usually divided into five portions or books, as follows: Book I, Psalms 1-41; Book II, Psalms 42-72; Book III, Psalms 73-89; Book IV, Psalms 90-106; and Book V, Psalms 107-150. The first four books end with the word "Amen," and the last book with "Hallelujah."

5. By whom was this collection made?—Probably by Ezra.

6. Who wrote the Psalms?—David is the author of over seventy of them; Solomon of one, perhaps two; Moses of one; Asaph of twelve; the sons of Korah of thirteen; Ethan of one; Heman of one; and Jeduthun of three. Many of them are anonymous.

7. What are the subjects of the Psalms?—They are historical, didactic, and prophetical, or contain praise, thanksgiving, and prayer, especially in trouble or affliction, for divine help, and in penitence, for mercy and pardon.

8. Do we know on what occasions these Psalms were written? —In only a few of them is the occasion mentioned.

9. Were any of these Psalms used in public worship?—Yes.

10. What does the word "Selah," which occurs frequently in the Psalms, signify?—It is supposed to be a musical direction, and to signify an "Interlude," equivalent to "Let the voices pause and the musical instruments sound."

PROVERBS.

1. What is a proverb?—A short and pithy saying, containing some practical truth or rule for conduct, and embodying the wisdom derived from experience and observation.

2. Who is the principal author of the Book of Proverbs?—Solomon. Prov. 1:1.

3. By whom were the proverbs collected?—By the men of Hezekiah. Prov. 25:1.

4. Are all of Solomon's proverbs contained in this collection?—No; for he spoke three thousand proverbs, and only a few appear here.

5. Why were these proverbs spoken?—"To know wisdom and instruction; to perceive the words of understanding; to receive the instruction of wisdom, justice, and judgment and equity; to give subtilty to the simple, to the young man knowledge and discretion." Prov. 1:2-4.

6. How many chapters are there in the Introduction of the Proverbs?—Nine.

7. With what is the Introduction mainly taken up?—With a personification of Wisdom.

8. What is Wisdom represented

as doing?—As inviting the simple and those lacking in understanding to come into her palace and eat at her table.

9. Why?—That their days may be multiplied and the years of their life increased.

10. Who is contrasted with Wisdom?—A foolish woman, sitting at the door of her house, and calling to those who pass by, "Whoso is simple, let him turn in hither," and saying to those void of understanding, "Stolen waters are sweet, and bread eaten in secret is pleasant."

11. What kind of abode is her house?—The dead are there, and her guests are in the depths of hell.

12. What does Solomon say is the beginning of wisdom?—The fear of the Lord. Prov. 1:7.

13. What reward is promised those who seek diligently after it? —That they shall find it.

14. How did Solomon estimate wisdom?—As more precious than rubies. Prov. 3:15.

15. What are wisdom's ways called?—Ways of pleasantness and peace. Prov. 3:17.

16. After this general introduction how are the proverbs arranged?—As distinct sentences containing observations on moral virtues and their contrary vices.

17. Is this kind of wisdom common in the East?—It is, and always has been. Oriental sages endeavored to compress much thought into few words, as being more easily remembered; and these detached sayings answered a better purpose than long treatises.

18. Did Solomon gather any wise sayings from other nations? —Quite likely he did.

19. Was he careful always to make wisdom his guide and keeper?—No.

20. Are there any other proverbs besides Solomon's in the Book of Proverbs?—There are the proverbs of Agur the son of Jakeh, and the sayings of King Lemuel; while the book closes with a glorification of a perfect woman.

ECCLESIASTES.

1. By whom was Ecclesiastes written?—The author is unknown though he personates Solomon.

2. What is the meaning of the term Ecclesiastes?—"The Preacher."

3. When was the book written? —Modern critics refer it to the post-exilian period of Hebrew history. It is certain that it could not have been written in the reign of Solomon.

4. Had the writer any means of knowing the subject on which he wrote?—He had personal experience, as he was probably brought up in Persia, and was acquainted with the usages of the Persian court.

5. What was the result of his knowledge?—That all is vanity under the sun. Eccles. 1:2, 3.

6. Was there anything the author found under the sun sufficient to satisfy the soul?—Nothing.

7. What is the meaning of that term "under the sun?"—Things that relate to this world alone.

8. What is the purpose of Ecclesiastes?—To set forth the quest of the chief good.

9. Wherein is the chief good found?—The author seeks it in human wisdom, and pleasure, in business, in wealth and worldly sufficiency, and finally finds it in the right use of the present life.

10. Where should we lay up our treasure?—In heaven. Matt. 6:20, 21.

11. Did "the Preacher" wish to impress this truth on us?—He did.

12. What argument does he use to urge this in early life?— The approach of old age and of death. Eccles. 12:1-7.

13. What does he say is the conclusion of the whole matter?— Let us hear the conclusion of the whole matter: Fear God and

keep his commandments: for this is the whole duty of man. For God shall bring every work into judgment, with every secret thing, whether it be good, or whether it be evil. Eccles. 12:13, 14.

14. Is the work, then, pessimistic or hopeful?—Hopeful.

15. How hopeful rather than otherwise?—During their captivity and by their contact with Persian thought, the Israelites learned as never before the great doctrine of immortality. Henceforth the immortality of the soul and the life beyond death entered prominently into their creed. This gave a new coloring to their sacred Scriptures, and they saw that the final awards of Jehovah were not limited to time and locality, but reached forward into eternity.

CANTICLES; OR, THE SONG OF SOLOMON.

1. What opinion was formerly held concerning Solomon's Song? —That it is a nuptial ode written on the occasion of Solomon's marriage with the daughter of Pharaoh, and by Solomon himself.

2. How is it regarded as a part of the scriptural canon?—As an allegorical poem, to denote the union of Christ and his Church; Christ being the bridegroom and the Church the bride.

3. What is the form or technic of the poem?—It is a series of eclogues, extending over a period of six days, in the form of a drama.

4. What is the plot?—A young maiden of Northern Palestine, betrothed to a shepherd lover, is one day walking in the fields, when Solomon, struck with her beauty, captures her, and carries her off in one of his chariots to Jerusalem to make her an inmate of his harem. Here he vainly attempts to gain her love, which resists all the blandishments of her royal admirer, and she is finally restored to her simple country life and her humble suitor,

who again pledges his affection, which she heartily accepts.

5. Who are the principal interlocutors?—Solomon, the women of his harem, the bride, her betrothed lover, and the bride's brothers. A few minor characters are introduced.

6. What is the moral of this poem?—It is the glorification of faithful married love, the betrothed lovers being regarded as already husband and wife.

THE PROPHETS.

1. What is a prophet?—A herald of divine truth, or a foreteller of future events.

2. By whom did the ancient prophecies come?—The prophecy came not in old time by the will of man: but holy men of God spake as they were moved by the Holy Ghost. 2 Peter 1:21.

3. Did the prophets always understand the scope and meaning of their own predictions?—They did not.

4. Who was the first of all the prophets?—Enoch. Jude 14.

5. When did prophecies cease? —Probably with the apostolic age. 1 Cor. 13:8.

6. How many prophetic books are there in the Old Testament? —Counting the Lamentations as a supplement to Jeremiah there are sixteen.

7. Into what classes are the authors of them divided?—Into two; the greater and the minor prophets.

8. Are they so called because of the importance and grandeur of their prophecies?—No; but because of the number and bulk of their recorded utterances.

9. Which are the greater and which the minor prophets?—Isaiah, Jeremiah, Ezekiel, and Daniel are the greater prophets; the others are the minor.

10. Are they arranged in the order of time?—They are not.

11. How may they be arranged?—As the prophets before

the captivity, during the captivity, and after the captivity.

12. Who prophesied before the captivity?—Jonah, Amos, Hosea, Isaiah, Joel, Micah, Nahum, Zephaniah, and Jeremiah, naming them in the order of their time.

13. Who prophesied during the captivity—Habakkuk, Daniel, Obadiah, and Ezekiel.

14. Who prophesied after the captivity?—Haggai, Zechariah, and Malachi.

ISAIAH.

1. Who is styled the Evangelical Prophet?—Isaiah.

2. Why?—Because he clearly and definitely predicts the coming of Messiah.

3. Who was Isaiah?—The son of Amoz.

4. In whose reigns did he prophesy?—In those of Uzziah, Jotham, Ahaz, and Hezekiah, kings of Judah.

5. Is any part of his book historical?—Yes, about four chapters, chaps. 36-39.

6. What are the subjects of his prophecies?—His chief prophecies relate to the judgment and captivities of Israel and Judah, the overthrow and desolation of Assyria, Babylon, Tyre, Syria, Moab, and Egypt; the domination of Cyrus whom he calls by name; the destruction of Edom; but especially the coming and kingdom of Christ.

7. How does Isaiah speak of Christ?—He minutely describes his divine character, his miracles, his peculiar qualities and virtues, his rejection by his own people, his suffering for our sins, his death, burial, and resurrection, and his final glory. He speaks also of the establishment, increase, and permanence of his kingdom, and its spread over the whole earth.

8. What prophecies designate the Saviour particularly?—Those that relate to his forerunner, his family, his birth, his name and kingdom, his preaching and wonderful works, his sufferings, his rejection by the Jews, and his reception by the Gentiles.

9. Why do certain modern critics believe that the prophecies of Isaiah were not all written by one person?—Because the style and subject of the later chapters differ so much from the earlier.

10. Is this any certain proof?—It is only presumptive, not convincing.

11. How is the supposed author of the later portion of these prophecies denominated?—As the Deutero-Isaiah; that is, the second Isaiah.

12. Are all the predictions of Isaiah fulfilled?—They are all fulfilled except those relating to Christ, some of which are still in process of being fulfilled, namely, those relating to the later glory and spread of his kingdom.

13. How did Isaiah end his life?—There is a tradition that he was put to death by order of Manasseh, being sawn asunder with a wooden saw. Heb. 11:37.

JEREMIAH.

1. In whose reign is Jeremiah first mentioned?—Josiah's.

2. In which year of his reign did this prophecy commence?—The thirteenth. Jer. 1:2.

3. Was this before or after Josiah's reformation?—The fifth year after.

4. How did Jeremiah at first feel when he found the Lord had appointed him to the prophet's office?—Timid and unfitted like a child.

5. Of what city and family was he?—He was a native of Anathoth, and belonged to a priestly family.

6. How long did he prophesy?—Upward of forty years.

7. What are the subjects of his prophecies?—His principal prophecies were the fate of Jehoiakim and Zedekiah, kings of Judah; the Babylonish captivity and its duration; the return of the Jews to Palestine; the downfall of Egypt,

Philistia, Moab, Ammon, Edom, Syria, Kedar, Hazor, Elam, and especially of Babylon; and the miraculous conception of Christ, the virtue of his atonement, his covenant, and his laws. His Lamentations consist of five distinct elegies concerning the woes of his people.

8. When Jerusalem was captured and its inhabitants carried away to Babylon, what became of Jeremiah?—He was taken as far as Ramah among the other captives, but was there dismissed to go back to Jerusalem, to Gedaliah, whom the king of Babylon had made governor of the city.

9. What happened to Gedaliah? —He was killed by Ishmael and others. Jer. 40:41.

10. What was the sad result of his death?—The carrying away as prisoners of those under his charge. Jer. 41:10.

11. Whither did the people purpose to bend their steps for fear the Chaldeans should revenge his death?—Toward Egypt. Jer. 41:17, 18.

12. What did the people pretend to desire after they had made up their minds to go down into Egypt?—Direction from God. Jer. 42:2, 3; 43:1-7.

13. Did they not prove this by their conduct?—Yes; they showed their hypocrisy by going into Egypt, notwithstanding Jeremiah's warning against it.

14. Did they take Jeremiah and Baruch with them or leave them behind?—They took them with them. Jer. 43:6, 7.

15. Had Jeremiah any message from the Lord to his rebellious people in Egypt?—He threatened them with destruction for their idolatry. Jer. 44.

16. Of what idolatry were the people guilty?—Of burning incense to the queen of heaven and to other gods. Jer. 44.

17. Were the people better off in Egypt than in Judea?—No, as its conquest by Nebuchadnezzar had been foretold and was soon accomplished. Jer. 46.

18. Where is it supposed Jeremiah died?—In Egypt, by the hands of the Jews.

EZEKIEL.

1. Who was Ezekiel?—A descendant of Aaron, and a prophet.

2. Where was he when he saw the wonderful vision his first chapter records?—By the river Chebar.

3. How came he there?—He was carried away with the Jews a captive to Babylon.

4. Where was the river Chebar?—In Mesopotamia, four hundred miles above Babylon.

5. Where are the cherubim first spoken of in the Bible?—In Gen. 3, in Eden.

6. For what were they placed in Eden?—To guard the tree of life.

7. What was always associated with the cherubim?—The glory of God. Ezek. 1:28; 3:23; 43:2.

8. Where is God said to dwell in Psalm 80:1; 99:1?—Between the cherubim.

9. How were the cherubim represented?—Most probably as winged calves, and perhaps having human heads.

10. When it was said (Gen. 4: 16), "Cain went out from the presence of the Lord," from what symbol of his presence is it supposed he departed?—From the cherubim.

11. How were the carved cherubim in the tabernacle and Solomon's temple connected with the glory of the Lord?—Because they were over the mercy seat, where the glory of the Lord was seen.

12. Where did God say he would meet his people?—Above the mercy seat between the cherubim. Ex. 25:22.

13. Have we any record of this? —Read Num. 7:89.

14. Are the cherubim ever spoken of in the New Testament? —Not by that name.

15. Are not the seraphim seen

126

by Isaiah (chap. 6) the same in appearance as the cherubim?—Very much the same.

16. In how many respects are the "cherubim" of Ezekiel, the "seraphim" of Isaiah, and the "living creatures" (translated "beasts") in Rev. 4, alike?—In having wings.

17. How does the Lord in Ezek. 2 describe the children of Israel to whom he sent Ezekiel to prophesy?—As "most rebellious."

18. How did the Lord prepare the prophet for his mission?—By encouraging and warning him not to fear. Ezek. 3.

19. How was the destruction of Jerusalem (which had not then taken place) described by Ezekiel?—Under the figure of a siege, with tokens of severe famine. Ezek. 4.

20. How long after Jehoiachin's captivity was Jerusalem taken by Nebuchadnezzar?—About eleven years. 2 Kings 25.

21. How was the utter dispersion of Israel described in Ezek. 5-7?—God said they should be scattered "into all the winds."

22. How was Ezekiel transported to Jerusalem?—In a vision by the Spirit of God. Ezek. 8:3.

23. What abominations did the Lord reveal to him there?—Those of the vilest idolatry. Ezek. 8-11.

24. What great honor does the Lord put on Noah, Daniel, and Job in Ezek. 14?—By distinguishing them as eminently righteous men.

25. To what does the Lord compare the inhabitants of Jerusalem in Ezek. 15 and 16?—To a useless vine branch and to a neglected infant.

26. To what is Nebuchadnezzar compared in Ezek. 17?—To a great eagle.

27. How does God show in Ezek. 18:19, 20, that the son shall not be punished for his father's sins?—The son shall not bear the iniquity of the father.

28. Which of the kings of Ju-

dah are spoken of under the figures of the young lions?—Jehoahaz and Jehoiakim. Ezek. 19; 2 Chron. 36.

29. To what animal did Jacob, in blessing his sons, compare the tribe of Judah?—A lion's whelp. Gen. 49:9.

30. Is the Lord Jesus ever spoken of under this symbol?—Yes, as the lion of the tribe Judah. Rev. 5:5.

31. How does Ezek. 21:22 show us the manner in which the ancient Chaldeans divined?—By casting lots with arrows bearing the names of their enemies' cities to be attacked, and by observing the appearances of the entrails of their sacrifices.

32. Against how many nations besides Israel did Ezekiel prophesy?—Eight: Ammon, Moab, Edom, Philistia, Tyre, Zidon, Egypt, and Assyria.

33. What is the "watchman's" duty?—To warn the wicked to turn from his evil way.

34. What is the duty of those who have the alarm sounded in their ears?—To turn at once from their evil ways.

35. Does this concern us?—Quite as much as it concerned them.

36. Against whom is the prophecy in Ezek. 34 uttered?—Against the priests, prophets, or religious teachers.

37. Who is the Good Shepherd?—Jesus Christ. Ezek. 34:23.

38. By what name is that glorious Person spoken of in chapter 34:29?—A plant of renown.

39. Are there any promises of future blessing in Ezekiel's prophecy?—Yes; of the restoration of Israel to their own land, and of great spiritual blessing, like a resurrection of the dead. Ezek. 36: 37.

40. What remarkable vision did the prophet see?—A valley of dry bones revived into an army of living men.

41. Of what was this vision a

symbol?—Primarily of the restoration of Israel from its captivity, and in general of the restoration of sinners to the favor of God.

42. In what state are our souls by nature?—Dead in trespasses and sins. Eph. 2:1.

43. By what means is life imparted unto them?—By being born again of the Spirit. John 3:1-8.

44. What means was the prophet to use to waken these dry bones?—To prophesy, or preach, and pray.

45. And what means are constantly being used to rouse us?—The teaching and preaching of God's word, and prayer for his blessing upon it.

46. What vision did Ezekiel see in the twenty-fifth year of the captivity of Judah?—Of a glorious temple and of healing waters issuing from it. Ezek. 40-48.

47. To what place was he in vision transported to see it?—To a mountain in the land of Israel.

48. As Jerusalem has never been built by this pattern to what must it refer?—To the future spiritual glory of Israel and the Church.

49. What great similarity is there between Ezek. 47 and Rev. 22?—The waters issuing from the temple are like the pure river of the water of life. And as in Ezekiel's vision there were on the bank of the river fruitful and healing trees, so in John's vision.

50. When and why was the tree of life prohibited?—At Adam's fall and spiritual death, lest he should live again without the atoning and restoring blood of Christ.

51. Will it ever be tasted again?—It will.

52. By whom?—By "him that overcometh." Rev. 2:7.

53. How can we overcome?—By the blood of the Lamb. Rev. 12:11.

DANIEL.

1. When was Daniel taken to Babylon?—With Jehoiakim king of Judah.

2. Where was Babylon?—On the Euphrates, in Chaldea.

3. What relationship did Jehoiakim bear to Josiah?—He was his son.

4. Was Daniel also of the royal family of Judah?—He was. Dan. 1:3.

5. How came he to Babylon?—With the captives Nebuchadnezzar made.

6. Who was Nebuchadnezzar?—King of Babylon.

7. What commandment did he give respecting the royal captives of Judah?—That some of the choicest and cleverest of them should be specially prepared for the king's service.

8. Why did Daniel and his companions object to eat the king's food?—Lest they should be defiled. Lev. 3:17.

9. What was the result of the experiment that Daniel requested might be tried on them?—They looked better than those who ate the king's food. Dan. 1:15.

10. How does this prove the truth of 1 Sam. 2:28-30?—It shows that God "will honor" those who obey and "honor" him.

11. What astonishing proof did Daniel give Nebuchadnezzar in Dan. 2 that God had endowed him with divine knowledge?—By telling him the dream that he had forgotten.

12. What was the dream?—Dan. 2:31.

13. Did Daniel take the honor to himself, or give it to God?—He gave it to God. Dan. 2:19, 23, 28.

14. Who did Daniel say was the head of gold?—Nebuchadnezzar himself. Dan. 2:38.

15. In what position did Nebuchadnezzar stand to the other kingdoms of the earth at this time?—He was a king of kings in glory and power. Dan. 2:37.

16. What kingdom was represented by the breast and arms of

silver?—The kingdom of the Medes and Persians.

17. In what respect were the two arms of the image a graphic representation of this kingdom?—They showed their united power.

18. What kingdom did the belly and thighs of brass represent?—The Macedonian or Grecian kingdom.

19. In what respect was brass an appropriate symbol for this power?—It was gained and held by force of arms.

20. How did the fourth kingdom differ from the former ones?—In strength.

21. What kingdom was symbolized by the legs and feet of iron mingled with clay?—The Roman empire.

22. When might this kingdom be said to be an iron power?—When it conquered the kingdom of Greece and other lands.

23. When was it in an enfeebled state?—When it joined the conquered nations to maintain its power.

24. What power was to be greater than all these kingdoms and crumble them into atoms?—The kingdom of Christ.

25. What does it mean when it says it was cut out without hands?—That it was formed by the power of God without the help of man. Isa. 63:1-6.

26. When was this kingdom to be set up?—In the days of one of these kingdoms or kings. Dan. 2:44.

27. At what time, as represented in this image, was Jesus born?—Under the iron or Roman kingdom.

28. What effect did the wonderful interpretation of this dream have on Nebuchadnezzar?—He worshiped Daniel as the messenger of God.

29. To what was Daniel promoted?—To be ruler over the whole province of Babylon.

30. About whom did he make request when himself was in pow-

er?—About Shadrach, Meshach, and Abed-nego.

31. How was the faith of these three friends of Daniel tried?—By Nebuchadnezzar's setting up a great image of gold, to be worshiped by all his people, and ordering them to fall down and worship with the rest.

32. Did they do this?—No.

33. What was the consequence?—They were cast into a burning fiery furnace.

34. Who walked with them in the furnace?—The Son of God.

35. What happened to the men that threw them in?—They were killed by the flames.

36. Were the three servants of God injured?—Not at all, nor even their clothes touched.

37. What effect did this wonderful deliverance have on Nebuchadnezzar?—He blessed and honored God and promoted his three faithful servants.

38. Did the Lord see the heart of Nebuchadnezzar humbled by what he had beheld of the true God or still proud?—He saw the pride within.

39. What dream did he give the king to warn him?—A vision of a lofty and flourishing tree hewn down, with its stump left for seven years among the grass and beasts of the field. Dan. 4.

40. Who interpreted this dream to Nebuchadnezzar?—Daniel.

41. Did the king take warning?—No. Dan. 4:30.

42. How was his pride humbled?—By his being deprived of reason and made a companion of beasts. Dan. 4:33.

43. What was the effect of this on the king?—At the end of seven years his reason returned and he acknowledged and praised God.

44. What wonderful vision does Dan. 7 record?—Of four great beasts that came up from the sea.

45. In which year of Belshazzar's reign did this happen?—The first.

46. Who was Belshazzar?—King

129

of Babylon.

47. What kingdom was represented by the first of these four beasts?—The kingdom of Babylon.

48. Do we see anything similar to this on the Nineveh sculptures lately discovered?—Yes; many winged lions are there portrayed.

49. What was the second beast like?—A bear.

50. What kingdom did that symbolize?—The kingdom of the Medes and Persians.

51. What was the third beast like?—A leopard.

52. How did the four wings symbolize this power?—Because the Grecian conquests were rapid as a bird's flight.

53. Who were represented by these four wings?—The kings of the four parts into which the Grecian kingdom was divided.

54. What was the fourth beast like?—It was terrible and strong, and had iron teeth and ten horns.

55. In what respect was this kingdom diverse from the others? —In having horns.

56. Who is meant by the Ancient of Days?—The eternal God.

57. When will his throne of judgment be set?—When the millennium begins, and God puts down his enemies' power.

58. What glorious Person under the name Son of man is introduced in this chapter?—Jesus Christ.

59. What kingdom is spoken of that the saints of God are to take and possess forever and forever? —The kingdom of Christ to the end of time.

60. What vision of Daniel's does Dan. 8 set forth?—Of the ram and he-goat.

61. In what year of Belshazzar's reign did this take place?— The third.

62. Do these two beasts represent any of the kingdoms of the former visions?—Yes; the ram the Median and Persian, and the goat the Grecian.

63. Whom do the two horns of the first of these two beasts symbolize?—The separate Median and Persian powers.

64. What effect did these visions have on Daniel?—He fainted and was greatly distressed.

65. How soon after this were they fulfilled?—In about sixteen years.

66. What impious act of profanity was King Belshazzar guilty of the very night in which his kingdom was taken?—Drinking out of the gold and silver vessels of the temple. Dan. 5.

67. Who took the city?—Cyrus, who made his grandfather Darius the Median (probably the same as Astyages) his viceroy.

68. How did God reveal to Belshazzar his impending fate?— By an awful handwriting on the wall.

69. Who came in and reminded the king of Daniel?—The queen.

70. How did Daniel interpret the mystic words, Mene, Tekel, and Peres, that appeared on the wall?—Mene; God hath numbered thy kingdom, and finished it. Tekel; Thou art weighed in the balances, and art found wanting. Peres; Thy kingdom is divided, and given to the Medes and Persians. Dan. 5:26-28.

71. What empty honor did Belshazzar put upon Daniel when he interpreted the handwriting?—A chain of gold and higher rank.

72. How soon after it was Belshazzar slain?—The same night.

73. What feelings did Daniel's prosperity under the reign of Darius Hystaspes excite in the minds of the king's other princes?—Jealousy, envy, and malice.

74. What trap did they lay for him?—They obtained a royal decree that no one should offer a petition or prayer for thirty days to anyone but the king, under penalty of being cast to the lions.

75. Did he forsake the worship of his God when he knew the

consequences?—No.

76. How did the king feel when he found what his edict had involved?—He was much displeased with himself.

77. Why would not the king alter the decree?—Because of a foolish law of the Medes that no decree of the king could be changed.

78. What became of Daniel in the den of lions?—He was unhurt.

79. How were Daniel's enemies punished by the king?—With the same punishment they had contrived for him.

80. What effect had this wonderful deliverance on the king?—He ordered reverence to be paid to the God of Daniel throughout his kingdom.

81. What revelation of God's future will concerning Israel does chapter 9 give?—The end of the Jewish sacrifices and the destruction of their city and temple. Verses 24-27.

82. Of what glorious Person does this chapter speak?—Of the Messiah.

83. Reckoning a day for a year, how soon might the Jews of that day anticipate his coming?—In about four hundred and ninety years.

84. Did Jesus come exactly when he was by Daniel's prophecy expected?—Yes, when Simeon and others were looking for him.

85. Where is Daniel supposed to have died?—At Susa, in Persia.

HOSEA.

1. Who was Hosea?—A prophet, son of Beeri.

2. In whose reigns did he prophesy?—In the reigns of Uzziah, Jotham, Ahaz, and Hezekiah, kings of Judah, and in the reign of Jeroboam, son of Joash, king of Israel.

3. What touching expostulation does the Lord address to Israel in Hosea 11:8?—How shall I give thee up, Ephraim? how shall I deliver thee, Israel? how shall I make thee as Admah? how shall I set thee as Zeboim? mine heart is turned within me; my repentings are kindled together.

4. What is meant by Ephraim?—Israel.

5. Why is the name of Ephraim given to Israel?—Because the tribe of Ephraim was the chief part of the kingdom of Israel.

6. What idolatries of Israel are alluded to in Hosea 13?—The worship of Baal and the golden calves.

7. What beautiful invitation is given in Hosea 14:1, 2?—O Israel, return unto the Lord thy God; for thou hast fallen by thine iniquity. Take with you words, and turn to the Lord: say unto him, Take away all iniquity, and receive us graciously.

8. Is this invitation for us also?—Yes. See Acts 2:39.

JOEL.

1. Of what family was Joel?—He was the son of Pethuel, or Bethuel, and supposed to be of the tribe of Reuben.

2. Is it known when he prophesied by his own writings?—No, not distinctly.

3. When is he supposed to have prophesied?—He is thought to have lived in the reigns of Uzziah, king of Judah, and of Jeroboam II, king of Israel.

4. Can we gather from his prophecy that he wrote it in a time of famine?—He speaks of the devourings by locusts and of the want of pasture, corn, wine, and figs; but the historical form may be used to express his prediction of God's judgments more definitely, and its accomplishment as more certain. Joel 1:4-20.

5. Of what was a famine in Israel ever a proof?—Of God's anger against sin.

6. What does he call on the people to do?—To fast, repent, and pray.

7. What are his principal predictions?—The judgments of the Almighty on Jerusalem, and its restoration; the calling of the Gentiles; and the descent of the Holy Ghost.

8. When was the Holy Ghost given in fulfillment of this prophecy?—On the day of Pentecost, after our Lord's ascension. Acts 2: 16-21.

9. With what glorious and consoling promises does the prophecy close?—Those of the future glory of Jerusalem and of the Church, in 3:16-21.

AMOS.

1. Who was Amos?—A resident of Tekoah, in Judah, and a prophet; but he was probably a native of Israel.

2. What was his occupation when the Lord called him to be a prophet?—That of a herdman, and a gatherer of sycamore fruit. Amos. 7:14.

3. Against how many nations does he prophesy besides Israel and Judah?—Against six — Syria, Philistia, Tyre, Edom, Ammon, and Moab.

4. What was probably the first of his predictions?—That against Israel in the seventh chapter.

5. Who reproved him for his predictions of evil things?—Amaziah, the priest of Beth-el, who ordered him to flee away into Judah. Amos. 7:12.

6. What was the evil predicted against the nation?—The captivity of Israel.

7. When was it threatened?— In the days of Jeroboam II.

8. What prophecy against the altar of Beth-el does Amos 3 contain?—In the day that I shall visit the transgressions of Israel upon him, I will also visit the altars of Beth-el; and the horns of the altar shall be cut off, and fall to the ground.

9. When was this fulfilled, and by whom?—About one hundred and sixty years after, by Josiah.

2 Kings 23:15.

10. What great similarity is there between Amos 4 and Deut. 28?—Amos 4 seems to be a fulfillment of the curses of drought, famine, and pestilence pronounced in Deut. 28 upon their national sins.

11. What prophecy in the lamentation of Amos (5:25-27) does Stephen quote in Acts 7?—See Acts 7:42, 43.

12. What proofs of Israel's luxury at this time does Amos 6 give us?—Read verses 4-6.

13. With what predictions of after-glory does the last chapter of Amos close?—The restoration of Israel to their own land in plenty and peace.

OBADIAH.

1. When did Obadiah prophesy? —It is not known, but probably about the time of the Babylonish captivity.

2. What is the subject of his prophecy?—The overthrow of the Edomites.

3. How had the Edomites always regarded the Israelites?—As enemies.

4. How did they exult when Jerusalem was captured by the Chaldeans?—They cried out, "Down with it, down with it, even unto the ground!" Psalm 137:7.

5. When was Obadiah's prophecy fulfilled?—It was partially accomplished a few years afterward, when Nebuchadnezzar overrun the entire continent between Egypt and Babylon.

6. Was Idumea again reduced to subjection?—It was, under John Hyrcanus, who utterly reduced the Edomites, and compelled them to leave the country or submit to circumcision, and to accept the Jewish rites. After this their nationality was forever lost.

7. How does the prophecy of Obadiah close?—With a vision of the future glory of Zion.

8. How are we to interpret this glory?—Spiritually.

132

9. Is it now manifested?—Yes, wherever the Gospel is preached.

JONAH.

1. Is their any prophesying of Jonah's recorded besides the book called by his name?—The prophecy of the reconquest, by Jeroboam, of the territory from Hamath to Damascus. 2 Kings 14:25.

2. Why is he styled "the disobedient prophet?"—Because he fled away when ordered by God to go to Nineveh.

3. Against whom was he commanded to prophesy?—Against the Ninevites.

4. Where is Nineveh?—On the river Tigris, in the ancient Assyria, and near the modern towns of Mosul and Bagdad.

5. How is Nineveh described in Scripture?—An exceeding great city, of three days' journey (or sixty miles) round.

6. Do the vast ruins lately discovered confirm or contradict this Scripture testimony?—They strongly confirm it.

7. Why did Jonah shrink from his errand?—From fear of being killed, or from a dislike to prophesy to a mere heathen nation.

8. Is it of any avail for a man to refuse to fulfill the will of God?—None. Isa. 45:9.

9. How did the Lord overtake Jonah in his rebellion?—By a storm at sea.

10. What did the mariners strive to do?—To save their lives by calling on their gods, lightening the ship, and rowing hard to reach the land.

11. Was it of any use?—No.

12. How did Jonah own God's righteous dealing?—By telling them of his flight, and that the storm was on his account.

13. When thrown overboard how did God preserve him?—By means of a great fish he had prepared.

14. Is God ever at a loss to fulfill his purposes?—Never.

15. How did Jonah feel when in the fish's belly?—Cast out of God's sight.

16. If the Lord could hear Jonah from the depths of the sea can we be in any circumstances beyond the reach of his arm to save?—Never.

17. When the Lord again commanded Jonah to go to Nineveh did he obey?—He did. Jonah 3.

18. What was the result of his preaching?—The king and people believed God, and repented and turned from their evil way.

19. How did Jonah regard this?—With anger, because his threatening was not fulfilled.

20. How did the Lord comfort and reprove Jonah?—By giving him a shade from the heat, and by rebuking his anger at its loss.

21. Is not God's mercy to the Ninevites a pledge to us of his mercy and his grace?—It is, if our repentance is as deep and sincere.

22. What attribute of the Lord's glorious character does his conduct toward Nineveh display?—His wonderful mercy.

23. Where is Nineveh first mentioned in Scripture?—In Gen. 10: 11, where Asshur is said to have built it.

24. How old was this great city at this time?—About fifteen hundred years.

25. Is the Book of Jonah a history or an allegory?—It is difficult to say, and both views have been maintained.

26. If we regard it as an allegory how are we to interpret it?—Jonah himself represents the nation; and as he was unfaithful to his trust, so Israel shrank from upholding the truth to all nations, and was swallowed up by Babylon. In exile the nation repented and sought the Lord, and was then restored, just as Jonah was swallowed up, and on repenting was thrown out of the fish's belly. And as Jonah was zealous for the Lord after his restoration, so the nation became zealots for God on

their return from exile, and never again relapsed into idolatry.

27. Is there any fish known that can swallow a man whole?—There are some species of sharks sufficiently large to do so.

MICAH.

1. In whose reigns did Micah prophesy?—In the reigns of Jotham, Ahaz, and Hezekiah, kings of Judah.

2. What were his chief predictions?—The invasions of Shalmaneser and Sennacherib; their triumphs over Israel and Judah; the captivities, dispersion, and deliverance of Israel; the destruction of Assyria and Babylon; but especially the birth of the Everlasting Ruler in Israel, the establishment of his kingdom, and its spread over the nations.

3. What prophecy of his is referred to in Jer. 26:18?—That contained in Micah 3:12.

4. How was it fulfilled?—The site of the temple was really plowed over by a Roman emperor; and Jerusalem has at different times been made heaps in the various sieges it has sustained.

5. In what state does he declare Samaria will be?—As a heap of the field. Micah 1:6.

6. What sins of Israel are enumerated in Micah 3:6, 7?—Cruelty, oppression, and idolatry.

7. What promises for the latter days does Micah 4:1-4 record?—The restoration of Zion and the reign of peace.

8. What glorious Person is prophesied of in Micah 5:2?—Jesus Christ.

9. Where was Jesus born?—At Bethlehem.

10. Where is Bethlehem first mentioned in the Bible?—In Gen. 35:19.

11. Where did Rahab (who was saved in Jericho) live?—At Bethlehem, after her marriage.

12. Whose wife was she?—Salmon's.

13. Whose mother was she?—Boaz's.

14. Where did Ruth live?—At Bethlehem. Ruth 1:1, 2, 19, 22.

15. Where was David born?—At Bethlehem.

16. What was Bethlehem called from this circumstance?—The city of David.

17. To what glorious event did the prophet allude when he spoke of Bethlehem's glory?—To the birth of Jesus.

18. Of whom alone can it be said in the words of Micah, 'Whose goings forth have been from of old, even from everlasting?" — Of God.

19. Who, then, must the Lord Jesus be?—God.

NAHUM.

1. Against whom did Nahum utter his prophecy?—Against the inhabitants of Nineveh.

2. Josephus says Nahum prophesied in the reign of Jotham, king of Judah; how long was this after Jonah's prophecy?—About sixty years.

3. In which reign of the kings of Israel did Jonah preach at Nineveh?—Jeroboam II's.

4. How long after Nahum's prophecy was his prediction fulfilled?—About one hundred years.

5. Of what tribe was the prophet Nahum?—Of the tribe of Simeon.

6. To what do his prophecies relate?—They relate solely to the fall of Sennacherib and the destruction of Nineveh by the Babylonians and Medes.

7. When were they uttered?—Probably between the Assyrian and the Babylonian captivities.

HABAKKUK.

1. What is meant by "burden," used by Habakkuk and other prophets in opening their predictions?—A heavy judgment.

2. When did Habakkuk prophesy?—The date is not known, but he is thought to be contemporary with Josiah, king of Judah.

3. What proof does Hab. 1:6 give us that he wrote before the captivity?—Because he there prophesies its coming.

4. Who were the Chaldeans?—The inhabitants of Babylon and the surrounding country.

5. What threatenings respecting them had Isaiah given to Hezekiah?—That they would come and carry away all his treasures.

6. What prediction does Habakkuk record in Hab. 2?—That in due time God would destroy the Chaldean power.

7. What promise is given in verse 14 of this chapter?—The earth shall be filled with the knowledge of the glory of the Lord, as the waters cover the sea.

8. How does the prophet close his prophecy?—With an anthem almost unequaled in Hebrew poetry, and nowhere surpassed.

9. In this anthem how does he express his confidence in God?—Read verses 17 and 18 of chapter 3.

10. Was this anthem adapted to singing?—It seems to have been, for like many of the psalms it contains the word "Selah," supposed to be a musical direction.

ZEPHANIAH.

1. In whose reign did Zephaniah prophesy?—Josiah's.

2. How does the first chapter show the abominations of the land before Josiah's reformation?—It speaks of the idolatry and indifference to God that prevailed. Zeph. 1:5, 12.

3. Against how many nations besides Judah is this prophecy uttered?—Five others: Philistia, Moab, Ammon, Ethiopia, and Assyria.

4. What proof is there in this book that Nahum's prophesy against Nineveh had not been fulfilled in the early part of Josiah's reign?—Its desolation is spoken of as yet to come. Zeph. 2:13.

5. With what glorious promises of Israel's restoration does the prophecy close?—With those of Zeph. 3:8-20, and especially verses 10-13, and the expression of God's joy and love in verse 17.

HAGGAI.

1. Who was Haggai?—A prophet, born during the captivity, and returning with the exiles to Jerusalem.

2. When did he begin to prophesy?—About fifteen years after the foundation of the temple was laid.

3. How does his first chapter show us that the Jews were more anxious to build their own houses than the temple of the Lord?—Is it time for you, O ye, to dwell in your ceiled houses, and this house lie waste?—Hag. 1:4.

4. What effect had it on Zerubbabel, the prince of Judah, and Joshua, the high priest?—Read Hag. 1:14.

5. Why had the building of the temple ceased?—On account of the interruptions of the Samaritans and others.

6. To whom did the prophet refer in Hag. 2:6, 7?—To Christ, as "the desire of all nations."

7. How was the new temple to exceed Solomon's?—Its glory was to be greater.

8. Why?—Because Christ would glorify it by his presence.

9. What promises did the Lord give to the Jews in connection with the building of his house?—That he would be with them, and give them glory and peace. Hag. 2:4. 9.

ZECHARIAH.

1. By what other prophet besides Haggai were the people of Jerusalem stirred up?—By Zechariah.

2. In which king's reign did these prophets utter their message?—In that of Darius.

3. Was this the same Darius who put Daniel into the den of lions?—Probably the same, Darius Hystaspes.

4. Whom does chapter 3 of this book (Zechariah) reveal to us as

135

the hidden adversary of Israel?—
Satan.

5. What is Satan called in Rev.
12:9, 10?—The great dragon, that
old serpent, called the Devil, and
Satan, which deceiveth the whole
world; the accuser of our brethren,
which accused them before our
God day and night.

6. What glorious Person did the
Lord speak of to comfort his people under the name of "the
Branch?"—Jesus Christ. Zech. 3:
8; 6:12.

7. What special promises to
Zerubbabel does Zech. 4 contain?
—The grace and help of the Holy
Spirit and the providential care of
God.

8. What further prophecy of the
Lord Jesus is there in Zech. 9:9?—
Rejoice greatly, O daughter of
Zion; shout, O daughter of Jerusalem; behold, thy King cometh
unto thee; he is just, and having
salvation; lowly, and riding upon
an ass, and upon a colt the foal of
an ass.

9. When was this fulfilled?—
When Jesus entered Jerusalem riding on an ass.

10. To what fountain does Zech.
13 refer?—To the blood of Jesus
Christ, that cleanseth from all sin.

11. To what does the Lord Jesus compare himself in John 10:
11, etc.?—To a good shepherd.

12. Of whom does the Lord of
hosts speak when he says (Zech.
13:7), "Awake, O sword, against
my shepherd, against the man
that is my fellow?" — Of Jesus
Christ.

13. How was the man Christ
Jesus God's fellow or equal?—
As himself also almighty and eter-
nal God.

14. When was this prophecy of
the smitten shepherd and the scattered sheep fulfilled?—When Jesus
was crucified and his disciples fled.

15. What prophecy is there in
Zech. 14:4 of the second coming
of the Lord Jesus?—His feet shall
stand in that day upon the Mount
of Olives.

16. From what part of Judea
did the Lord Jesus ascend to
heaven?—From the mount called
Olivet. Acts 1:12.

17. What did the angels say to
his disciples who had seen him go
into heaven?—This same Jesus,
which is taken up from you into
heaven, shall so come in like manner as ye have seen him go into
heaven. Acts 1:11.

18. In verse 8 of this chapter
(Zech. 14) living waters are spoken of; where else in Scripture are
these described?—In Ezek. 47:1-
12, in Joel 3:18, and in Rev. 22:1.

19. What glorious promises does
this prophecy contain of future
blessings in store for Israel?—
That God would bring them again
to their own land (Zech. 10:6-12),
and would dwell among them,
(Zech. 2:10-12), and pour his
Spirit upon them (Zech. 12:6-14),
and that they should be holiness
unto the Lord (Zech. 14:16-21),
and be a blessing. Zech. 8:3-23.

20. What effect did they have
on them?—They began to build
the house of God, and prospered
and finished it. Ezra. 5:2; 6:14.

21. How did they withstand
their adversaries?—Through "the
eye of their God" upon them.
Ezra 5:5.

22. What new edict did they
obtain from the king?—That the
Persian governors should furnish
them supplies for the building
and the sacrifices. Zech. 6:6-12.

23. How had this been brought
about?—Through the discovery of
the former decree of Cyrus. Ezra
5:3; 6:5.

24. When was the temple fin-
ished?—In the sixth year of King
Darius and about the year 515
B.C.

MALACHI.

1. When did Malachi prophesy?
—Probably after the captivity, and
during the time of Nehemiah.

2. What reason is there for so
thinking?—Because he reproves the
corruptions which the priests had

136

fallen into of marrying heathen wives, and which Nehemiah put down with a strong hand.

3. What is the tradition concerning his family and birthplace? —That he was of the tribe of Zebulun, and a native of Sopha.

4. Of what sins does he reprove the people?—Of scanty and mean sacrifices and offerings to God. Mal. 1.

5. Of whom does Malachi speak in chapter 3:1?—Of John the Baptist.

6. How is he described?—As God's messenger, to prepare his way.

7. Does not this chapter reveal yet further Israel's sin at that time?—Yes. See Mal. 3:5-9.

8. Were there any faithful ones left among this general corruption?—Yes, some that feared God, and met together to speak about him for their mutual comfort and help, and who were all written down in his book of remembrance. Mal. 3:16, 17.

9. What awful day does the prophet speak of in chapter 4: 1, 5?—The great and dreadful day of judgment. -

10. Is this day mentioned in any other part of Scripture?—Yes, in Joel 2:31, as "the great and terrible day of the Lord."

11. Who is spoken of under the figure of the "Sun of righteousness?"—Our Lord Jesus Christ.

12. What warning is spoken to God's people?—To remember the law of Moses, which was given to him in Horeb for all Israel, with the statutes and judgments.

13. What name is given to God's messenger who shall turn the hearts of parents and children to each other?—Elijah the prophet.

14. When was this prophecy fulfilled?—See Mark 9:13.

15. How was Judea governed in Malachi's time?—As a province of Persia.

16. How long before Christ was this?—About four centuries.

17. What are these centuries called?—The four centuries of silence, because in them no prophet arose in Israel.

18. Who is the prophet next named after Malachi?—Zacharias, the father of John the Baptist, who prophesied concerning his son. Luke 1:67-80.

THE NEW TESTAMENT

THE GOSPEL NARRATIVE: NATIVITY AND CHILDHOOD OF JESUS. (Luke 1, 2; Matt. 1, 2.)

1. To whom was the angel Gabriel sent?—To Zacharias.

2. Where did the angel find him?—In the temple as he ministered in the priests' office.

3. What message did the angel bring?—That his wife Elisabeth should bear him a son, who was to be called John, and that he should be a Nazarite from his birth, and by his preaching turn many of the people to the Lord.

4. How did Zacharias receive the message?—With distrust.

5. What sign did the angel give him that the message would come

true?—That he should from that time remain dumb until after the birth of the child.

6. What occurred six months after?—The same angel was sent to Mary at Nazareth, a maiden espoused to Joseph, to announce to her that she was to become the mother of the Messiah.

7. What was Mary's reply to the angel after he had saluted her and calmed her fears?—Behold the handmaid of the Lord; be it unto me according to thy word.

8. When John was born what did Zacharias do?—His tongue was loosed, and he broke out into a psalm of praise and thanksgiving, and prophesied concerning the

career of his son.

9. What word came from the Lord to Joseph?—Not to hesitate to take Mary as his wife, for that, though a virgin, she should become the mother of the Messiah, and that he should name him JESUS.

10. What is meant by the name Jesus?—Saviour.

11. Who was the emperor of Rome at this time?—Caesar Augustus.

12. What decree went out from him?—That all the world should be taxed.

13. What does the phrase "all the world" signify?—The Roman empire.

14. When this decree was published what did Joseph do?—He went up with Mary, his espoused wife, from Nazareth to Bethlehem, to be enrolled there.

15. Why?—Because he was of the house and lineage of David.

16. Where did he lodge?—At an inn.

17. What happened while he was here?—Mary brought forth her firstborn child, and wrapped it in swaddling bands, and laid it in a manger.

18. What is said of the shepherds that were watching their flock in the fields near Bethlehem?—The angel of the Lord came upon them and the glory of the Lord shone round about them, and they were sore afraid.

19. What did the angel say to them?—Not to fear, for he brought to them good tidings of great joy, which should be to them and to all people.

20. What were these tidings?—That to them a Saviour, Christ the Lord, was born in the city of David, and that they would find him at the inn lying in a manger.

21. Why was Bethlehem called the city of David?—Because David was born there.

22. What song did the shepherds hear?—The song of a multitude of the heavenly host praising God and saying, "Glory to God in the highest, and on earth peace, good will toward men."

23. Did the shepherds go to Bethlehem to see what was come to pass?—They did.

24. What effect did their story have on the hearers?—They all wondered at the things told them.

25. How did it affect Mary?—She kept all these things, and pondered them in her heart.

26. When Jesus was brought to the temple to be offered to the Lord, who received him?—Simeon, a devout man, and Anna, an aged prophetess. Both spoke of him as the Redeemer or Saviour of Israel.

27. Who was king of Judea at this time?—Herod.

28. Who came to Jerusalem on a special errand?—A company of wise men from the East.

29. Why did they come to Jerusalem?—Because that was the capital of the nation.

30. Who were these wise men?—Magi, probably from Persia.

31. What was their object in coming?—To inquire where he was born that was to be King of the Jews.

32. Why did they ask about the newborn King?—Because they saw his star in the east, which they believed indicated the expected birth.

33. Why was Herod, and all Jerusalem with him, troubled when they heard these things?—They were afraid lest he should overthrow the reigning dynasty.

34. What answer did they receive?—That the prophecies concerning the Messiah showed that he was to be born in Bethlehem of Judea.

35. When this answer was given what did Herod do?—He called the wise men privily to inquire when they saw the star, and then sent them to Bethlehem, charging them that when they found

138

the young child they should bring him word, so that he, too, might go and pay him homage.

36. Did the wise men have any trouble to find the babe?—No; for the star which they saw in the east guided them.

37. When they found the child what did they do?—They worshiped him, and presented him gifts of gold and frankincense and myrrh.

38. Did they return to Herod?—No; for God warned them in a dream not to do so.

39. When they were departed what did Joseph do?—Being warned by the angel of the Lord that the child was in danger from Herod, he arose in the night and took him and his mother and fled at once into Egypt.

40. Of what act of cruelty was Herod then guilty?—He sent and slaughtered all the young children of Bethlehem and vicinity from two years old and under.

41. How long did Joseph remain in Egypt?—Until the death of Herod.

42. On returning, where did he dwell?—In Nazareth, his former home.

43. What prophecy was thus fulfilled?—Perhaps that Jesus should, by being known as a Nazarene, be an object of contempt, since Nazareth was regarded with contempt by educated Jews (John 1: 46), and thus fulfill the prophecy of Isaiah: "He was despised, and we esteemed him not." Isa. 53:3.

44. How old was Jesus when he next visited the temple?—Twelve years.

45. Upon what occasion?—With his parents, to attend a feast of the passover.

46. How did they happen to lose him?—By their supposing he was in the company of friends returning from Nazareth they went a day's journey before they missed him.

47. Where and when did they find him?—On the third day, in the temple.

48. What was Jesus doing when they found him?—Sitting in the midst of the doctors, both hearing them and asking them questions.

49. How did Jesus spend the remaining years of his childhood?—He went down with his parents to Nazareth, and was subject to them. He also worked at Joseph's trade. Mark 6:3.

THE PREACHING OF JOHN THE BAPTIST. (Matt. 3; Mark 1; Luke 3; John 1.)

1. Who was John?—A man sent from God to be the messenger and forerunner of Christ, to prepare his way before him.

2. When did he begin his preaching?—In the fifteenth year of the reign of Tiberius, the emperor of Rome.

3. How was Judea then governed?—By a Roman procurator, Pontius Pilate.

4. How old was John at that time?—Thirty years.

5. Where was he until he entered upon his ministry?—In the deserts or the hill country of Judea.

6. What was the character of John?—He was a Nazarite.

7. What was the tenor of his preaching?—Repent ye; for the kingdom of heaven is at hand.

8. What is repentance?—A godly sorrow for sin, accompanied with a change of purpose and of life.

9. How did John initiate his disciples into his doctrine?—By baptism.

10. Was baptism a familiar rite among the Jews?—It was.

11. What was John called?—The Baptist.

12. What was John's raiment and food?—His raiment was camel's hair fastened with a leathern girdle, and his food was locusts and wild honey.

13. Was it lawful for the Israelites to eat locusts?—It was. Lev.

11:22.

14. Is such food still used?—The Arabs eat dried locusts fried in butter and mixed with honey.

15. Where did John baptize?—In the river Jordan.

16. Who came to him for baptism?—All the land of Judea, and they of Jerusalem, and all the region round about Jordan.

17. Was John surprised to see many of the Sadducees and Pharisees come to him?—He was.

18. What did he say to them?—Who warned you to flee from the wrath to come?

19. Who were the Sadducees and Pharisees?—The two leading religious sects of the Jewish people; the former denying the doctrine of the resurrection and the existence of angels and of spirits, and the latter confessing both.

20. What did John mean by "the wrath to come?"—God's impending judgment on the land and nation.

21. What further did he say to the Pharisees and Sadducees?—Bring forth fruits meet for repentance.

22. What did John say of his baptism?—That he baptized only with water; but that Christ should baptize with the Holy Ghost and with fire.

23. What did the people that came to him ask?—What they should do then.

24. How did he answer?—He told them to be kind and neighborly, and to give to the needy.

25. What was his reply to the publicans?—Exact no more than that which is appointed you.

26. Who were the publicans?—Native collectors of the imperial revenue serving under Roman officers.

27. What did he say to the soldiers?—To do violence to no man, to accuse no one falsely, and to be content with their wages.

28. Who specially came to John to be baptized?—Jesus.

29. Was John personally acquainted with Jesus?—Probably not until that time. John 1:31.

30. How did he receive Jesus?—With humility and reverence, saying: "I have need to be baptized of thee; and comest thou to me?"

31. How did Jesus remove his scruples?—He said: "Suffer it to be so now, for thus it becometh us to fulfill all righteousness."

32. What was the design of the ceremony in this case?—As a public consecration of Christ to his work of bringing in the kingdom of heaven.

33. What attestation was given to Jesus by the Father?—The Spirit of God descended like a dove and rested upon him, and a voice from heaven said: "Thou art my beloved Son; in thee I am well pleased."

34. What was Jesus then doing?—Praying.

35. Is there here any proof of the doctrine of the Trinity?—Yes; for the three divine Persons of the Godhead were manifesty present.

36. How old was Jesus at this time?—About thirty years.

37. Why is Jesus called the Word?—Because he is the medium of communication between God and man.

38. How else is he designated?—As the true Light, which lighteth every man that cometh into the world.

39. In what way does the Divine Spirit enlighten every man?—By inspiration, by providence, by the works of nature, by revelation, and by the preaching of the Gospel.

40. To whom did the true Light come?—He came unto his own, and his own received him not. John 1:11.

41. In what form did he come?—As a man, in the likeness of sinful flesh. Rom. 8:3.

42. Of what family was Jesus born?—Of David's.

43. How is this shown?—By the

tables of genealogy, one in Matthew and one in Luke.

44. Do these two tables correspond?—Not exactly. Matthew copies the official register, and traces the descent of Jesus through the line of the kings and the heirs to the throne, while Luke copies the private register, showing the actual parentage.

45. Whose genealogy is given, Joseph's or Mary's?—Ostensibly Joseph's in both tables. Mary was probably the cousin of Joseph, and her offspring was the heir of David on both sides, as Joseph was counted to be his legal father.

46. How long did John's ministry continue after Christ's baptism?—Only a few months at most.

47. What became of John's disciples?—A few of them followed Jesus.

THE TEMPTATION IN THE WILDERNESS. (Matt. 4; Mark 1; Luke 4.)

1. After his baptism, whither did Jesus go?—Into the wilderness of Judea.

2. For what purpose?—Doubtless to prepare for his mission.

3. How did these themes occupy him?—He was absorbed in their contemplation.

4. What happened at the end of the forty days?—The tempter came to him.

5. Who was the tempter?—The devil.

6. Had the devil been with Jesus during all the forty days?—He probably had been all the time trying to exercise his malignant influence. Mark 1:13.

7. Did he appear in a bodily shape?—This cannot be told; but he was personally present.

8. Of what physical want was Jesus now sensible?—The want of food.

9. What did the tempter say?—If thou art the Son of God, command that these stones be made bread.

10. As it is right to eat when hungry, wherein lay the force of this temptation?—To distrust divine providence, and to use unworthy means to supply his necessities.

11. How did the Saviour answer the tempter?—It is written, Man shall not live by bread alone, but by every word that proceedeth out of the mouth of God.

12. Where is this written?—Deut. 8:3.

13. Where did the devil then take him?—To the holy city, and set him on the pinnacle of the temple.

14. What was this pinnacle?—The eastern porch of the temple, the roof of which was two hundred feet high.

15. What suggestion did the tempter now make to him?—If he was the Son of God, to cast himself down, because it was written, "He shall give his angels charge concerning thee; and in their hands they shall bear thee up, lest at any time thou dash thy foot against a stone."

16. Did the devil quote the Scripture accurately?—No; he omitted the clause, "To keep thee in all thy ways." Psalm 91:11, 12.

17. In what did this temptation consist?—To secure fame by this act of presumption.

18. What did Jesus answer?—It is written again, Thou shalt not tempt the Lord thy God. Deut. 6:16.

19. What did he mean by this?—That to expect God to deliver us when we run rashly into danger is to tempt him.

20. What was the third temptation?—Satan took Jesus into an exceeding high mountain and showed him all the kingdoms of the world and the glory of them, and promised to give them all to Jesus if he would fall down and worship him. This appealed

to his ambition.

21. How did the Saviour rebuke him?—He said: "Get thee hence, Satan; for it is written, Thou shalt worship the Lord thy God, and him only shalt thou serve." Deut. 10:20.

22. What then followed?—Satan's departure and the ministry of angels.

23. Why was it necessary for Jesus to undergo these temptations?—In order that he might conquer Satan and redeem man from the fall.

24. Were these all the temptations our Lord endured?—No. See Luke 4:13; 22:28.

25. What encouragement does this history afford us?—See Heb. 2:18; 4:15.

26. How may we properly estimate the force of these temptations?—By considering Jesus as a man, subject to all the conditions of humanity (Phil. 2:7, 8), as a patriot (Matt. 23:37), and as a world conqueror (1 Cor. 15:25, 28); and these temptations as presented to him in each of these characters.

27. What should we learn from Christ's example?—To resist Satan. James 4:7.

28. Can any temptation befall us from which God cannot deliver us?—No. 2 Peter 2:9.

CHRIST'S EARLIER MINISTRY. (John 1, 2.)

1. To what place did Jesus go after the temptation?—To Galilee. Luke 4:14.

2. Was his coming known to many?—A fame of him went through all the region round about.

3. Why?—Because he taught and preached in the synagogues.

4. What testimony did John bear to Jesus?—Behold the Lamb of God, which taketh away the sin of the world.

5. Did John regard Jesus as the Messiah?—He did. John 1:23.

6. How did he know him as such?—By the Spirit of God. John 1:33.

7. What opinion did he have of the Messiah's mission?—The same which the Israelites in general held, with a more lofty spiritual conception of the Lord's kingdom.

8. Whom did John introduce to Jesus on the next day?—Two of his disciples, of whom Andrew was one, and perhaps John the son of Zebedee the other.

9. What did the two disciples do?—They followed Jesus to his home and remained with him the rest of the day.

10. How were they impressed?—They accepted Jesus as the Messiah, and Andrew brought Peter his brother to Jesus.

11. What did Jesus do on the day following?—He went forth to preach, and found Philip, and asked him also to follow him.

12. What did he mean by this?—For him to become his disciple.

13. What did Philip do?—He found his brother Nathanael, and told him that they had found him of whom Moses and the prophets wrote, Jesus of Nazareth.

14. Did Nathanael believe his report?—He was incredulous, and asked, "Can any good thing come out of Nazareth?"

15. How did Philip reply to his objection?—Come and see.

16. What better answer can a saved sinner make to other sinners?—None. Psalm 34:8. Personal experience is the best argument.

17. When Jesus saw Nathanael coming, what did he say?—Behold an Israelite indeed, in whom is no guile.

18. What response to his did Nathanael make?—Whence knowest thou me?

19. How did Jesus show that he knew him?—By telling him that before Philip called him he saw him under the fig tree.

20. Was Nathanael convinced

that something good could come out of Nazareth?—Yes; for he exclaimed: "Rabbi, thou art the Son of God, thou art the King of Israel!"

21. How did Jesus confirm his faith?—He said he should see greater things than these, and that hereafter he should behold the angels of God ascending and descending upon the Son of man.

22. Why does Jesus call himself the Son of man?—Because he was a man, and belonged to the whole human race rather than to one nation or family.

THE MARRIAGE FEAST AT CANA OF GALILEE. (John 2.)

1. What happened on the third day after Philip and Nathanael came to Jesus?—There was a marriage feast in Cana.

2. Who was present at the feast?—The mother of Jesus.

3. Who were invited as guests?—Jesus and his disciples, Andrew, Simon, Philip, and Nathanael.

4. How long did a wedding feast continue?—A whole week.

5. How did Mary happen to be present?—She may have been the mother of the bride or some near relative.

6. What interest did Mary have in this marriage feast?—She seems to have had charge of the entertainment.

7. Of what did she find a deficiency?—Of wine.

8. What did she say to her Son?—They have no wine.

9. What did Jesus respond?—Woman, what have I to do with thee? Mine hour is not yet come.

10. Was the word he used to address his mother harsh?—No; it was one of the highest dignity and respect.

11. Was there any reproof in what he said?—No, but possibly a hint that his conduct as Messiah was not to be controlled by earthly relationships and considerations.

12. Did she so understand him?—She did.

13. What directions did she give to the servants?—For them to do whatsoever Jesus directed.

14. What vessels were set there?—Six waterpots of stone, holding from sixteen to twenty-four gallons each.

15. For what were they used?—For purification, or for washing the hands before meals.

16. Were the Jews very particular in thus washing their hands?—They were; as they used no knives or forks, and served both themselves and others with their fingers. Mark 7:3, 4.

17. What order did Jesus give to the servants?—To fill the waterpots with water full to the brim.

18. What further order did he make?—To dip out and take to the governor of the feast.

19. Who was the governor of the feast?—Usually "the friend of the bridegroom," who took charge of all the guests and saw that they lacked nothing for their comfort.

20. What did the ruler of the feast do and say?—He tasted the water that had become wine, and not knowing whence it came, said to the bridegroom: "Every man at the beginning doth set forth good wine, and when the guests have well drunk, then that which is worse; but thou hast kept the good wine until now."

21. Why was so much wine made?—That the miracle might be complete.

22. What may we learn from the Lord's presence at this wedding feast?—That he came to sanctify all life, its joys as well as its sorrows.

23. What was the effect of this miracle upon his disciples?—They believed on him.

24. Of what was this first miracle a symbol and a promise?—Of the Lord's ministration of life. He came to bring joy and gladness to the hearts of men.

143

25. Did Jesus work any other miracle at Cana?—He healed the son of a nobleman there, without seeing him, because of the faith of the father. John 4:46-54.

THE FIRST PASSOVER OF THE LORD'S MINISTRY.
(John 2, 3.)

1. What great feast was celebrated at Jerusalem in the spring? —The passover.

2. Of what was it a memorial? —Of the angel's passing over the homes of the Israelites in Egypt when the firstborn were slain.

3. Who were expected to attend the feast?—All the men of the Israelites.

4. Did Jesus attend this feast after his baptism?—Yes.

5. What did he do at Jerusalem?—He purged the temple by casting out all the dealers, with their sheep and oxen, and overthrowing the tables of the money changers, pouring out the money.

6. What did he say to those who sold doves?—Take these things hence; make not my Father's house a house of merchandise.

7. What did the Jews who saw this say to him?—They asked him what sign he showed that he had the right to do these things.

8. What did they mean by this?—The proof that he was sent by God.

9. Was not this action itself a sufficient proof?—They did not seem to think so.

10. Did the worshipers at the temple approve the Lord's action?—Probably they all did; only the priests and the getters of gain found fault.

11. Why should the priests find fault?—They were worldly-minded, covetous, and self-seeking.

12. What sign did Jesus offer in proof of his authority?—He said: Destroy this temple, and in three days I will raise it up.

13. Of what temple did he speak?—Of the temple of his body.

14. Did the Jews understand his prophetic riddle?—No; they supposed he meant the temple of Herod, where they were assembled.

15. What use did they make of it afterward?—It was perverted, and alleged aginst him on a charge of blasphemy, when he was on trial before the high priest. Mark 14:58.

16. While Jesus was in Jerusalem did he work any miracles? —Yes.

17. What was the effect of these miracles?—Many believed in his name.

18. Did they believe him to be the expected Messiah?—Not then; only a prophet and teacher.

19. Who was Nicodemus?—A ruler of the Jews and a Pharisee.

20. Why did he come to Jesus by night?—To escape observation or for the sake of privacy.

21. What acknowledgment did he make?—Rabbi, we know that thou art a teacher come from God; for no man can do these miracles that thou doest, except God be with him.

22. How did Jesus answer him? —Verily, verily, I say unto thee, Except a man be born again, he cannot see the kingdom of God.

23. What is the kingdom of God?—The spiritual kingdom of Christ on earth, the invisible Church.

24. What is meant by being born again?—A change of heart and life, so as to love God supremely.

25. How did Nicodemus understand him?—Literally; and he asked, in astonishment: "How can a man be born when he is old?"

26. What answer did Jesus make?—He repeats the statement; but distinguishes between being born of the flesh, as Nicodemus understood it, and being born of the Spirit.

27. Did Nicodemus see into this mystery?—No; for he asks,

144

perplexed, "How can these things be?"

28. Ought he not to have perceived the meaning?—Yes; for he was a master of Israel, and was a student of the Scriptures.

29. What is the substance of the Gospel as spoken to Nicodemus?—God so loved the world, that he gave his only begotten Son, that whosoever believeth in him should not perish, but have everlasting life.

30. Did Nicodemus embrace this great truth?—He certainly became a follower of Jesus, and showed his great love for him at the burial of his body. John 19:39.

31. Do we know anything of the subsequent history of Nicodemus?—There is a tradition that he at last publicly professed the doctrines of Christ, and suffered much persecution on that account.

32. After this interview of Nicodemus whither did Jesus go?—Into Judea.

33. Where was John the Baptist at this time?—In Enon, baptizing.

34. What controversy arose between some of John's disciples and the Jews?—A question about purifying.

35. When it was told to John that Jesus was baptizing what did John say?—That he was not himself the Christ, but was sent before him, and was like the friend of the bridegroom, rejoicing in the bridegroom's voice; but that henceforth he must decrease while Jesus should increase.

36. In returning home to Galilee what route did Jesus take? —The one that led through Samaria.

37. At what point did Jesus stop on the way?—At Sychar, or Shechem, a village of Samaria.

38. How far is this from Jerusalem?—About thirty-four miles north.

39. Why did he tarry there? —Because he was wearied and hungry. His disciples had gone into the city to buy food.

40. Where did he rest?—At the well of Jacob.

41. What is the condition of this well, as it now exists?—It is about nine feet in diameter and perhaps seventy-five feet in depth, without much water, cut in firm limestone rock. It is near the road on the south side of the valley of Shechem.

42. Who dug this well?—Jacob.

43. Who came, while Jesus was there, to draw water?—A woman of Samaria.

44. What did he ask of her?— A drink of water.

45. What surprise did the woman express?—That a Jew should ask a favor of a Samaritan.

46. To this what did Jesus reply?—That if she knew the gift of God, and who it was that asked her for a drink, she would instead have asked of him, and he would have given her living water.

47. How did this excite her curiosity?—She knew that Jesus could not obtain water from the well, as he had nothing to draw with, and she asked from whence he had that living water.

48. What did Jesus assure her? —That the water which he had to give should be a well of water within one, springing up into everlasting life.

49. Did the woman quite apprehend his meaning?—She did not; yet she asked him for this water which he had offered.

50. What did Jesus tell her to do?—To go and call her husband.

51. What did she say?—That she had no husband.

52. How did Jesus disclose to her his knowledge of her life?— By his saying that she had had five husbands, and that he with whom she was now living was not her husband.

53. What did she take Jesus to be?—A prophet, and so told

him.

54. What further did she say? —She said: "Our fathers worshiped in this mountain; and ye say that in Jerusalem is the place where men ought to worship."

55. What mountain did she refer to?—Mount Gerizim, where the Samaritans had built a temple not long after the new temple of Zerubbabel was built, and in which they worshiped.

56. What did Jesus say to her? —That true worship was to be offered in spirit and in truth, that the place where it was offered was indifferent, and that national rites were of no importance.

57. Was she willing to accept this teaching?—Scarcely; for she said that the Messiah, when he should come, would tell them all things.

58. What answer did Jesus make?—That he was himself the Messiah.

59. What did the woman do? —She went to the city and said to the men: "Come, see a man that told me all things that ever I did; is not this the Christ?"

60. Did the Samaritans go to see?—They did.

61. What did the disciples of Jesus do in the meanwhile?— They returned with food, and besought him to eat; but he said: "My food is to do the will of him that sent me, and to finish his work."

62. What did the Samaritans think of Jesus when they came to him?—The same as the woman did; and they besought him to tarry with them.

63. How long did Jesus stay in the city?—Two days.

64. What were the results of his stay?—Many believed on him, and accepted him as the Christ.

65. What four disciples did Jesus call on his return to Galilee?—Simon and Andrew, and James and John.

66. What was their occupation?

—They were fishermen.

67. Were there many people with Jesus at the seashore?—Yes.

68. How did he teach them?— Out of a ship.

69. When he was done speaking what did he tell Simon?—To launch out into the deep water and cast their nets.

70. Had the fishermen been successful during the night's toil? —No; and they were now on the shore washing their nets.

71. Did they obey the order of Jesus?—Yes.

72. When they had done this what was the result?—They inclosed a great multitude of fishes, and the net broke.

73. How many did they catch? —They filled both ships so full that they began to sink.

74. What impression did this miracle make on Simon?—He was astonished, and fell down at Jesus' knees, saying: "Depart from me, for I am a sinful man, O Lord."

75. What did Jesus say to him? —Fear not: from henceforth thou shalt catch men.

76. When Jesus called these disciples what did they do?—They brought their ships to land, and forsook all and followed him.

77. When Jesus calls us what should we do?—Obey at once.

JESUS IN GALILEE.

1. Where did Jesus go to reside?—To Capernaum.

2. Who went with him?—His mother, his brethren, and his disciples.

3. Why did he prefer Capernaum for his home?—It was on the Sea of Galilee, and was the center of a larger population than Nazareth. Besides, the people of Nazareth had rejected him.

4. Under what circumstances?— He went into the synagogue at Nazareth and stood up to read. When the book of the prophet Isaiah was handed to him he found the place where was writ-

ten a prophecy concerning the Messiah, and after reading it sat down, and said: "This day is this prophecy fulfilled in your ears." For a while they were charmed with his words; but when he began to make a personal application of the truth they were filled with wrath, and expelled him from the city, and tried to fling him down a precipice; but he passed unharmed through the midst of them and went on his way.

5. How was he received at Capernaum?—As he taught in the synagogue on the Sabbath days they were astonished at his doctrine, and his word was with power.

6. What miracle did he perform?—He cast out the spirit of an unclean devil and healed the demoniac.

7. What effect did this miracle have?—His fame went out into every place of the country round about.

8. Where did he lodge?—He entered into Simon's house to stay.

9. How was the mother of Simon's wife affected?—She was taken ill with a great fever.

10. What did the family do?—They besought Jesus for her.

11. Did Jesus attend to their request?—He came and stood over the sick woman and rebuked the fever, and it left her; and immediately she arose and ministered to them.

12. What happened when the sun was setting?—He healed many and cast out many devils.

13. Why did they come in the evening?—Because the Sabbath was then ended.

14. What did Jesus do the next morning?—He departed and went into a desert place.

15. When the people missed him what did they do?—They besought him that he should not depart from them.

16. Was Jesus willing to remain?—No; for he said that he must preach the kingdom of God to other cities also; because for that purpose he was sent.

17. Where did he preach?—In the synagogues of Galilee.

18. What miracles did he perform in this tour?—He cleansed a leper and healed a paralytic.

19. Were they both healed through their own faith?—They were.

20. Was Jesus afraid of being defiled when he touched the leper?—No.

21. How was the paralytic brought to Christ?—On a couch or mat.

22. Did his bearers find ready access to Jesus?—No; on account of the multitude around him they could not come to him; but they went to the top of the house and broke up a portion of the tiling and let the man down into the room or court where Jesus was.

23. What did Jesus say to the paralytic when he saw their faith?—Man, thy sins are forgiven thee.

24. What did the Pharisees and scribes present think when they heard this?—They began to reason within themselves, saying: "Who is this that speaketh blasphemies? Who can forgive sins but God alone?"

25. How did Jesus show his divine power?—He asked what they reasoned in their hearts, thus showing that he knew their secret thoughts; and then commanded the paralytic to arise and take up his couch and go to his house; which command he instantly obeyed, glorifying God.

26. What was the effect on the people who saw this miracle?—They glorified God, saying, "We have seen strange things to-day."

27. Whom did Jesus next call to be his disciple?—Levi, otherwise named Matthew.

28. Who was Levi?—A publican, or taxgatherer.

29. How did he answer the call?—He immediately rose up and left all and followed Jesus.

30. What was the receipt of custom?—The place where the taxes imposed by the government of Rome were paid.

31. How did Levi entertain Jesus?—He made him a feast, to which was invited a great company of publicans and of others.

32. When the scribes and Pharisees knew of it what did they say?—They murmured against the disciples of Jesus, asking why they ate and drank with publicans and sinners.

33. How did Jesus vindicate them and himself?—He said that they which are whole do not need a physician, but they that are sick; and that he had come to call, not the righteous, but sinners to repentance.

CHRIST'S SECOND PASSOVER AT JERUSALEM.
(John 5; Matt. 12.)

1. What pool was at Jerusalem?—Bethesda.

2. What peculiarity was there about it?—Its waters were supposed to be curative of disease.

3. Was it much frequented?—Yes.

4. At what times?—When the water was agitated by an overflow of the fountain that supplied it.

5. Who was there waiting to bathe in the pool?—A man that had an infirmity thirty-eight years.

6. When Jesus saw him what did he say?—Wilt thou be made whole?

7. What answer was returned?—The man said that he had no one to help him into the water, and that others crowded him out; thinking, perhaps, that Jesus would assist him.

8. How did Jesus help him?—"Rise, take up thy bed, and walk." And immediately the man was healed, and took up his couch, and walked.

9. On what day was this miracle performed?—On the Sabbath.

10. What did the Jews say to the man?—That it was not lawful on the Sabbath for him to carry a burden.

11. How did he excuse himself?—By saying that he who healed him directed him to do so.

12. Did he know who was his healer?—No; because Jesus had withdrawn.

13. When Jesus afterward found him in the temple what did he say?—Sin no more, lest a worse thing happen unto thee.

14. Were the disciples allowed to take and eat growing corn?—They were while passing through it, but not to carry any away. Deut. 23:25.

15. Why was fault found with them then?—Because they did it on the Sabbath.

16. Did the priests profane the Sabbath and remain blameless?—They did so by killing the sacrifices on that day as on other days.

17. What did Jesus teach concerning the nature of the Sabbath?—That the Sabbath was made for man, and not man for the Sabbath.

18. What other miracle did Jesus work on the Sabbath?—He healed a man with a withered hand, in the synagogue.

19. How did the Jews look upon this miracle?—They were filled with madness, and communed with one another what they might do to Jesus.

20. Why did they oppose him?—Because he paid no regard to their traditions, and acted contrary to their prejudices and teachings.

21. Where was this opposition begun?—In Judea.

CHRIST'S MINISTRY EXTENDING.

1. On his return to Galilee what did Jesus do?—He selected twelve disciples, whom he named

148

apostles, that they might be with him and that he might send them forth to preach.

2. What immediately preceded this selection?—A night spent in prayer on a mountain.

3. What summary of doctrine did the Saviour give?—The Sermon on the Mount.

4. What miracle did Jesus perform for a stranger at Capernaum?—He healed the servant of a centurion.

5. What was a centurion?—A Roman officer, having the command of a hundred soldiers.

6. What did Jesus say of the centurion's faith?—That he had found nowhere, not even in Israel, so great faith.

7. What occurred the day after this?—The raising to life of the son of the widow of Nain.

8. When John, in prison, heard about Jesus what did he do?—He sent two of his disciples to Jesus to inquire whether he was really the expected Messiah or whether they were to look for some one else.

9. What answer did Jesus return?—He made no direct reply, but referred John to the evidences of his (Jesus') Messiahship.

10. What testimony did Jesus give of John?—That among those born of women there was no greater prophet than John the Baptist.

11. To whose house was Jesus invited to dine?—To the house of a Pharisee named Simon.

12. What occurred while at the meal?—The anointing of Jesus' feet by a woman that was a sinner.

13. What did Simon think of this?—That Jesus was not a prophet, or otherwise he would have known what kind of a woman this was, and would not have allowed her to touch him.

14. How did Jesus reprove and instruct Simon?—By a parable, the application of which Simon could not help perceiving.

15. What did Jesus say to the woman?—"Thy sins are forgiven;" and he continued, "Thy faith hath saved thee; go in peace."

16. What did he say of her to Simon?—That she loved much.

17. What wonderful works did Jesus do in pursuing his ministry in Galilee?—He healed a dumb man possessed with a devil, cured Mary Magdalene, stilled a tempest on the lake of Galilee, cast out the devils from two demoniacs at Gadara, restored the daughter of Jairus to life and healed a woman diseased with an issue of blood, gave sight to two blind men, and cast out a dumb spirit.

18. How did the Lord teach? —By parables.

19. What parables did he speak while on this circuit?—The parables of the rich husbandman, the bridegroom, the unfaithful steward, the sower, the tares, the mustard seed, the leaven, the treasure hid in the field, the goodly pearl, the net, and some others. Matt. 13; Luke 12.

20. What denunciations did Christ utter?—Against the practices of the scribes and the Pharisees, and their doctrines. Luke 11.

21. Why did the Lord teach in parables?—See Matt. 13:10-13.

22. Were the truths that he taught always palatable?—By no means; they stirred up much opposition. Matt. 15:6-9.

THE APOSTLES SENT FORTH.
—THE HEIGHT OF CHRIST'S MINISTRY. (Matt. 10-16; Mark 6-8; Luke 9.)

1. When the Lord saw the multitude flocking to him how did he feel?—He was moved with compassion, because they fainted and were scattered abroad as sheep having no shepherd.

2. What did he say to his disciples?—Pray ye the Lord of the harvest, that he will send forth laborers into the harvest.

149

3. What power did he confer on his apostles?—The power to heal diseases and to cast out devils.

4. What did he bid them do?—To go throughout the land of Israel and preach, saying, "The kingdom of heaven is at hand," and to perform miracles.

5. After they went forth what did Jesus do?—He continued his journeying through Galilee.

6. Had the people of Nazareth changed their opinion of Christ?—No; they nearly all rejected his claim as the Messiah.

7. Did Jesus at first make the claim that he was the Messiah?—Not at the first.

8. Why did they resist this claim?—Because they believed that the Messiah would come as an earthly monarch and conqueror.

9. What kind of a kingdom did the Lord come to estabish?—A spiritual kingdom.

10. Who were the chief opposers of Jesus?—The scribes and priests, who were generally Sadducees, and many of the leading Pharisees.

11. What success attended the labors of the apostles?—They cast out many devils and healed many that were sick.

12. What did they tell Jesus when they returned from their mission?—They told him the things they had done and taught. Mark 6:30.

13. What did the Lord tell them?—To come apart into a desert place and rest awhile.

14. Why?—Because there were many going and coming, and they had not so much leisure as to eat.

15. To what place did they go, and how?—They took ship privately and went into a desert place.

16. Did they escape the crowd?—No.

17. How did Jesus receive them?—Compassionately.

18. When the day was far spent what did the disciples do?—They prayed him to send away the people, that they might go into the villages and the country adjoining and buy bread for themselves.

19. What did Jesus say?—He said, "Give ye to them to eat."

20. How did they reply?—They inquired whether they should go themselves and buy two hundred pennyworth (about thirty dollars) of bread to give them.

21. What question did Jesus ask?—How many loaves have ye? Go and see.

22. When they answered that they had five loaves and two fishes, what did Jesus do?—He bade them seat the multitudes by companies on the grass.

23. What was then done?—The Lord took the five loaves and the two fishes, and looked up into heaven and blessed and broke the loaves and gave to his disciples to set before them; and he divided the two fishes among them all.

24. After all had eaten was anything left?—Yes; they took up twelve basketfuls of the loaves and the fishes.

25. What did the multitudes wish to do?—To make Jesus king by force; for they said: "This is of a truth that Prophet that should come into the world."

26. To what place did the Lord send his disciples?—To Bethsaida, by ship.

27. What did he do himself?—He remained behind and dismissed the multitudes, and then departed into a mountain to pray.

28. How did he rejoin his disciples?—He came to them about the fourth watch of the night, before they landed, by walking over the sea.

29. When they saw Jesus walking on the sea what did they suppose him to be?—A spirit, and they cried out for fear.

30. What reassured them?—

150

The Lord said: "Be of good cheer; it is I; be not afraid." And he went up unto them into the ship.

31. What power did the Lord show over nature?—The sea became calm.

32. What did Herod the tetrarch think of Jesus?—He said it was John the Baptist, whom he had beheaded, that was risen from the dead.

33. Why had he beheaded John?—John had reproved him for his sins, and he imprisoned him. But when he held a birthday feast the daughter of his wife Herodias, being instructed by her mother, asked for the head of John the Baptist, and Herod sent and beheaded him in the prison.

34. What did John's disciples do?—They took the body of John and buried it, and came and told Jesus.

35. When the Lord reached the land of Gennesaret what did he do?—He healed many that were sick. Mark 6:55.

36. To what place did Jesus go next?—To Capernaum. John 6:24, 25.

37. What did he do in Capernaum?—He delivered a remarkable discourse in which he taught such strange doctrines concerning his person and his work that many of his disciples went back and walked no more with him. John 6:26-66.

38. Did Jesus seem disappointed at the result?—He did; for, turning to the twelve, he asked, pathetically, "Will ye also go away?"

39. What was Peter's response? —He said: "Lord, to whom shall we go? thou hast the words of eternal life; and we believe and are sure that thou art that Christ, the Son of the living God."

THE DEPUTATION FROM JERUSALEM. (Matt. 15.)

1. Who came to Jesus to dispute with him?—A number of scribes and Pharisees from Jerusalem.

2. What question did they ask? —Why the Lord's disciples transgressed the traditions of the elders.

3. In what particular did they transgress?—In eating with unwashed hands.

4. How did Jesus answer?—He inquired why they also transgressed the commandment of God by their traditions.

5. What transgression did he mention?—The case of a son who pretended to dedicate property to God, so as to avoid supporting his parents. The property so dedicated was called "corban," or "gift."

6. Was this dedication accepted by the scribes as a reason for not keeping the fifth commandment?—Yes; although they knew it to be only a subterfuge.

7. How did the Lord rebuke them?—He called them hypocrites.

8. What did Jesus say defiles a man?—The evil thoughts that proceed from the heart, murders, adulteries, fornications, thefts, false witness, blasphemies—these are the things that defile a man; but to eat with unwashen hands defileth not a man.

9. When Jesus was told that the Pharisees were offended at what he said, what was his answer?—He said: "Let them alone; they be blind leaders of the blind."

MISSIONARY TOURS OF JESUS. (Matt. 15, 16; Mark 7, 8.)

1. What long missionary tour did Jesus make?—He went into the coasts of Tyre and Sidon.

2. Were Tyre and Sidon Jewish cities?—No; they were on the seacoast, to the northwest.

3. What woman came to him for a favor?—A woman of Canaan, a Syrophenician.

151

4. What was her request?—The healing of her daughter, who was vexed by an evil spirit.

5. Did the Lord pay any attention to her cry?—He seemed to be indifferent, and said: "I am not sent but unto the lost sheep of the house of Israel."

6. Was the woman easily repulsed?—No; she was in earnest.

7. What did she do?—She came to Jesus and worshiped him, saying: "Lord, help me."

8. Was Jesus moved by her entreaty?—He said: "It is not meet to take the children's bread and cast it to dogs." ·

9. What was the woman's reply?—Truth, Lord; yet the dogs eat of the crumbs that fall from their masters' table.

10. What was the Lord's answer?—O woman, great is thy faith; be it unto thee even as thou wilt.

11. When was the child healed? —At once; it was made whole from that very hour.

12. Does this incident afford any encouragement to parents to pray for the conversion of their children?—It does; God will be entreated of his people.

13. To what place did Jesus come next?—He came nigh to the Sea of Galilee, and went up into a mountain.

14. Who came to him there? —Great multitudes, bringing with them those who were lame, blind, dumb, maimed, and many others, and laying them at Jesus' feet.

15. What did Jesus do?—He healed them.

16. Who is specially mentioned as having been healed on this occasion?—A deaf man, having an impediment in his speech.

17. Why did Jesus sigh?—He was either physically worn out or was oppressed with their unbelief. Mark 7:34.

18. What does the word "Ephphatha" show us of the language which the Lord generally used? —That it was the Aramaic, or ancient Syriac. Mark 5:41.

19. Did Jesus and his disciples speak Greek?—They probably did, but not in their familiar intercourse with each other and with the native Jews.

20. How did the Lord treat the multitudes after he healed their sick?—He had compassion on them, because they had been with him three days and were faint through fasting.

21. What did he propose to do? —To feed them.

22. On what?—On seven loaves and a few little fishes.

23. How did he proceed to do this?—The same as in a former case of feeding a multitude in the desert.

24. How many were fed?—Four thousand men, besides women and children.

25. To what place did Jesus go next?—To the coasts of Magdala, on the west side of the lake.

26. What did the Pharisees and Sadducees require of him? —A sign from heaven.

27. What did they mean by this?—Perhaps some public attestation of his Messiahship, such as was given at Sinai when the law was proclaimed.

28. What sign was offered them?—The sign of the prophet Jonah.

29. What did the Lord mean by the leaven of the Pharisees and of Herod?—Their doctrines and political principles.

30. How did Jesus heal a blind man at Bethsaida?—By moistening and touching his eyes with spittle.

31. Why did the Lord resort to this method?—Probably to establish more effectually the blind man's faith.

32. What confession does Peter again make concerning Jesus?— That he was the Christ, the Son of the living God.

33. What commendation does Jesus give to him?—He calls him blessed, and pronounces him a

Rock.

34. In what sense was Peter a Rock?—With the other apostles and prophets he was a foundation stone, upon which the Church was built. Eph. 2:20.

35. Was the Church built on Peter as a corner stone?—No; Christ is the chief corner stone.

36. When was the Church founded?—By God himself in the garden of Eden.

37. What great honor was conferred on Peter?—He was made the instrument of first admitting Gentiles into the Christian Church.

38. What is signified by the keys of the kingdom of heaven?—The power of admitting or excluding members in the Church.

39. Was this power given to Peter alone?—No; it was given to all the apostles.

40. Who are the successors of the apostles?—All ministers of the Lord Jesus Christ.

41. After this confession of Peter and his receiving the name of Rock, what took place?—Jesus began to show to his disciples the necessity of his suffering and dying at Jerusalem, and his resurrection on the third day.

42. How did Peter receive this communication?—He began to rebuke the Lord, saying: "Far be it from thee, Lord; this shall not be to thee."

43. What did the Lord say to Peter?—He bade him get behind him.

44. How did Peter savor the things that are of men?—His thoughts of Christ's kingdom were worldly; he had no idea as yet of a purely spiritual kingdom.

45. What views did the Jews generally have of the Messiah?—That he was to come as a national king and conqueror.

THE TRANSFIGURATION. SUNDRY TEACHINGS. (Matt. 17, 18; Mark 9; Luke 9-17.)

1. What apostles did Jesus take with him privately into the mountain?—Peter, James, and John.

2. What mountain was this?—Without doubt one of the peaks of Mount Hermon.

3. What change was shown in his person?—He was transfigured before his disciples.

4. How did he appear?—His face shone as the sun, and his raiment was white as snow.

5. Who appeared with him?—Moses and Elijah.

6. What did Moses and Elijah represent?—The law and the prophets.

7. How did these two represent both the living and the dead?—Elijah was translated into heaven alive; Moses died and was buried. The two worlds come together.

8. On what subject did they converse?—On the Lord's decease, or departure, at Jerusalem.

9. What effect did this vision produce on the disciples?—They were heavy with sleep.

10. What did Peter say?—He said it was good for them to be there, and proposed to make them tabernacles, one for each of them, not knowing what he said.

11. Why did he say this?—Because there was a tradition among the Jews that Moses and Elijah would both appear when the Messiah did.

12. What overshadowed them? —A bright cloud.

13. Of what was this a symbol?—Of the divine presence.

14. What voice was heard?—A voice which said: "This is my beloved Son, in whom I am well pleased; hear ye him."

15. Why not hear the law and the prophets?—Because Christ was the end of the law for righteousness to them that believe, and the accomplisher of the prophecies.

16. How were the disciples affected?—They fell on their faces and were sore afraid.

17. What reassured them?—The words and touch of Jesus, who said: "Arise, and be not afraid."

153

18. Had the vision now passed? —When they lifted up their eyes they saw no man save Jesus only.

19. Did the disciples tell this vision?—They kept it close, and told no man in those days of any of those things which they had seen.

20. Why did they not speak of it to others?—It was a mystery which they could not explain, and the Lord cautioned them not to tell the vision until after he was risen from the dead.

21. Did Peter and John then refer to it?—Yes. See 2 Peter 1: 16-18; John 1:14.

22. Were they now able to understand it?—Yes; what before had been only a belief was now a certainty — the resurrection of the dead—of which this vision was an anticipation.

23. When Jesus and the three disciples descended from the mountain who met them?—A certain man whose son was a lunatic, sore vexed with an evil spirit and epilepsy.

24. What did he do?—He kneeled down to Jesus and asked him to have mercy on his son.

25. What had he already done? —He had brought him to the disciples of Christ, but they could not cure him.

26. Why?—Because of their lack of faith.

27. Did Jesus effect a cure?— Yes.

28. When they came to Capernaum how did Jesus pay the tribute money?—He directed Peter to cast a hook into the lake, and take the fish that first came up, and he should find in its mouth a coin of sufficient value to satisfy the claim for them both.

29. What was the tribute money?—The amount assessed on every Israelite for the temple service. Exod. 30:13.

30. How much was assessed on each person?—Half a shekel (twenty-six cents).

31. What is the meaning of the word "prevented?"—Anticipated.

32. What lesson of considerateness does the Lord of all teach us?—Not to give needless offense, especially in little matters.

33. What do we learn from the "piece of money" being the exact amount claimed for Peter and our Lord?—Perhaps that Jesus had miraculously brought the exact coin required into the fish's mouth.

34. What questin did the disciples ask Jesus?—Who is the greatest in the kingdom of heaven?

35. How did the Lord answer the question?—By placing a little child in the midst of them and saying that those who would enter into the kingdom of heaven must be converted and become as little children.

36. Why had they asked this question?—Because they had been disputing among themselves in the way who should be greatest.

37. What request did the mother of James and John once make? —That her two sons might be the chief ministers of state in the Lord's kingdom.

38. What is conversion?—A change of heart.

39. What is it to become like little children?—To be teachable, guileless, forgiving, and humble.

40. Are children naturally good? —They inherit a fallen nature, but until they begin to practice sin they are innocent.

41. What is meant by offending one of these little ones?—Leading any of Christ's disciples into sin.

42. What kind of a millstone does Christ speak of?—A heavy millstone requiring an ass or other large beast to turn it.

43. Why must offenses come?— Because of the depravity of men.

44. What denunciation did Christ pronounce on this account against one of his own disciples?— See Matt. 26:24.

45. Whom did the Lord commission besides the twelve apostles?— Seventy of his other disciples.

46. For what purpose?—To pre-

154

pare the people in every place to which he might come to receive him.

47. How did he send them?—Two and two.

48. Why?—For company, counsel, and aid to one another.

49. What did he say to them?—Carry neither purse, nor scrip, nor shoes, and salute no man by the way.

50. What is a scrip?—A leathern bag or wallet to hold provisions.

51. Why were they to make no provision for their journey?—That they might throw themselves on the hospitality of their brethren and win their confidence.

52. Why were they to salute no man by the way?—Because oriental salutations are formal and consume time. The Lord's business was urgent.

53. What salutation were they to use in entering into a house?—Peace be to this house.

54. What is meant by the son of peace?—In Jewish style every one possessing a good or bad quality was called the son of it; as "sons of Belial," or wickedness; "sons of light." Son of peace means a peaceable man.

55. How long were they to remain?—Until their mission was accomplished.

56. Why were they not to go from house to house?—Because it would show that they were more desirous for their own comfort than to attend to the Lord's work.

THE FEAST OF THE TABER-NACLES.—GROWING OP-POSITION. (John 7, 8.)

1. What feast did Jesus now attend at Jerusalem?—The feast of tabernacles.

2. When was this feast kept?—It began on the fifteenth day of the seventh month (parts of September and October) and lasted seven days.

3. Why did Jesus come secretly to the feast?—Because the Jews

sought to kill him.

4. At what time did Jesus come?—About the middle of the feast.

5. What did he do?—He went up into the temple and taught.

6. What effect did his teaching have?—Many of the people believed on him.

7. What did the Pharisees and chief priests do?—They desired to get rid of Jesus and sent officers to take him.

8. Did these officers take him?—No; they were astonished and returned, saying: "Never man spake like this man."

9. How did the Pharisees receive this report?—They were indignant.

10. What did Nicodemus say?—Doth our law judge any man before it hear him and know what he doeth?

11. What was their reply?—They answered and said: "Art thou also of Galilee? Search and look; for out of Galilee ariseth no prophet."

12. On the next morning what was done?—While Jesus was teaching in the temple a woman taken in adultery was brought to him for his judgment; but instead of pronouncing judgment he convicted her accusers of sin, and they all left him and the woman in the midst, when Jesus dismissed her, bidding her to sin no more.

13. When Jesus left the temple whom did he see as he passed by?—A man blind from his birth.

14. What did the disciples think was the cause of this man's blindness?—Sin either in his parents or himself.

15. What made them think this?—The Jews taught that every affliction and disease was a punishment of sin.

16. How did Jesus teach on this subject?—That this blindness came to the man providentially, and not as a penalty for sin; but that the works of God should be manifest in him.

17. Could God's works have

155

been manifest in him had he always remained blind?—Undoubtedly, as we now understand them.

18. How?—In the spiritual results, as patience, gentleness, devotion, joy, and the like fruits of good living.

19. But what physical work of God was specially manifest in him?—Jesus gave him sight.

20. How did Jesus cure him?—He spat on the ground, made clay of the spittle, anointed the eyes of the blind man, and sent him to the pool of Siloam to wash; and he went and washed and received sight.

21. When the seventy returned to Jesus what report did they bring?—That even the devils were subject to them through his name.

22. What did Jesus say?—Not to rejoice so much in this power which he gave them as that their names were written in heaven.

23. What question did a certain lawyer put to Jesus?—He inquired what he should do to inherit eternal life.

24. Was he sincere?—He desired to prove Jesus, or put him to the scrutiny.

25. How did Jesus answer?—He asked what was written in the law.

26. When the lawyer responded what did Jesus say?—Thou hast answered right; this do, and thou shalt live.

27. How did the Lord show the lawyer who his neighbor was?—By the parable of the Good Samaritan.

28. Who is our neighbor?—Anyone who stands in need of help.

29. What prayer did Jesus teach his disciples?—What is known as the Lord's Prayer. Luke 11:2-4.

30. What act of healing did Jesus soon after this perform in a synagogue?—He healed a woman that had a spirit of infirmity eighteen years.

31. And what at the house of a chief Pharisee?—He cured a man who had the dropsy.

32. What parable did the Lord speak in this connection?—The parable of the Supper.

33. What other parables did he speak after leaving the Pharisee's house?—The parables of the Lost Sheep, the Lost Piece of Money, the Prodigal Son, the Unjust Steward, and the Rich Man and Lazarus.

34. Were there any additional instructions?—Yes.

TOURING IN GALILEE AND ELSEWHERE. (Luke 17, 18; John 10.)

1. After our Lord's return from the feast of tabernacles, where did he go?—To his own country.

2. Did he remain here long?—No; for shortly afterward he returned to Jerusalem.

3. What feast did he wish to attend?—The feast of dedication, occurring in the winter.

4. What was this feast?—It was one kept in memory of the Lord's delivery of the temple from King Antiochus.

5. When Jesus passed through Samaria and entered into a village did the inhabitants receive him?—No.

6. Why?—Because he was going to Jerusalem, and was not willing to tarry there.

7. What did James and John want to do?—To call down lightning from heaven to consume them.

8. What name did Jesus give to these two disciples?—Sons of Thunder.

9. How did he rebuke them?—By telling them that the Son of man was come to save men's lives, not to destroy them.

10. As Jesus left this village and entered into another, who met him?—Ten lepers.

11. What was done?—On their crying for mercy, Jesus directed them to go and show themselves to the priest, and as they went they were cleansed.

12. When Jesus entered Judea

where was he entertained?—At the home of Martha and Mary in Bethany.

13. When he came to Jerusalem what did he do?—He conversed with the Jews in Solomon's porch; but his teachings angered them, and he left the city.

14. To what place did he go?—To Bethabara, beyond Jordan.

15. What message was sent to him?—That his friend Lazarus, the brother of Martha and Mary, was sick.

16. When did Jesus come to Bethany?—After Lazarus was dead.

17. What great truth did Jesus teach Martha?—That he was the resurrection and the life.

18. How did he show this truth?—By restoring Lazarus to life after he had been dead and buried four days.

19. Did this great work convince the Pharisees and chief priests that Jesus was the Christ?—No; they sought the more to kill him.

THE LORD'S LAST VISIT TO JERUSALEM. (Matt. 21; Mark 11; Luke 22; John 12.)

1. How did our Lord enter Jerusalem?—Riding on an ass.

2. Why did he do this?—It was customary for kings thus to ride, and he now claimed and manifested his royal authority and prerogative.

3. Was he welcomed?—Yes; they cried: "Hosanna: Blessed is the King of Israel that cometh in the name of the Lord."

4. What did he do on the next day?—He again purged the temple.

5. What parables did he speak?—The parables of the Vineyard, the Marriage Feast, the Ten Virgins, and the Talents.

6. What other things did Jesus say?—He denounced the scribes and Pharisees, foretold the destruction of the temple, confuted the Sadducees, forewarned his disciples, and bewailed the coming fate of the city and nation.

7. When was the temple destroyed and the nation scattered?—About the year 70 A.D., by Titus.

8. Did any of the Christians perish at the fall of Jerusalem?—No; forewarned by Christ, they escaped betimes from the city.

9. Where did Jesus keep the passover?—In an upper room, at the house of an acquaintance and friend.

10. What contention arose among the disciples?—As to who should be greatest.

11. How did the Lord settle the question?—By showing that the greatest among them should be the servant of all, and by washing their feet.

12. Was Jesus aware of the intended treachery of Judas?—He was, and did his best to save him.

13. What memorial did Jesus substitute for the passover?—The Lord's Supper.

14. What did he say to Peter?—That Satan had desired to sift him as wheat; but that he had prayed for him that his faith might not fail.

15. What self-confidence did Peter exhibit?—He said he was ready even to die with Jesus.

16. What did the Lord reply?—That Peter should that very night deny him thrice.

17. After Judas had gone out what discourse did Jesus have with the eleven?—He gave them his last instructions, spoke words of comfort, and prayed with and for them.

18. Did they understand the purport of this talk?—Not at the time.

19. How did they conclude the feast?—With the singing of a hymn.

20. What did Jesus do then?—He went with his disciples to the garden of Gethsemane.

21. Where was this garden?—On the western slope of the Mount of Olives, near the foot.

157

SUFFERINGS, DEATH, AND BURIAL OF JESUS. (Matt. 26, 27; Mark 14, 15; Luke 22, 23; John 18, 19.)

1. How did the agony of Jesus in the garden affect him?—His sweat was as it were great drops of blood falling down to the ground.

2. How was he enabled to endure it?—An angel from heaven appeared unto him, strengthening him.

3. When the multitude came to arrest Jesus how did they recognize him?—Judas betrayed him with a kiss, and Jesus also said that he himself was the one they wanted.

4. What became of the disciples?—They all forsook him and fled. Zech. 13:7.

5. To what place did the officers take Jesus?—To the high priest's house, where an examination was held between midnight and dawn.

6. When the morning dawned what was done?—The Sanhedrin was hastily summoned, and Jesus was put on trial before it.

7. To what decision did this council come?—That Jesus should die.

8. How did they secure this result?—They brought Jesus to Pilate, who, though he could find no fault in Jesus, yielded to their clamors, and gave orders to crucify him.

9. To whom was Jesus then committed?—To a company of Roman guards, who mocked him, treating him with unwonted cruelty before they led him away for execution.

10. Where was Jesus crucified? —On Golgotha, or Calvary.

11. Who were crucified with him?—Two malefactors.

12. On what day did this take place?—The day before Sabbath.

13. How long did he hang on the cross?—Six hours.

14. What natural phenomena accompanied the crucifixion?—The sun was darkened, and there was an earthquake which rent the veil of the temple from top to bottom; the rocks were split, and the graves were opened.

15. Where was Jesus buried, and by whom?—In a new tomb in a garden near to Calvary, by Joseph of Arimathea.

THE RESURRECTION AND ASCENSION OF JESUS. (Matt. 28; Mark 16; Luke 24; John 20, 21.)

1. When did Christ rise from the dead?—On the third day after his death, very early in the morning.

2. What day was this?—The first day of the week.

3. How was the tomb opened? —By an angel, accompanied with a great earthquake.

4. What did the guards who watched the tomb do?—They shook with fear and became as dead men.

5. To whom did Christ first appear?—To Mary Magdalene.

6. What message did he give her?—To go and tell his brethren that he was about to ascend to their common Father and God.

7. How many other appearances are recorded?—Eleven or twelve are mentioned.

8. What proof did Jesus give of his identity?—He allowed the disciples to handle him; he ate food in their presence; he showed them the prints of the nails in his hands and feet, and of the spear in his side; and called to their remembrance words which he had spoken while he was yet with them.

9. Was the resurrection of Jesus made known in the city?—The keepers of the tomb came and told it to the chief priests and rulers.

10. Did the chief priests believe their statement?—They could not do otherwise.

11. What did they do?—They bribed them to tell a different

story.

12. Why?—Because, since they had rejected Jesus, they desired to conceal from the people all the evidence that went to establish his Messiahship.

13. Did they succeed in this?—They failed miserably.

14. How long did Jesus remain on the earth after his resurrection?—Forty days.

15. Why did he not appear oftener to the disciples?—Perhaps to teach them to live by faith, and to think of him as being continually present with them though they could not see him.

16. Who were the two disciples whom the Lord met on the way to Emmaus?—Cleopas was one of them; the other was probably Luke, the author of the Gospel.

17. Why did they not at first recognize him?—Because he appeared to them in another form. Mark 16:12.

18. Where did above five hundred brethren at once see him?—On a mountain in Galilee.

19. Why did the Lord not show himself more publicly?—The proof of the resurrection would not have been more clearly established thereby; but he appeared openly, not to all the people, but unto witnesses chosen before of God. Acts 10:41.

20. Who were these witnesses?—Those who knew him intimately and could not be mistaken in his person, as mere acquaintances or strangers might have been.

21. Is the fact of the Lord's resurrection, then, clearly established?—It is more clearly established than most facts in history, and admits of no doubt.

22. What is paradise?—The place into which righteous souls go after death, and where they remain between death and the resurrection.

23. Did Jesus go into paradise?——Yes. Acts 2:31.

24. Have any souls been redeemed from paradise?—Yes; for after the Lord rose from the dead, many bodies of the saints which slept arose and came out of the graves and went into the holy city, and appeared unto many. Matt. 27:52, 53.

25. What is death called in the New Testament?—A sleep. John 11:11; Acts 7:60; 1 Cor. 15:6; 1 Thess. 4:14.

26. What became of these saints which arose with Christ?—They probably ascended into the heavens with him, though invisible to the disciples.

27. Will there be a general resurrection?—The Scriptures so teach. Isa. 26:19; Dan. 12:2; Acts 24:15.

THE ASCENSION OF THE LORD.

1. When did the last interview between Jesus and his disciples take place?—On the fortieth day after his resurrection.

2. Where?—At Jerusalem.

3. What question did the apostles ask Jesus?—Whether he would at that time restore the kingdom to Israel.

4. What did he respond?—That it was not for them to know the times or the seasons which the Father hath put in his own power.

5. Did he correct their erroneous views?—He opened their mind that they might understand the Scriptures; but their erroneous views were fully corrected by the Holy Ghost.

6. What promise did he give to them?—That they should receive power after the Holy Ghost was come upon them.

7. What power did he confer upon them?—The power to work miracles. Mark 16:17, 18.

8. From whom does all power proceed?—From the Lord himself, because all power in heaven and earth is given to him. Matt. 27:18.

9. What commission was given to the disciples?—To go into all the world, and preach the Gospel

159

to every creature.

10. Does this order still bind the Church?—Yes.

11. What were they directed to do before they went forth?—To tarry at Jerusalem until they should be endued with divine power.

12. When God calls men to go forth and preach must they go at once?—Not necessarily; they should first qualify themselves to preach.

13. To what place did Jesus lead his disciples?—To Bethany, on the eastern slope of the Mount of Olives.

14. What happened there?—He was parted from them and carried up into heaven, a cloud receiving him out of their sight.

15. What was his last act of love to his disciples before his ascension?—He lifted up his hands and blessed them.

16. What act of homage did they immediately perform?—They worshiped him.

17. While still gazing and worshiping, who stood beside them?—Two angels, in white apparel.

18. What did the angels ask?—Why they stood gazing up into the heavens.

19. What did they mean by this?—That the Lord's immediate return need not be looked for.

20. What promise did they give?—That in like manner as they had seen him go into heaven so should he come.

21. What did the disciples do?—They returned to Jerusalem.

22. Where is Jesus now?—At the right hand of God. Heb. 12:2.

23. What is he to those who have sinned?—Our Advocate with the Father and the propitiation for our sins. 1 John 2:1, 2.

24. What is Jesus to those who believe?—The Saviour of all men, especially of those who believe. 1 Tim. 4:10.

THE ACTS OF THE APOSTLES—PREACHING AND LABORS OF PETER. (Acts 1-12.)

1. Who wrote the Book of Acts?—Luke, who also wrote one of the gospels.

2. What is the subject of this book?—It is chiefly the histories of Peter and Paul.

3. What did the apostles first do after the ascension of Jesus?—They returned to Jerusalem and engaged in daily worship in an upper room with the other disciples.

4. How many disciples were there in Jerusalem?—One hundred and twenty.

5. What was their first act?—The election of Matthias as successor of Judas.

6. What took place on the day of Pentecost?—The disciples received the gift of the Holy Spirit.

7. How were they affected?—They began to speak with other tongues, as the Spirit gave them utterance.

8. How were the multitudes affected when they heard of it?—They were amazed, and wondered how these Galileans could speak in so many different tongues.

9. How did Peter explain it?—That it was a fulfillment of a prophecy of Joel. Joel 2:28-32.

10. What was the theme of Peter's sermon?—Jesus of Nazareth, both Lord and Christ.

11. What was the effect of this sermon?—Three thousand souls were converted and baptized the same day.

12. Did the disciples then cease to work?—No; and the Lord added daily to their number.

13. What miracle did Peter and John perform at the gate of the temple?—The healing of a lame man in the name of Jesus.

14. What did the rulers and priests do?—They imprisoned Peter and John until the next day.

15. What was then done?—The apostles were charged by the rulers to preach and teach no more in the name of Jesus; but they kept on doing so.

16. How was the Church early

taught integrity and righteousness?
—By the judgment that befell
Ananias and Sapphira his wife for
lying and deceiving.

17. Who was the first martyr
for Jesus?—Stephen.

18. What followed the death of
Stephen?—A general persecution of
the infant Church.

19. Who was one of the chief
persecutors?—Saul of Tarsus.

20. How was Saul arrested in
his mad career?—By a light from
heaven which appeared to him on
his way to Damascus and by the
words which Jesus spoke to him.

21. Did Saul give up all for
Christ?—He did, and began forthwith to preach Christ in the synagogues of Damascus.

22. What miracles did Peter
now perform?—He healed Eneas
of the palsy at Lydda, and restored Dorcas to life at Joppa.

23. Who was the first Gentile
convert to Christ?—Cornelius, a
Roman centurion of Caesarea; for
the chamberlain of Queen Can-
dace, led to the truth by Philip,
was either a foreign Jew or a
proselyte who had come to Jerusalem to worship.

24. By whom was Cornelius led
to Christ, and how?—By Peter, as
he preached before him and a
company of Gentiles in Caesarea.

25. What was the effect of the
persecution at Jerusalem?—The
disciples there were scattered
abroad, and some of them went
to Cyprus and Phoenicia and Antioch, and preached Christ there
to the Jews.

26. Was fault found with Peter
for preaching to Gentiles?—Yes;
but when he made his defense
before the brethren at Jerusalem
they held their peace and glorified
God, saying, in their amazement:
"Then God hath granted to the
Gentiles also repentance unto
life!"

27. Who was the second martyr
for Jesus?—James, the brother of
John, who was slain by Herod.

28. Did Herod intend to put
other disciples to death?—Yes; he
apprehended Peter and put him
into prison, with the intention of
slaying him after the feast of
unleavened bread.

29. How was Peter delivered?—
By an angel of the Lord.

30. After his deliverance whither
did Peter go?—To Caesarea, where
he remained.

SAUL AND BARNABAS.
(Acts 9-15.)

1. How was Saul received by
the Christians in Jerusalem?—
They were afraid of him and did
not believe that he was a disciple
until Barnabas brought him to
the apostles and told them the
story of his conversion.

2. When Saul himself was persecuted by the Grecians, or Hel-
lenistic Jews, what did the disciples do with him?—They brought
him to Caesarea, and from there
sent him to Tarsus.

3. Was the preaching of the
disciples at Antioch attended with
success?—It was; and the brethren
at Jerusalem sent Barnabas to
their assistance.

4. What did Barnabas do when
he saw the grace of God there
displayed?—He went to Tarsus
and brought Saul back with him
to Antioch, where they labored an
entire year.

5. For what purpose did Barnabas and Saul go to Jerusalem?—
To carry alms for the relief of
the poor.

6. On their return to Antioch
who went with them?—John, sur-
named Mark, supposed to be the
author of one of the gospels.

7. What name was given to the
disciples at Antioch?—Christians.

8. On what mission were Barnabas and Saul sent?—To labor in
outlying cities and countries.

9. What places did they first
visit?—Seleucia and Cyprus.

10. What occurred in Paphos?
—Elymas the sorcerer withstood
them as they were preaching to
the deputy Sergius Paulus, and

Saul pronounced upon him a judgment from the Lord, the effect of which was that the deputy believed, being astonished at the word of the Lord. Saul now took the name of Paul, which, as he began to preach to Gentiles, was probably preferred by him as being his Roman name; for Saul was a Roman citizen as well as a Jew.

11. After going through Cyprus what places did they visit?—Perga; Antioch in Pisidia; Iconium, where Paul and Barnabas were thought by the Gentiles to be Jupiter and Mercury; and Derbe; and thence they returned to Lystra, Iconium, and Antioch in Pisidia, and came to Attalia, from which point they sailed to Antioch.

12. Where did Mark part company with them?—At Perga.

13. What controversy sprang up between Paul and Barnabas, and certain Jewish Christians?—A dissension about the manner of receiving the Gentiles into the Church.

14. How was the controversy settled?—The apostles and brethren in Jerusalem, guided by the Holy Ghost, decreed that no other burden was to be put upon the Gentile Christians than these: To abstain from meat offered unto idols, from blood, from things strangled, and from fornication.

15. To what new places did Paul now go?—After revisiting Derbe and Lystra, he went through Phrygia, Galatia, Mysia, and Troas.

16. Who accompanied Paul?—Silas and Timothy.

PAUL'S MISSIONARY TOURS.
(Acts 16-20.)

1. Why did Paul go into Europe?—While he was at Troas he had a vision of a Macedonian man asking him to come over to Macedonia and help them; from which he inferred that the Lord had called him to preach there.

2. What city did Paul and his companions first visit in Macedonia?—Philippi.

3. Did they make any converts there?—Yes; among them Lydia and her household.

4. How were Paul and Silas treated?—They were cast into prison and cruelly treated by the jailer.

5. What happened?—A great earthquake opened the prison doors and loosened the stocks; and when the jail·r, supposing the prisoners had all escaped, was about to kill himself, Paul cried out that they were all there. The jailer's conversion and the release of the prisoners speedily followed.

6. What other cities did Paul visit?—Thessalonica, Berea, and Athens.

7. Where and what did Paul preach in Athens?—He stood on Mars' Hill and preached the resurrection of the dead.

8. Was this a new doctrine to the Athenians?—It was; but while some mocked, others desired to hear more concerning it.

9. To what city did Paul go next?—To Corinth.

10. How long did Paul remain there?—A year and a half.

11. What places did he next visit?—Some of the chief cities in Syria and Asia Minor.

12. Which was the most important of these?—Ephesus.

13. Was Paul there long?—About two years.

14. Whither did Paul go from Ephesus?—He returned to Macedonia, and then came into Greece, where he remained three months. At Troas he restored Eutychus to life; then went to Assos and took ship to revisit Jerusalem. He stopped at several points on the voyage and met the disciples, confirming them in the faith.

15. What were the results of these missionary labors?—Churches were planted in all the principal cities and provinces, and many souls were converted to Christ. The more important of these

churches were those at Philippi, Colosse, Laodicea, Corinth, Thessalonica, Ephesus, and in Galatia.

PAUL AT JERUSALEM.
(Acts 21-23.)

1. How far was Caesarea from Jerusalem?—About sixty miles.

2. Why did Paul wish to go to Jerusalem?—To be present at the feast of Pentecost.

3. How was he received?—With gladness.

4. Whom did Paul visit?—James and the elders of the Church.

5. Who was James?—The Lord's brother.

6. Was he an apostle?—He was not one of the twelve, but he was the leading spirit in the apostolic Church.

7. What tumult took place in the temple?—A riot of the Jews, who supposed that Paul had brought a Greek into the temple and so polluted it.

8. What was the law about Gentiles entering the temple?—On the fence, or "the middle wall of partition," dividing the court of the Gentiles from that of the Israelites there was an inscription in Greek and Latin, that no Gentile should enter within under penalty of death.

9. What did the furious mob do to Paul when they saw him in the temple?—They dragged him out of the temple and forthwith the gates were shut.

10. What was their intention?—To kill him.

11. How was he rescued?—The chief captain of the Fortress Antonia took soldiers and centurions, and ran down into the crowd and took him.

12. Where was this fortress?—At the northwest corner of the temple, of which it was the citadel. A large troop of Roman soldiers were stationed there, and some of the sentinels saw the tumult and reported it to the chief captain.

13. Whom did the chief captain think Paul to be?—An Egyptian ringleader of four thousand seditious men.

14. What permission did Paul have from the chief captain?—To address the crowd from the stairs leading up to the castle.

15. Did he speak in Greek?—No; in the popular Hebrew, or Aramaic.

16. What did Paul say?—He began to give an account of his life; but when he spoke of his being sent to the Gentiles they made such an uproar that he could no longer speak.

17. When this uproar was at its height what did the chief captain do?—He commanded the soldiers to bring Paul into the castle, where he would have examined him by scourging; but learning that Paul was a Roman citizen he was afraid and desisted.

18. What was done on the morrow?—The commandant summoned the chief priests and all their council to appear, and brought Paul down and set him before them.

19. When Paul perceived that the council was composed of both Sadducees and Pharisees how did he take advantage of that fact?—He declared himself to be a Pharisee, and that he was called in question on the resurrection of the dead.

20. What were the results?—There was so great a dissension between the two sects that the commandant rescued Paul and brought him again into the castle.

21. Why was Paul sent to Caesarea?—Because of a conspiracy to kill him.

22. To whom was Paul sent?—To Felix, the governor of the province.

23. What did Felix do?—He ordered the accusers of Paul to come to Caesarea and present their case before him at that place.

24. After they had presented their accusation and Paul had replied to it, what did he do?—He

said that he would hear the matter more fully when the chief captain should come down.

25. When Felix and Drusilla afterward conferred with Paul what effect had Paul's address on Felix?—As Paul reasoned of righteousness, sobriety, and the coming judgment, Felix trembled, but put him off to a "convenient season."

26. How long was Paul kept in confinement at Caesarea, and why?—During the remainder of the term that Felix served as governor, Felix hoping that Paul or his friends would pay money for his release.

PAUL'S VOYAGE TO ROME.
(Acts 27, 28.)

1. Who succeeded Felix as governor?—Porcius Festus.

2. How did he treat Paul?—He desired to take Paul back to Jerusalem to be tried by the Jewish council, but Paul refused, and appealed to the emperor.

3. Who came to visit Festus?—King Agrippa and his wife, Bernice.

4. What did Festus tell them?—He declared Paul's cause to the king.

5. What did the king say?—That he would like to hear Paul himself.

6. Was his wish gratified?—It was; for on the next day Paul was brought before the governor and his visitors, and allowed to speak for himself.

7. What did Paul's hearers think of Paul's speech?—Festus said that he was mad; and Agrippa, when Paul appealed to him, replied: "Almost thou persuadest me to be a Christian!"

8. What did Festus do with Paul?—He sent him to Rome.

9. On what ship was he put?—A ship of Adramyttium.

10. Why in this ship?—It was a coasting vessel then in port, and the centurion expected to meet on the way some ship bound for Italy.

11. What kindness did Julius show to Paul?—He gave him his liberty and allowed him to visit his friends in Sidon.

12. What route did they pursue from Sidon?—They sailed to the leeward of Cyprus over the Sea of Cilicia and Pamphylia, and came to Myra, a city of Lycia.

13. What vessel did the centurion find at Myra?—A ship of Alexandria, sailing into Italy, on board of which he put his prisoners.

14. Why did it take such a roundabout way to sail into Italy?—In the winter season a strong northwest wind blows along the coast of Africa; so the vessel preferred to tack north toward Asia Minor, and then west among the Aegean Islands.

15. What was the character of this ship?—It was one of the largest vessels afloat, and used for bringing corn from Egypt.

16. At what place did they stop?—At Fair Havens, a port near the southern extremity of Crete.

17. Why did they not winter at Fair Havens?—Because the south wind was then blowing, and the centurion thought they could reach Phenice, a more commodious harbor on the same island.

18. What hurricane arose?—A tempestuous wind called Euroclydon, probably the same as is now called a Levanter.

19. Why did the seamen let the ship drive?—Because they lost control of it, and the open sea was in the direction of the wind.

20. Near what island did they run?—Clauda, on the leeward side.

21. What did they do here?—They undergirded the ship; that is, they slipped a stout cable under the vessel from the prow, and when they reached the middle of the keel the two ends of the rope were drawn up on the deck, and then tied.

22. What quicksands were feared?—The Syrtis, on the coast

164

of Africa.

23. How did they lighten the ship?—The least valuable wares and stores were first thrown overboard.

24. Did Paul and his companions assist?—Yes.

25. How long did the storm continue?—Many days.

26. Did they know where they were?—No; for neither sun nor stars appeared, and the mariner's compass was not then discovered.

27. What feeling did the crew have?—All hope that they would be saved was lost.

28. Who encouraged them?—Paul exhorted them to be of good cheer, saying that an angel of God had stood by him and assured him that he should be brought before Caesar, and that the whole company of them should be saved.

29. What did the shipmen do?—They sounded and found twenty fathoms, and going a little farther they found fifteen fathoms; and thinking they were near to land they waited for day.

30. What did they then try to do?—To escape from the vessel in a boat which they were letting down.

31. How was this prevented?—Paul saw through their purpose, and declared to the centurion that it was necessary for them to stay.

32. How did the soldiers decide the matter?—They cut the ropes and let the boat fall off.

33. What was done as soon as the day broke?—Paul took food and ate it, and exhorted the others to eat, because they had continued so long without regular meals.

34. When they had eaten what did they do?—They lightened the ship and made for the shore, where they ran the ship aground.

35. Upon what land were they wrecked?—On the island of Malta.

36. How did they escape from the ship?—By swimming or floating on boards and pieces of the ship that was being broken by the violence of the waves.

37. When they all reached land how did the inhabitants treat them?—With kindness, kindling a fire for them because of the rain and the cold.

38. How long were Paul and his company on the island?—Three months.

39. What hospitality did Publius, the chief man of the island, show them?—He received them into his house and lodged them three days courteously.

40. What miracles did Paul work here?—He healed the father of Publius of a fever; others also who had diseases in the island came and were healed.

41. How did they requite the favors thus shown them?—They honored Paul and his friends with many honors; and when they departed, they laded them with such things as were necessary.

42. How did they get to Rome?—They sailed in a ship from Alexandria, whose sign was Castor and Pollux.

43. What route did they take?—They sailed to Syracuse on the island of Sicily; thence to Rhegium in Italy, and thence to Puteoli, where they disembarked.

44. At Rome what became of Paul?—He was delivered to the captain of the guard, who suffered him to dwell by himself with a soldier that kept him.

45. How long was Paul here before he was brought before the emperor?—Two years.

46. How did he employ himself?—In preaching the kingdom of God and teaching those things which concern the Lord Jesus Christ.

47. Who was then the Roman emperor?—Nero.

48. How was Christianity planted in Rome?—So deeply that no persecution was ever able to root it out.

THE EPISTLE OF PAUL TO THE ROMANS—PAUL'S INTEREST IN THE ROMANS.
(Rom. 1.)

1. What is the theme of the book of Romans?—The Gospel of Jesus Christ.

2. What is the book of Romans sometimes called?—The great systematic statement of Christianity.

3. About what time in Paul's life was this book written?—Near the end of his earthly life.

4. With what does the first chapter deal?—God's wrath against sin, Man's responsibility. World apostasy. Sin and the present state.

5. How did Paul introduce himself to the Romans?—As a servant of Jesus Christ.

6. For what purpose was Paul called?—To be an Apostle, separated unto the Gospel of God. Rom. 1:1.

7. Upon what did Paul base his right to Apostleship?—Obedience to his faith in Jesus Christ.

8. How did Paul greet the Christians in Rome?—Beloved of God, called to be saints: Grace to you and peace from God our Father, and the Lord Jesus Christ. 1:7.

9. For what did he thank God?—That their faith was spoken of throughout the whole world.

10. For what did he call God to witness?—That without ceasing he made mention of them always in his prayers.

11. How did Paul prepare for his proposed visit to Rome?—He prayed for a prosperous journey.

12. What did he hope to gain by such a journey?—Power to impart and receive spiritual uplift. 1:10, 11, 12.

13. How did Paul regard his ministry among the Greeks and the Barbarians?—A debtor to both.

14. Who were the Barbarians?—The Greeks and afterward the Romans called all nations except themselves barbarians.

15. Was Paul eager to proclaim the good news in Rome?—As much as in me is, I am ready to preach the gospel to you that are at Rome also. 1:15.

15. What important text is in verse 16?—For I am not ashamed of the gospel of Christ.

17. Why was Paul so bold in this statement?—For it is the power of God unto salvation . . .

18. How far-reaching is this power of the Gospel to save?—To every one who believeth.

19. What is the secret of the Gospel's power?—It is the revelation of God's righteousness to those who have faith. 1:17.

20. Upon what principle do the righteous live?—The principle of faith.

21. What is God's attitude toward them that defy him?—For the wrath of God is revealed from heaven against all ungodliness and unrighteousness of men. 1:18.

22. What is ungodliness?—A disregard of God. Wickedness, sinfulness.

23. After the Gentiles received a knowledge of the true God, what was their attitude?—They did not glorify him, nor worship him, neither were they thankful.

24. What was the result of such rejection?—Professing themselves to be wise, they became fools. 1:22.

25. How did they insult God?—They made images or idols to resemble man, beasts, birds, and the like. 1:23.

26. What was the result of their apostasy?—God gave them up to the lust of their own hearts.

27. Were the Gentiles aware that such evil practices made them worthy of death?—They were, but they continued on in their depravity, taking pleasure in so doing.

GOD'S JUDGMENT IMPARTIAL. (Rom. 2.)

1. What subjects are discussed in the second chapter of Romans?—Man's state before God, without

excuse, without escape, sinners judged by law and conscience.

2. What did the Apostle say about those who judge others?—They condemn themselves for they also are guilty.

3. What is the first principle of God's judgment?—It is according to truth.

4. How does God's goodness react in our daily life?—He provides for us, preserves us, and protects us.

5. How does the impenitent heart accumulate guilt?—It treasures up wrath against the day of wrath.

6. How will God reward each one?—He will render unto every man according to his deeds. 2:6.

7. To whom are granted the gift of eternal life?—To those who, in patient well doing, seek for God's glory and honor.

8. What is the fearful visitation upon the impenitent?—Tribulation and anguish.

9. To whom shall such tribulation and anguish come?—To the Jew and Gentile alike. 2:8, 9.

10. Is any class excluded?—No, for there is no respect of persons with God. 2:2.

11. Is the hearing of the law an advantage?—Not without obedience.

12. Who shall be justified?—The doer of the Word.

13. How far-reaching is the judgment of God?—He shall judge the secrets of men.

14. By what standard shall such judgment be made?—By Jesus Christ according to the Gospel. 2:16.

15. Whether Jew or Gentile, in what way does religion help us?—In its reality.

THE JEW'S ADVANTAGE.
(Rom. 3.)

1. Chapter three comprises what subjects?—Advantage of the Jew. All guilty. God's salvation in Christ.

2. What advantage had the Jews over other nations?—That nation was entrusted with the Oracles of God. 3:2.

3. Was the unbelief of some of the Jews detrimental to the believing Jews?—No, God with all faithfulness will fulfill his promises.

4. How can we benefit by God's promises?—We must fulfil the conditions of the promises.

5. Does humanity by nature understand the things of God?—There is none that understandeth.

6. Can we be justified before God by keeping the law?—No. There is none righteous.

7. Did the Gentiles seek after God?—They did not.

8. How universal was their apostasy?—They all abandoned the way.

9. What was their condition without God?—They became unprofitable. (The Greek word means useless, good for nothing).

10. What does the all-wise Physician say about the throat of the sin sick world?—Their throat is as an open sepulchre. 3:13.

11. What does the inspired writer say about their tongue?—They have used deceit.

12 What is said about the lips of the sin sick race?—The poison of asps is under their lips.

13. What about their mouth?—Full of cursing and bitterness.

14. What about their feet?—Swift to shed blood.

15. What does the all-seeing God see in fallen man?—Destruction and misery.

16. Of what are they ignorant?—The way of peace.

17. What do they sorely need?—The fear of God.

JUSTIFICATION BY FAITH.

18. Are we made righteous by the law?—No. By the deeds of the law shall no flesh be justified. 3:20.

19. What is the purpose of the law?—To make known to men their sins and their need of salva-

tion.

20. Why is there no difference between the Jew and the Gentile?—Because all have sinned and come short of the glory of God.

21. What provision has God made for our salvation?—Through the redemption that is in Christ Jesus.

22. How does the propitiation of Christ become effectual?—Only through the faith of him who appropriates it.

23. Can great works save us?—No. While they are a part of a Christian's life, good works alone cannot save us.

ABRAHAM JUSTIFIED BY FAITH. (Rom. 4.)

1. In what two great characters did the Jews especially glory?—Abraham and David.

2. How were these two great men accounted righteous?—By faith, not by law or by works.

3. Do righteousness and ordinances go hand in hand?—No. They stand apart.

4. Did Abraham's heirship depend upon the law?—No.

5. Upon what did it depend?—Upon the Promise.

6. Can we share such blessing?—Yes. Believers can also share this blessing.

7. Who has been called the father of the faithful?—Abraham.

8. What did he exemplify?—The way and walk of faith.

9. How is our justification connected with Christ's resurrection?—He was raised for our justification. 4:25.

JUSTIFICATION. (Rom. 5.)

1. This chapter falls into how many parts?—Into two parts.

2. What is shown in the first eleven verses?—The blessed results of justification by faith.

3. What else do we find in these eleven verses?—The great love and grace of God, in giving Christ for sinners.

4. What do we learn in the second part of the chapter?—About Adam, as our representative head whose sin became condemnation.

5. What further do we learn?—About Christ, who by his act of death on the cross, brought us justification and life.

6. What is the first blessing we notice in this part of the chapter?—Peace with God, in looking back to Calvary where Christ made peace by his blood.

7. What is the second blessing we find here?—A present standing in grace, and Divine favor.

8. What is the third blessing we find here?—Hope of Glory, and of being glorified with Christ when he comes.

9. How then do we have peace with God?—Through our Lord Jesus Christ. 5:1.

10. "Peace with God" what does this involve?—That God has judged sin, upon Christ our substitute.

11. Was God satisfied with Christ's sacrifice?—He was, and will forever remain so.

12. In what should we rejoice?—In the hope of Glory. 5:2.

13. Having this great peace through Christ in what further do we glory?—In tribulations which beset us.

14. How is tribulation a blessing?—If endured, tribulation worketh patience.

15. What further blessing comes through patient endurance?—Experience.

16. How is hope aroused within us?—By a sense of God's approval.

17. Why is it that our hope is not put to shame?—Because the love of God is shed abroad in our hearts, by the Holy Ghost which is given unto us. 5:5.

18. When did God command his great love to us?—While we were yet sinners.

19. How many "Much mores" are there in this chapter?—Four.

168

20. Where do we find them?—Two are in this first section; and two in the second. 5:9, 10, 15, 17.

21. What does grace do for us?—Turns our sorrow into joy. 5:2.

22. Who has the privilege of sharing such joy?—Every believer.

23. What was our state in previous chapters?—Sitting in the presence of the Judge, guilty.

24. What is God's plan?—The reign of grace through Christ. 5:12, 21.

25. What two men are mentioned in this chapter?—Adam and Christ.

26. What act of Adam reflected on all mankind?—One trespass. 5:12, 15, 17, 18, 19.

27. What important act of Christ benefited the whole world?—One righteous act (on the cross). 5:18.

28. What was the result of Adam's trespass?—Condemnation, guilt, death.

29. What was the result of Christ's one act on the cross?—Justification, life, kingship.

30. To what extent has the Grace of Christ abounded?—To many.

31. How far is that?—Beyond the sin of Adam.

32. How does the King of Sin reign?—Through Death. 5:21.

33. How does the King of Grace reign?—Through Righteousness. 5:21.

34. What two abundances do we find in verse 17?—Abundance of Grace, and abundance of the gift of righteousness.

35. What is the contrast between the condemned men and justified men?—Condemned men, slaves of death, by Adam. Justified men, reigning in life, by Christ.

VICTORY OVER SIN.
(Rom. 6.)

1. How are Christians to regard themselves?—As dead unto sin and alive unto God in Christ Jesus. 6:1, 2.

2. How should we yield ourselve unto God?—As risen, not under law, but under grace.

3. What is the result of such consecration?—Sin loses its dominion over us. 6:12-14.

4. Is it possible to abuse grace?—Yes.

5. What is a consequence of sin?—Slavery.

6. What is the end of sin?—Death.

7. What is the result of obedience?—Freedom.

8. What else is the result of obedience?—Eternal life.

9. How do we obtain God's free gift?—Through Jesus Christ our Lord. 6:15-23.

10. How does the second part of Romans identify us?—With Christ's death.

11. What became of the old nature?—The old man was crucified with him. 6:6.

12. How should Christians regard themselves?—Dead unto sin, but alive unto God in Christ Jesus.

13. How should we present ourselves before God?—As alive from the dead.

14. What does walking in newness of life presuppose?—The possession of life.

15. Does it mean more than a mere manner of living?—Yes, a new kind of life.

16. Who was the first-born of death?—Christ was the first-fruits of them that slept.

17. If we died in Christ what should be our expectation?—The expectation of a blessed life in Christ.

18. What was the cause of Paul's thanksgiving?—Because those who were once the servants of sin had accepted the Gospel of Christ. 6:17.

19. Becoming servants of God tends to what?—To holiness and the end everlasting life.

20. What is the pay a sinner

earns and receives?—The wages of sin is death.

21. What is the gift of God to them that follow him?—Eternal life.

LIMIT OF THE LAW.
(Rom. 7.)

1. How long does law have dominion over a man?—As long as he lives.

2. How does the Apostle illustrate this general principle?—By reference to the case of a married woman.

3. How do we know that the law is spiritual?—Its requirements reach the spirit.

4. What did Paul mean by carnal, sold under sin?—A conflict between the flesh and the spirit.

5. What did Paul mean by a "law" that when I would do good, etc.?—A tendency to that which is wrong.

6. What does it mean to delight in the law after the inward man?—All of God's saints love his law from their hearts.

7. Why was Paul so wretched?—Because his imperfection made him prone to sin.

8. Who is able to bring deliverance?—Jesus Christ the Lord.

THE LAW OF THE SPIRIT.
(Rom. 8.)

1. Who are free from condemnation?—Those who are in Christ Jesus.

2. How do they walk?—Not after the flesh but after the spirit.

3. From what did the law of the spirit of life in Christ Jesus free Paul?—From the law of sin and death.

4. Why was the law inadequate?—It was weak through the flesh.

5. How did the Son of God come to earth?—In the likeness of flesh.

6. What condemnation did this bring?—Condemnation of sin in the flesh.

7. For what purpose was such condemnation?—That the right-eousness of the law might be fulfilled in us.

8. How is such righteousness fulfilled?—By walking after the spirit, and not after the flesh.

9. What is the result of carnality?—Death.

10. What follows spirituality?—Life and peace.

11. Why cannot the unregenerated please God?—Because the carnal mind is enmity against God.

12. In what way are we debtors to the spirit?—We are obligated to follow the impulse of the spirit, and not the flesh. 8:12.

13. What is the sure sign of spiritual life?—The spirit of Christ within.

14. Who are the children of God?—Those who are led by the Spirit of God.

15. What is the assurance that we are the children of God?—His Spirit bears witness with our spirit.

16. What follows hope?—Patience.

17. To whom do all things work together for good?—To those who love God.

18. What is the advantage of God on our side?—If God be for us, who can be against us? 8:31.

19. Is God able to see us through?—God shall freely give us all things. 8:32.

20. What consolation do we have when condemned by others?—Christ maketh intercession for us.

21. Where does Christ make intercession for us?—At the right hand of God.

22. How strong is the love of God?—Stronger than tribulation, distress, persecution, famine, nakedness, peril, or sword.

23. How can we be conquerors in these things?—Through him that loved us.

24. About what was Paul persuaded?—That neither death, nor life, nor angels, nor principalities, nor powers, nor things present, nor things to come, nor height, nor depth, nor any other crea-

ture, shall be able to separate us from the love of God, which is in Christ Jesus our Lord. 8:38, 39.

SORROW FOR THE JEWS.
(Rom. 9.)

1. How did Paul say he spoke the truth?—In Christ.

2. What did Paul say about his conscience?—It acted under the influence of the Holy Spirit.

3. For whom did Paul have such great sorrow?—For those to whom he was related by ties of blood.

4. Who were the Israelites?—Abraham's descendants through Jacob.

5. What is meant by the word adoption here?—The Israelites had been divinely chosen and in a sense were God's adopted people.

6. What significance in the expression, "For he saith unto Moses?"—Any thing said to Moses was all important to the Jews.

7. What power has the potter?—To fashion the clay at will.

8. What are the riches of God's glory?—The riches of his Grace.

9. What is the meaning of vessels of mercy?—The saved, indebted to mercy for their salvation.

10. What is meant by "afore prepared"?—That the preparation for salvation is Divine.

11. What do we understand by "even us whom he hath called"?—The regenerated are vessels of mercy, and comprise all believers whether Jew or Greek. 9:24.

12. How far-reaching was the rejection of the Jews?—It was general but not universal, a remnant was to be saved.

13. How did the Gentiles attain to righteousness?—By faith in the Messiah whom the great body of the Jews rejected.

SALVATION.
(Rom. 10.)

1. What is true prayer?—An expression of the heart's desire.

2. What was Paul's prayer for Israel?—That they might be saved.

3. What did Paul say they lacked?—Knowledge.

4. How is Christ the end of the law?—In fulfilling its types by satisfying its demands by his obedience and death, he is the end of ceremonial law.

5. What is indispensable to justification?—Faith.

6. What lesson is taught in verses 6, 7, 8?—Salvation is easily attainable by faith in Christ.

7. How near to us is the word of faith?—As near as our heart.

8. How should such faith be openly avowed?—Shalt confess with thy mouth the Lord Jesus.

9. What prompts such confession?—Believe in thy heart.

10. What shall we believe?—That God has raised him from the dead. 10:9.

11. Our faith should include what?—Assent of the intellect, and the consent and love of the heart.

12. What it the meaning of, "There is no difference between the Jew and the Greek"?—The Gospel abolishes national distinctions.

13. Who shall be saved?—Whosoever shall call upon the name of the Lord shall be saved. 10:13.

14. We shall be saved from what?—Saved from sin, from wrath; saved eternally in heaven. Matt. 1:21; Rom. 5:9; Heb. 5:9.

15. What should precede our calling upon the Lord?—Belief.

16. The preciousness of the Gospel message brings what poetical description of the bearer?—How beautiful are the feet of them that preach the gospel of peace, and bring glad tidings of good things. 10:15.

17. How does faith come to us?—The Word of God preached is the means of inspiring faith in Christ. 10:17.

NOT CAST OFF FOREVER.
(Rom. 11.)

171

1. What do we learn from verses 1 to 6?—Israel was not finally cut off.

2. What proof did Paul offer?—Himself.

3. Why was it that Elijah did not make any plea for Israel?—He considered the nation hopelessly apostate.

4. What was God's answer to Elijah?—I have reserved to myself seven thousand men who have not bowed the knee to the image of Baal.

5. What was the image of Baal?—A Phoenician idol worshipped in the days of Elijah by most of the Israelites.

6. What is meant by a remnant?—Not many, a minority.

7. What is the meaning of the phrase, "Israel has not obtained"?—The Jewish nation, in its entirety, has not secured justification before God.

8. What blessing came to the Gentiles through Israel's temporary fall?—The blessing of salvation. 11:11.

9. Where else besides in verse 13 is Paul called the Apostle to the Gentiles?—In Acts 22:21 and Eph. 3:1.

10. "If the first fruit be holy" refers to what?—To the honored ancestors of the Jews: Abraham, Isaac, and Jacob. 11:16.

11. What are the "branches"?—The descendents.

12. What does the wild olive tree symbolize?—A Gentile not having had the moral culture of the Jew.

13. What people were warned to boast not against the branches?—The Gentiles were in danger of indulging a boastful spirit.

14. Why was there danger of such boasting?—Because the Gentiles had been exalted to that position in God's favor from which the Jews had been displaced because of their sins.

15. In what way did the unbelief of the Jews reveal itself?—In the rejection of Christ.

16. What is the meaning of: "if the believer stands by faith, spiritual attitude develops"?—He will not be high-minded, but will fear God.

17. In what manner is the Goodness and Severity of God exemplified?—Severity: justly merited punishment inflicted on unbelieving Jews. Goodness: undeserved kindness to the believing Gentiles.

18. What was the secret mystery to which Paul refers in verse 25?—That the Gentiles should be partakers of the blessing of salvation through the Messiah.

19. What is the supreme source of all gifts?—God.

GOD'S MERCIES.
(Rom. 12.)

1. What should inspire us to please God?—His mercies.

2. What are God's mercies?—Specially manifested in the justification, sanctification, and adoption of believers, through Jesus Christ.

3. In what way can we glorify God?—By presenting our bodies a living sacrifice.

4. What is a living sacrifice?—Opposite of the sacrifices of the law, which had to be slain, and therefore dead.

5. What is the meaning of "be not conformed to this world"?—Yield not to its spirit, which conflicts with love to God. 1 John 2:15.

6. What should we guard against?—Not to think too highly of self. 12:3.

7. How should we think?—Think soberly according to facts.

8. What kind of love should we have?—Free from hypocrisy.

9. In what hope should we rejoice?—The hope of heaven.

10. How should we act in tribulation?—With patience.

11. How should we share joy with the joyful?—Rejoice with

them that do rejoice.

12. How should we show our sympathy?—By weeping with those who weep, entering into the troubles of the sorrowful. 12:16.

13. How should we live?— United in our views and feelings; of the same mind, in Christian harmony. 12:16.

14. In what way are we admonished against worldly greatness?—Mind not high things.

15. Is it right to injure others because they have injured us?— Recompense to no man evil for evil. 12:17.

16. How should we strive to live?—Live peaceably with all men.

17. How can we overcome evil?—With good. This is the only way it can be overcome. 12:21.

DUTIES TO RULERS.
(Rom. 13.)

1. To what should we yield obedience?—The higher powers, such as Government.

2. What does Paul say about debt?—Meet every obligation. Pay the debts. Owe no man any thing. 13:8.

3. Under what great principles should we seek to live?—The Ten Commandments.

4. What great underlying principle would be of great benefit to the world?—Love. It worketh no ill to his neighbor. 13:10.

5. What night is far spent?— The night of sorrow and trial in this world.

6. What day is at hand?—The bright day of heavenly blessedness and the glory of God.

7. What are the works of darkness?—So called because they are sinful. Many bad deeds are often committed in the dark.

8. How should we walk?— Honestly, becomingly, consistently with our heavenly destiny.

9. How can we put on the Lord Jesus Christ?—Imbide his spirit, appropriate unto ourselves

his character, and follow his example.

JUDGE NOT.
(Rom. 14.)

1. What is meant by, "him that is weak in the faith"? Verse 1.—Refers to the inability of some members of the Church at Rome to give up scruples which lead them to distinguish between certain food, and some days as sacred.

2. How were the stronger to receive such?—In Christian fellowship.

3. What were they to avoid? —Doubtful disputations or discussions with a view to remove the scruples of the weak brother, leaving Christian kindness to do its work.

4. What is the Christian attitude?—Condemn not one the other. 14:3.

5. Who is the Christian's master?—Christ, and he is supreme and all conclusive. His decisions are final.

6. How were the Christians in the Church at Rome to act in regard to the observance of days? —Let every man be fully persuaded in his own mind. Let him follow his own convictions, and not those of another.

7. What did Paul say both of these classes were doing?—Both were trying to please the Lord. They gave thanks to the same God and there should be respect for each others' feelings. 14:6.

8. What great fact did Paul present in verse 7?—None of us liveth to himself, and no man dieth to himself.

9. What does this seventh verse mean?—No one lives alone, then we should not forget our brother's rights. Neither do we die alone. We are not our own, neither in death nor in life. Therefore we should not be so selfish as to forget our brother's right.

10. Whether living or dying

173

the Christian belongs to whom? —The Lord. We are the Lord's; we are his property.

11. What is the basis of Christ's lordship of the dead and the living?—Christ's death and resurrection, followed by his life in heaven. 14:9.

12. How will God judge the world?—In righteousness by that man whom he hath ordained. Acts 17:31.

13. "For it is written" in verse 11 refers to what Prophecy?—In Isa. 45:23.

14. What is the meaning of "as I live"?—Equivalent to an oath based on the certainty of Divine existence.

15. For whom shall we have to give an account before God? —Every one of us shall give account of himself to God.

16. What important matter should we judge and decide?— That no man put a stumbling block or occasion to fall, in his brother's way.

17. Of what was Paul fully convinced?—That nothing was unclean of itself.

18. What is the Kingdom of God?—Righteousness, peace, and joy in the Holy Ghost.

19. What are the things we should follow after?—The things which make for peace.

PATIENCE.
(Rom. 15.)

1. How are the strong to treat the weak?—Bear the infirmities of the weak. Allow for their weakness and be patient with them.

2. Should we seek first to please ourselves?—Let every one of us please his neighbor.

3. With what object in view should we please our neighbor? —For his good.

4. What should be our example?—For even Christ pleased not himself. He became the man of sorrows and bore heavy burdens.

5. What is the patience and comfort of the Scriptures?—The patience and comfort which the Scriptures inspire.

6. Who is the author of patience and comfort?—God. 14:5.

7. How should we glorify God? —By unity of mind and speech. 15:6.

8. How should we treat one another?—As servants of the same master.

9. What is the meaning of the God of hope?—That God inspires his people with hope.

10. What is the means of joy and peace to the soul?—Faith, for we receive joy and peace in believing. 15:13.

11. What was the meaning of minister to Paul?—The servant of Jesus Christ.

12. What was the Gospel of God?—Clothed with divine authority.

13. Why had Paul been much hindered from visiting the Church at Rome?—By his labors which extended over a wide field.

14. For what purpose was he on his way to Jerusalem?—To take with him the contributions of the Gentile churches to the "poor saints."

CONCLUDING ADVICE.
(Rom. 16.)

1. Who was Phebe?—A sister, not in the flesh, but in the Lord.

2. What is meant by a servant of the church?—Probably a deaconess who labored for the poor and sick.

3. What others were helpers of Paul?—Priscilla and Aquila.

4. What did Paul say that Priscilla and Aquila had done especially?—They had risked their lives to save his. 16:4.

5. Why did the Gentile churches feel thankful?—Because those two helpers had risked their lives to save the Apostle from danger.

6. To whom did Paul refer as fellow "prisoners"?—Those who had been shut up with him when and where is not known.

7. What do verses 3 to 16

174

comprise?—Loving salutations to particular saints and assemblies in Rome.

8. What are found in verses 17 to 20?—Warnings against those who cause divisions and stumbling.

9. What do verses 21 to 23 comprise?—Salutations from Paul's fellow workers.

10. In the closing verses 25 to 33, what topics are used?—Ascription of praise through Jesus Christ to God the only Wise, who is revealing, through Paul's Gospel, the mystery heretofore concealed.

11. This Epistle was written to the Romans from what place?—From Corinth.

12. By whom was it sent?—By Phebe, a deaconess in the church in the town of Cenchrea, the eastern seaport of Corinth.

13. Why was it sent by this Christian woman?—Because of her trustworthiness, and probably because she had to go to the world metropolis about her own affairs.

INTRODUCTION.
(1 Cor. 1.)

1. What was the status of the city of Corinth in Paul's day?—A city of importance and wealth.

2. Where is it prominently mentioned?—Both in Grecian and Roman history.

3. About what time was this Epistle written?—A. D. 57.

4. Where was it written?—At Ephesus.

5. In what condition was the church at this time?—An unhappy condition.

6. Why was this?—There were divisions among its members.

7. What else was wrong?—There was toleration of unchristian conduct, and neglect of discipline.

8. What else contributed to unhappiness? — Irregularities connected with the Lord's supper.

9. What further caused fric-

tion?—Some questioned the doctrine of the resurrection of the dead.

10. How did Paul write to them?—As a father to his children.

11. Upon what does Paul base his Apostleship?—Divinely appointed. Through the will of God. 1:1.

12. Who was Sosthenes?—One of the brethren; first mentioned in Acts 18:17.

13. What was the church of God to which Paul refers?—The congregation of believers at Corinth.

14. Who are the saints?—Holy persons set apart from the world.

PREACHING OF THE CROSS.
(1 Cor. 1.)

1. How did Paul salute the Church at Corinth?—Grace: divine power be unto you, and peace, resulting from Grace. 1 Cor. 1:3.

2. What does Paul mean "waiting for the coming"?—The first Christians looked and waited for the second coming. 1 Thess. 1:10-13. 2 Thess. 3:3. Titus 2:13. Heb. 9:28. 2 Peter 3:12.

3. What does Paul mean: "In the day of Jesus Christ"?—When Christ comes in his glory. 1:8.

4. How does Paul beseech the Corinthians?—By the name of our Lord Jesus Christ.

5. To whom is the Gospel foolish?—To them that perish.

6. To whom does it mean power?—To them that are saved.

7. What did the Jews seek?—A sign—miracles.

8. What did the Greeks seek after?—Wisdom, philosophy. 1:23.

9. What did Paul say he preached?—Christ crucified; his atoning death as the only salvation of men.

10. What was this preaching to the Jews?—A stumbling block.

11. What did it mean to the Greeks?—Foolishness.

12. What is the Gospel to those who are regenerated either Jews or Greeks?—The power of

God and the wisdom of God,
1:24.

13. What is God to those who are in Christ Jesus?—Wisdom, righteousness, sanctification, and redemption.

PAUL'S METHOD OF PREACHING. (1 Cor.2.)

1. What did Paul say about the manner of his preaching?—Not with the excellency of speech: elaborate rhetoric prevalent among the Greeks.

2. Upon what course had Paul fully decided?—Not to know anything among them but Jesus Christ, and him crucified.

3. What was the central theme of Paul's preaching?—The cross and related truths to the death of Christ. 2:2.

4. How did he feel in approaching this task?—Incompetent, in weakness, in fear, and in much trembling.

5. What was the secret of his success?—Demonstrations of the spirit and of power. 2:4.

6. What kind of wisdom did Paul speak?—The wisdom of God in a mystery.

7. Why a mystery?—Because it is concealed, hidden until revealed by the spirit.

8. Who are the princes of the world who crucified the Lord of Glory?—Probably Pilate, Herod, and the Jewish Sanhedrin.

9. Can man in his natural state without the help of the spirit realize the full and complete blessings of salvation on earth and in heaven?—Eye hath not seen, nor ear heard, neither have entered into the heart of man, the things which God hath prepared for them that love him. 1:9.

10. How do we receive such blessings?—God has revealed them unto us: made known what could not be found out by human knowledge. 2:10.

THE SURE FOUNDATION.
(1 Cor. 3.)

1. What did Paul mean when he said they were "Babes in Christ"?—Spiritual infancy. They had not advanced in the divine life.

2. What kind of teaching did Paul present to them?—The plainest kind of truth, fed them with milk, not with meat.

3. Upon what did Paul base his conclusion that they were carnal (the opposite of spiritual)?—Their divisions expressed in the words, "I am of Paul," "I am of Apollos," proved their lack of spirituality.

4. What is a minister in the literal sense?—A servant.

5. What shall we then say of Paul and Apollos?—They were Christ's servants through whom the Corinthians believed.

6. In reference to his first ministry in Corinth what did Paul say?—I have planted, and Apollos watered; but God gave the increase. 3:6.

7. For what was Apollos known?—His eloquence.

8. In what sense are we laborers together with God?—Engaged in promoting one and the same thing.

9. Why did Paul regard himself as a wise master builder?—Because he had laid the foundation, and first preached Christ in his sacrificial death as the basis of rest, and hope for a guilty sinner.

10. What about other foundations?—Christ is the only Saviour. Peter taught this years before. Acts 4:12.

11. How are gold, silver, and precious stones some times symbolized?—To represent the truths of the Gospel.

12. What do wood, hay and stubble represent?—Doctrinal and practical error in many forms.

13. What did Paul mean when he said the day will declare it?—The last day, the day of final judgment.

176

14. Whose work will abide?—Such as is fully represented by gold, silver, and precious stones; fire will not injure it.

15. What is the promise to such?—They shall receive a reward.

16. What is the nature of such award?—A reward of grace according to the work done.

17. What did Paul call the Corinthian Church?—The temple of God.

18. To what did this refer?—To the Temple at Jerusalem which was God's house.

19. What is meant by "all things are yours"?—All things mentioned in verse 22; World, life, death, things present, or things to come.

MINISTERS AND STEWARDS.
(1 Cor. 4.)

1. How did Paul want the people to consider himself and his helpers?—As ministers of Christ; his servants under solemn obligation to do his will.

2. They are stewards of what?—The mysteries of God.

3. What are the mysteries of God?—The gracious secrets revealed in the gospels.

4. What did Paul say about premature judgment?—Judge nothing before the time.

5. Why did Paul refer to himself and Apollos in verse 6?—To avoid giving personal offence to any factions.

6. How were some rejoicing?—Without giving God credit for the gifts they had received from him.

7. In what way were the Apostles considered fools for Christ's sake?—Because they were devoting their time to God's work in the midst of trial and suffering.

8. What did Paul mean about Apostles being appointed to death?—They were destined to martyrdom.

9. What does Paul give some details of in verses 11, 12, 13?—The privations and sufferings of the Apostles.

10. Why did Paul write these things to the Corinthians?—To promote their spiritual interests.

PURGING THE CHURCH.
(1 Cor. 5.)

1. What did Paul say of some of the Corinthians?—That they were puffed up when they should be deeply humbled.

2. What causes him chief concern in this chapter?—The incestuous person.

3. What instructions did he give for action?—In the name of the Lord Jesus Christ; that is, by his authority, gathered together as a church, acting collectively.

4. What did he urge them to do further?—Purge out the old leaven.

5. And what else?—Put away from among you the wicked person. 5:7, 13.

REDEEMED.
(1 Cor. 6.)

1. What is Paul's chief concern in the first part of the chapter?—That they vex not their brethren by going to law with them.

2. What is the meaning of "and such were some of you" in verse 2?—Some of the Corinthians were before their conversion great sinners before God and men.

3. What was their standing when Paul wrote this Epistle?—Washed: morally cleansed.

4. What further?—Sanctified, consecrated to God.

5. What else was involved in their salvation?—Justified, accepted in Christ.

6. What should we do in the presence of sin?—Get away from it.

7. What was the price of our redemption?—The Son of God's death on the cross.

MARRIAGE.
(1 Cor. 7.)

1. What do we have in the

177

first part of this chapter?—A treatise on marriage.

2. Is marriage to be taken seriously?—Yes, it should not lightly be dissolved.

3. Every man should be content with what?—His vocation. Of course if it is lawful.

4. What do we find in verses 35-40?—With what respects we may either marry or abstain from marriage.

CHRISTIAN LIBERTY.
(1 Cor. 8.)

1. What does this chapter treat of principally?—Meats offered to idols.

2. What about our liberty as Christians?—We should not abuse it to the offence of our brethren.

3. What noble gesture of self denial did Paul make?—See verse 13.

RECOMPENSE.
(1 Cor. 9.)

1. How does Paul show his liberty?—See verse 1.

2. When had Paul seen the Lord?—On the road to Damascus, Acts 26:19.

3. What was the seal of his Apostleship?—The conversion of those with whom he labored.

4. How should ministers live?—By the Gospel. 9:7-14.

5. Was Paul compelled to preach the gospel?—Yes, Woe is unto me if I preach not the gospel. 9:16.

6. Why did Paul make himself the servant of all?—That he might be able to save more souls.

7. To what did he compare life?—To a race. 9:24-27.

ALL FOR GOD'S GLORY.
(1 Cor. 10.)

1. Of what was the cloud a symbol?—Of Divine presence.

2. What is meant by spiritual meat?—Food, especially manna, which symbolized Christ, the bread of life. John 6:31-35.

3. What is meant by "the same spiritual drink"?—Called spiritual as was the manna, because supernaturally supplied from the rock smitten by Moses.

4. That rock was a type of what?—Of Christ. He is referred to, not as a fountain in this connection, but as the source whence flow the refreshing streams of salvation.

5. What happened to many of the children of Israel?—They were overthrown in the wilderness. God was not well pleased with them.

6. Elevated opinion of one's security is apt to lead to what? —A fall. Let him that thinketh he standeth, take heed lest he fall. 10:12.

7. Are our temptations unusual? —No, they are such as are common to man.

8. Will God help us bear our temptations?—He will because He is faithful to his word.

9. What is meant by the cup of blessing?—Used in the Lord's Supper.

10. What does this represent?— The communion of the blood of Christ, representing his blood and their fellowship with him.

11. What does the bread represent?—The communion of the body of Christ. This symbolizes the crucified body and their union with him.

12. What is the meaning of one bread?—One loaf; symbolic of Christ's body and of church unity.

13. What should be our great object in life?—Whatsoever ye do, do all to the glory of God.

14. Why should we seek to give no offence?—So that there should be no reasonable ground for complaint.

15. To whom should we seek to give no offence?—To the Jews, holding some particular views. To the Gentiles, differing widely from the Jews.

16. What does it mean to give no offence to the Church?—It is neither a Jewish nor a Gentile organization distinctively, but a

body of believers, Jews and Gentiles.

17. Why was this carefulness not to offend?—That they may be saved. Paul never forgot the salvation of men.

METHODS OF WORSHIP
(1 Cor. 11.)

1. How far may we go in being like men?—As far as they are like Christ.

2. Is it right to bestow praise on others?—Yes, if they deserve it.

3. What does church mean in the New Testament?—Not the place of worship, but the congregation. Church in the New Testament never means house of worship.

4. What had Paul heard about them?—That there were divisions among them.

5. How could the Corinthians show themselves on the Lord's side?—By resisting and condemning heresies.

6. What exclamation of surprise do we find in verse 22?—What! Despise ye the church of God.

7. What had Paul received of the Lord Jesus Christ?—The institution and design of the Lord's Supper.

8. What is the meaning of the words "Take, eat: this is my body"?—A memorial of his body.

9. What is the meaning of "This cup is the New Testament in my blood"?—The new covenant: new, as distinguished from Sinai, which was ratified by the blood of animals, whereas the new covenant was ratified by the blood of Christ. 11:25.

10. What is the meaning of "shew the Lord's death till he come"?—Proclaim his death, and observe the ordinance of the Lord's Supper till Christ shall come the second time.

11. Then this ordinance is prophetic of what?—The Lord's second coming.

12. What does unworthily mean in verse 27?—Taking part in this solemn service irreverently; eating as one would a common meal.

13. To whom did Paul address himself thus, "let a man examine himself"?—The church member.

14. Who are they who eat and drink to condemnation?—Those who do not discern the Lord's body.

15. What is meant by, "Judge ourselves"?—Make a test of our Christian character. We should act according to our profession.

16. What does it mean, "should not be judged"?—Subjected to God's judgments.

SPIRITUAL GIFTS.
(1 Cor. 12.)

1. What did Paul mean by spiritual gifts?—Most probably gifts miraculous, endowments by the Holy Spirit.

2. Can there be unity in diversities of gifts?—Yes, because of the same Spirit.

3. What illustration did Paul use to show that, with many different gifts, all should work in unity?—The human body with many members and yet one body.

4. What is the more excellent way which Paul points out to us?—The next chapter.

LOVE.
(1 Cor. 13.)

1. What does Paul mean by "tongues of men"?—Languages of men.

2. And what by "of angels"?—The angels method of expression.

3. What is the meaning of the word charity here?—Love. The word love should be used in every part of this chapter.

4. What does Paul mean by "all mysteries"?—Things secret and profound and beyond human comprehension.

5. What is the meaning of "all faith"?—The faith by which miracles are wrought.

179

6. What is meant by "bestow all thy goods to feed the poor"? —Worldly possessions.

7. "And though I give my body to be burned"?—As a sacrificial offering. Though I die at the stake.

8. What would all this profit if one had not love?—Nothing. It would be of no avail.

9. What is the endurance of love?—Suffers long. He who has this love endures trials and injuries with patience.

10. Is love disturbed over the prosperity of others?—Love envieth not. 13:4.

11. What is the spirit of love? —Love is kind both to friends and to enemies.

12. What is the meaning of "vaunteth not itself"?—Love is not boastful. Is not puffed up.

13. What about the manners of love?—Doth not behave itself unseemly, or unbecomingly.

14. Is love unselfish?—Seeketh not her own. 13:5.

15. What do you know about the temper of love?—Is not easily provoked nor excited to evil.

16. Does love question the motives of others?—No, love "thinketh no evil."

17. What is love's attitude towards iniquity?—Takes no pleasure in such; "rejoiceth not in iniquity."

18. What is love's attitude towards the truth?—Rejoiceth in or (with) the truth.

19. What does "beareth all things" mean?—The Greek means "Covereth." Love is proof against all that would provoke.

20. What does "believeth all things" mean?—Has the most favorable view of things.

21. How does love hope all things?—Has hope when it is difficult to believe all things.

22. How does love endure all things?—Bears the crosses and burdens without complaint.

23. Is love permanent?—"Love never faileth." Verse 8.

24. What is the extent of our knowledge on earth?—Limited. We know in part.

25. What about our prophecies? —They are incomplete.

26. When will we have full knowledge?—In the heavenly state, when that which is perfect has come.

27. What did Paul say he had done since he reached manhood? —Put away childish things.

28. How does this illustrate verses 9 and 10?—The difference between childhood and manhood illustrates the difference between what Christians now are, and what they will be in the future state.

29. What does "now we see" mean in verse 12?—While here on earth.

30. How do we see?—As through a glass, rather a mirror, darkly, obscurely.

31. What does the "but then" mean in verse 12?—When we reach the heavenly state.

32. How shall we then see?— Face to face. Distinctly and without any obstructions.

33. What then shall I know?— That I do not now know.

34. How clear will my knowledge be then?—I shall know even as I am also known.

35. Of the three, faith, hope, and love, which is the greatest? —Love.

36. Why is love the greatest?— It is the fulfilling of the law. Rom. 13:10.

37. On what "hang all the law and the prophets"?—On the two commandments, love to God, and love to man.

PROPHECY.
(1 Cor. 14.)

1. What did Paul urge the Corinthians to follow after?—The love described in the preceding chapter.

2. What else were they to seek? —Spiritual gifts.

3. What else should they espe-

180

cially seek?—The gift of prophecy.

4. What was prophecy in this sense?—The exposition and the application of divine truth.

5. What should be the result of prophesying?—Edification of the Church. 14:4.

6. Why is he who prophesies a greater servant?—He performs a more useful service. Note the dignity of service as taught by Jesus. Matt. 20:26.

7. What gifts should be sought? —Those that promote the spiritual interests of the Church. 14:12.

8. How should we pray and sing?—With understanding. 14:15.

9. How should we teach others?—By using words that are understood. 14:19.

10. How should all things be accomplished?—Decently and in order.

RESURRECTION.
(1 Cor. 15.)

1. What did Paul declare unto the Corinthians?—The Gospel.

2. What was their reaction?— They received it and accepted it as true.

3. What is the heart of the Gospel?—That Christ died for our sins, according to the Scriptures. Isa. 53.

4. Christ appeared to whom first?—To Peter.

5. Then to whom?—To all the Apostles.

6. After that Christ was seen of how many?—Above five hundred. A large number of witnesses.

7. Then Christ was seen of whom?—James.

8. Why did Paul say he (Paul) was the least of all Apostles?— Because he persecuted the Church.

9. What made Paul what he was?—The grace of God. 15:10.

10. What did Paul assume with regard to the Resurrection of Christ?—That it was inseparable from the resurrection of the dead.

11. What grand fact did Paul utter?—Now is Christ risen from the dead. 15:20.

12. What verse refers to a general resurrection?—Verse twenty-two.

13. In what other part of the Scripture is this doctrine taught?— John 5:28, 29. Acts 24:15, and other places.

14. The resurrection of what class does this chapter specially treat?—The pious dead.

15. What does "first fruits" mean in verse 23?—First to rise from the grave never to die again.

16. What guarantee does this give his followers?—A guarantee of their resurrection.

17. What does "then cometh the end" mean?—End of the world, followed by the day of judgment.

18. What kingdom will Christ deliver up?—The mediatorial kingdom which he received from the Father. Psalm 2:6.

19. How long shall this kingdom continue?—Till he hath put all enemies under his feet. 15:25.

20. What is the last enemy that shall be subdued?—Death. 15:26.

21. In verse 27 who is expected?—God, the Father.

22. When Christ has delivered his kingdom what will happen?— Then shall the Son also himself be subject.

23. What does "God may be all and in all" mean?—God, in his eternal threefold unity.

24. What are the three fundamental facts of the Gospel?—The death, burial, and resurrection of Christ.

25. What does resurrection mean?—The raising up of the fallen body.

26. What will be the highest distinction and glory of the saints? —Bearing the image of the Lord Jesus.

27. How should Christians stand?—Firm; and should not be moved away from the hope of the Gospel. Col. 1:23.

181

RELIEF OF BRETHREN.
(1 Cor. 16.)

1. Where were the saints for whom Paul took the collection?—In Jerusalem and Judea.

2. What method were they to follow?—That which he had given to the Galatian churches.

3. What was this method?—Upon the first day of the week, recognized as the Lord's day, to lay by as God had prospered.

4. For what did he commend Timothy?—For his work for the Lord.

5. Why were the Corinthians warned to watch?—Against all enemies and to stand fast in the faith.

6. What did Jesus say about the poor?—The poor ye have with you always.

INTRODUCTION.
(2 Cor. 1.)

1. When was second Corinthians written?—Probably less than a year after the first.

2. Whom had Paul sent to Corinth?—Titus.

3. What was the purpose of such visit?—To emphasize the advice of the first epistle.

4. What else was the reason for his visit?—To learn if the instructions had been followed.

5. What was the nature of the report of Titus?—Good. It was highly gratifying to Paul, and is the reason for the second Epistle.

6. Why was there a minority unfriendly to Paul?—This was instigated by some Judaizing teachers.

7. How did they seek to harm Paul?—By assuming that his credentials of Apostleship were not satisfactory.

8. In this letter what do we have?—Love, commendation, indignation, rebuke, and severity.

TRIALS AND REJOICING.
(2 Cor. 1.)

1. In writing to Timothy what does Paul call him?—Son.

2. In writing of Timothy what does Paul call him?—Brother.

3. Why did Paul call God "the Father of mercies"?—Because God is the source of mercies.

4. What is the meaning of "the God of all comfort"?—God is the fountain from whence streams of consolation flow.

5. Who are more able to comfort others?—Those whom God has comforted. 1:4.

6. What trouble does Paul refer to in Asia?—Maybe a trouble which has not been recorded. Some think it refers to Acts 19: 23-31.

7. Was the trouble, referred to by Paul, severe?—It was; "we were pressed out of measure and we despaired of our lives." 1:8.

8. To whom should thanks be given for such deliverance?—To God.

9. Why did Paul rejoice?—Because the approval of his conscience was such as would bear the scrutiny of God and approval by him.

10. What is the meaning of conversation in verse 12?—This refers to conduct, deportment. We behaved ourselves.

REASONS FOR WRITING.
(2 Cor. 2.)

1. What reason did Paul give for not visiting Corinth as he had planned?—He would have had personal sorrow.

2. What effect would this have had on them?—He would have inflicted sorrow upon the whole church. He looked to them to make him glad.

3. What did "the many tears" in verse 4 express?—His deep grief and, at the same time, his abundant love.

4. What did Paul mean by "grieved in part"?—The incestuous man (1 Cor. 5:1.) had grieved Paul but not him alone.

5. Why did Paul say, "such a man"?—Delicately indefinite, ab-

staining from describing the offender.

6. What should be their next step?—Forgive and comfort him.

7. How should they confirm their love?—Restore to fellowship the penitent man.

8. What was Paul anxious to know?—Whether the Corinthian brethren had the spirit of obedience. 2:9.

9. Why was Paul so anxious to know this?—Lest Satan should get an advantage in the matter of excessive severity which would be injurious to the offender and also to the cause of Christ.

10. What do we see in Paul?—A majestic intellect and a tender heart.

11. How would his intelligence compare with the Greeks?—He could measure mental strength with any of the philosophers of Greece.

12. Why is it a great crime to corrupt the Word of God?—Immortal souls are put in jeopardy.

COMMENDATIONS.
(2 Cor. 3.)

1. What brought up the matter of commendation?—Probably because false teachers paraded before the Corinthians letters of commendation.

2. What did Paul say were his letters?—Ye are our Epistle.

3. How did Paul explain his love for them?—Written in our hearts. verse 2.

4. By whom are these read?—By all men.

5. What kind of epistles did he call them?—Epistles of Christ.

6. How were they ministered?—By the Apostles or through their instrumentality.

7. On what kind of tablets were they written?—Fleshly tablets of the heart. See Heb. 8:10.

8. From whom did Paul get his sufficiency?—From God.

9. What kind of ministers had God made them?—Able ministers. Sufficient ministers.

10. They were made ministers of what?—The New Testament or better, the New Covenant.

11. Why is the ministration of the spirit much more glorious?—Because the Gospel excels the law.

12. What is the glory that excelleth?—The glory of the Gospel.

13. What did Paul mean by the words "such hope"?—Hope of the superior achievement of the Gospel to the end of the world.

14. What is meant by that which remaineth?—The Christian dispensation which will not end until the Lord Jesus comes in his Glory.

15. Why did Paul use such plain speech?—So that nothing would be obscure or hard to understand.

16. What did the veil over the face of Moses symbolize?—The darkness of the age.

17. What is the most charming style of the ministry?—Simplicity.

LIGHT OF THE GOSPEL.
(2 Cor. 4.)

1. What did Paul mean by this ministry?—Referred to in verse 6 of the preceding chapter.

2. To whom is the Gospel hid?—To those who are lost.

3. How or in what manner did God command the light to shine?—Let there be light, Gen. 1:3.

4. How does the light shine in our hearts?—Spiritual light disperses the moral darkness.

5. Where does Glory appear greater than that which shone in the face of Moses?—In the face of Jesus Christ.

TROUBLES AND PERSECUTIONS. (2 Cor. 4.)

6. What did Paul mean about being troubled but not distressed?—There were troubles on every side, but they had not reached the point of distress.

7. What about perplexed, but not in despair?—While men are perplexed, God sustains.

8. What about persecution but not forsaken?—Men persecute but God does not forsake.

9. What do you understand by, "Cast down but not destroyed"?—Able after being stricken, to renew the good fight.

10. How did Paul experience the dying of the Lord Jesus? 4:10.—Suffering a kind of living death for Christ's sake and always exposed to peril of martyrdom.

11. What kind of life did he crave to manifest?—A life like Jesus—presented so clearly as to be seen by all.

12. How did death work in his life and that of the rest of the apostles?—At all times subject to suffering and death for Christ.

13. How did life work in the Corinthians?—The apostles' work in face of death contributed to their spiritual and eternal life.

14. How did Paul contrast affliction in verse 17?—With glory, light affliction with a weight of glory.

15. Upon what are we to fix our attention?—Upon things that are not seen.

16. How should we believe?—In the things that are eternal rather than those that are temporary.

CONSTRAINING LOVE.
(2 Cor. 5.)

1. Of what was Paul assured?—Immortal glory.

2. What did Paul mean by earthly house?—The body, made of the earth, sustained by productions of the earth, and destined to return to the earth.

3. What is a tabernacle?—A temporary abode. 2 Pet. 1:13-14.

4. What is a building of God?—A permanent place. A body that will not be dissolved.

5. How does this compare with our earthly house?—It is eternal not temporary.

6. While we are at home in the body we are absent from what?—From the Lord's glorious presence in heaven.

7. How should we walk?—By faith, not by sight.

8. Why did Paul say, he was willing to be absent from the body?—He would be present with the Lord which he thought was "far better." Phil. 1:23.

9. What is the controlling motive of saints either on earth or in heaven?—A desire to please the Lord.

10. Who must appear before the judgment seat of Christ?—All, everybody,

11. How will we be judged?—According to that we have done, whether it be good or bad. 5:10.

12. Knowing the terror of the law, how did Paul seek men?—By persuasion tenderly entreated them to seek Christ and his salvation.

13. What was the constraining influence in Paul's work?—The love of Christ.

14. If there is spiritual union with Christ what is the result?—A new creation. Old views and old ways have passed away.

FAITHFULNESS.
(2 Cor. 6.)

1. How are we working together with God?—Working in harmony.

2. "I have heard thee" refers to what?—God the Father, to his Son, the Messiah. Isa. 49:8.

3. Why is this the day of salvation?—We now have every facility for obtaining salvation.

4. How did Paul endure trials?—In much patience.

5. What are some of the things he endured?—Afflictions, distress, stripes, imprisonment. . . .

6. What is the meaning here of unknown?—Unknown to the world of unbelievers.

7. What is the meaning here of well known?—Well known to those

184

known?—Well known to those who are saved.

8. What does Paul mean by "as dying, and behold, we live"?—In danger of death yet preserved by divine power.

9. What is the meaning of "chastened and not killed"?—The discipline which Paul had thus far received did not result in his death.

PAUL'S COMFORT.
(2 Cor. 7.)

1. To what promises did the Apostle refer?—The gracious assurances in the last three verses in the preceding chapter.

2. What did Paul mean by, "receive us"?—Give us room. Let us have a place in your affections.

3. Why was Paul filled with all comfort?—Because they had been obedient to his instructions.

4. Why was Paul troubled in Macedonia?—Without were fightings, contest with heathen unbelievers. Within him were fears, lest his work would not be successful.

5. How were the Corinthians, in the Apostles' hearts, "to die and live with them"?—Their love for the Corinthians would make it a pleasure to live and die with them.

6. Why was Paul comforted by the coming of Titus?—Because he brought good news from Corinth.

7. Why did Paul further rejoice?—Because their sorrow had resulted in repentence and correction of evils in the church. 7:9.

8. What is godly sorrow?—Sorrow which carries with it a sense of sin committed against God.

9. How does godly sorrow worketh repentance to salvation? —It is indispensable to and results in salvation.

10. What is the meaning of "not to be repented of"? 7:10.—Such repentance carries with it no regrets for time and eternity.

11. What is worldly sorrow? —Sorrow for the losses and failure of worldly plans.

12. How does such work death? —It hastens man's natural death and sometimes is the forerunner of death eternal.

13. What was the joy of Titus? —He rejoiced that the letter from Paul to the Corinthians had been received in the proper spirit resulting in accomplishing that for which it had been written.

14. Why was Paul not ashamed?—Because he had expressed to Titus a favorable opinion of the Corinthians. Their actions justified his good opinion of them.

15. What was the reason for Paul's confidence in them?—Because they acted according to their Christian profession.

CONTRIBUTION.
(2 Cor. 8.)

1. How did Paul stir up the Corinthians to a liberal contribution for the poor saints at Jerusalem?—By the example of the Macedonians.

2. What other example did he use?—The example of Christ. 8:9.

3. Whose willingness and integrity did Paul commend unto them?—Titus, and the other brethren who assisted in this work.

CHEERFUL GIVING.
(2 Cor. 9.)

1. What is meant by "Forwardness of your mind"?—Readiness.

2. Where was Achaia?—A province of Greece, Corinth being its chief city.

3. How does God reward his people for their services in his cause?—Proportionate to what they do.

4. What is a cheerful giver?—One who finds delight in giving. 9:7.

5. What is God's unspeakable gift?—Jesus Christ.

6. What should be our reaction for such a gift from such a giver?

185

—A devout gratitude and sincerest service.

WEAPONS OF WARFARE.
(2 Cor. 10.)

1. What two attractive traits of the Master's character did Paul present?—His meekness and gentleness.

2. For what should Christ's followers seek?—They should strive to be like him in these two traits of character.

3. What should encourage Christian ministers?—That their weapons in the Christian warfare are "mighty through God."

4. How mighty are those weapons?—Can pull down the strongholds. 10:4.

5. How else are they effective?—Casting down imaginations and every high thing that arrays itself against the cause of Christ.

6. What should ministers ever remember?—That the authority they possess is "for edification and not for destruction." 10:8.

7. What is the result of men measuring themselves by themselves?—They assume that they have in themselves the standard of moral excellence.

8. By what should the standard be supplied?—By the Word of God.

9. Self commendation is usually the sign of what?—Weakness.

10. What is the commendation of others?—A snare.

11. Define the commendation of the Lord.—Of infinite value.

12. What commendation should every one seek?—Well done, good and faithful servant.

GROUNDS FOR GLORY.
(2 Cor. 11.)

1. Under the guidance of the Spirit, what Mosaic narrative did Paul endorse?—That the serpent beguiled Eve.

2. In what manner does the Old and the New Testament stand or fall together?—They are so connected that the New is the fulfilment of the Old.

3. What three ideas did Paul strongly express?—No greater Saviour, no superior Spirit, no better Gospel. 11:4.

4. Whom did the Corinthians seem to admire?—False apostles.

5. What did this influence Paul to do?—Commend himself.

6. What equality did Paul claim?—With the chief Apostles. 11:5.

7. Of what did he remind the Corinthians?—His preaching the Gospel to them without pay.

8. In what other respect did he claim superiority to those false apostles?—He showed that he was not inferior to those deceitful workers in any legal prerogative.

9. How else did Paul show himself superior?—In the service of Christ, and in all kinds of sufferings for his ministry.

THORN IN THE FLESH.
(2 Cor. 12.)

1. What did Paul say about his taking glory to himself in the previous chapter?—It was not expedient—Not becoming nor profitable.

2. What did Paul mean when he said, "exalted above measure"?—Extravagantly elated.

3. What was the thorn in the flesh?—May have been a grievous bodily affliction, the nature of which we cannot know therefore useless to conjecture.

4. What did Paul mean by the word "buffet"?—Satan made use of the thorn in annoying and humiliating the great Apostle.

5. How many times did he pray about this?—Three times.

6. Praying three times was in imitation of whom?—The Saviour, who in Gethsemane prayed three times that the cup might pass from him.

7. What was the answer to Paul's prayer for deliverance?—My grace is sufficient for thee.

8. What does sufficient Grace mean in this respect?—Power to

bear the trial with Christian patience.

9. What else does sufficient Grace mean?—To extract from the trial such comfort as no external prosperity can give. Every child of God should strive to attain this spiritual elevation.

10. What was Paul's reaction?—Most gladly therefore will I rather glory in my infirmities, that the power of Christ may rest upon me. 12:9.

11. Why did Paul thus glory?—Larger communication of Grace was open to him to prepare him for greater usefulness in the cause of Christ.

12. What did Paul mean by "the third time I am ready to come to you"?—He may have made a second visit to Corinth of which we have no account.

13. What should be the chief joy of ministers of the Gospel?—When those who are converted under their labors walk humbly before God.

CONTRASTS.
(2 Cor. 13.)

1. Where else do we find the expression "two or three witnesses"?—This number given by Christ in Matt. 18:16, and Moses in Deut. 14:6.

2. What impressive contrast does Paul make?—The difference between what Christ was, crucified, and what he is, glorified. 13:4.

3. Explain this further?—There were striking proofs of weakness in his crucified mortality and also striking proofs of his majestic power in his resurrected life in heaven.

4. What of our evidences of piety?—They are defective, unless Christ is in us.

5. What is of supreme importance?—To have Christ in our hearts as the hope of glory. Col. 1:27.

6. In the benediction, what positive proof is there that in the Godhead three persons are equal in glory?—They are revealed as the Father, the Son, and the Holy Spirit.

GALATIANS INTRODUCTION.
(Gal. 1.)

1. Where was Galatia?—A province near the central part of Asia Minor.

2. From whence did it derive its name?—Probably from the Gauls who took possession of the country about 280 years before Christ.

3. Where in the Scriptures do we find the first mention of the name, Galatia?—Acts 16:6 where we are told that Paul and Silas went throughout Phrygia and the region of Galatia.

4. What did they do in that region?—Churches were formed which Paul afterward visited, as we learn from Acts 18:23.

5. What hindered the progress of these churches?—Judaizing teachers.

6. How did they hinder the churches?—By saying to the Gentile converts "except ye be circumcised after the manner of Moses ye cannot be saved."

7. What did Paul think about this?—Regarded this as a vital error which would pervert and nullify the Gospel.

8. What did these false teachers insinuate?—That Paul was not an Apostle, or at least he did not stand on an equality with the other Apostles.

9. Why did Paul find it necessary to refute this?—To preserve his influence among the churches.

10. In this Epistle what then is his first thought?—To vindicate his Apostleship.

11. What was his next step?—To establish the doctrine of justification by faith.

12. What effect did this have?—It utterly demolished the position of the Judaizing teachers.

FALSE TEACHERS.
(Gal. 1.)

187

1. To whom did Paul trace his Apostleship?—To Christ, and God the Father. 1:1.

2. How did Paul introduce himself to the Galatians?—Grace be to you and peace from God the Father and from our Lord Jesus Christ. 1:3.

3. What was Paul's wonderment concerning the Galatians? —That they so soon left him and the Gospel.

6. What did Paul consider a great sin?—The preaching of any other Gospel.

7. From whom did he learn the Gospel?—Not of men, but of God. 1:11, 12.

8. How is God glorified?—In his servants.

9. For what are we indebted to God?—For gifts, and graces, and for whatever success comes to us.

10. Did the brethren glorify Paul?—No, they glorified God in him.

REASON FOR GOING TO JERUSALEM.
(Gal. 2.)

1. When Paul went up again to Jerusalem with Barnabas, whom did they take with them?—Titus.

2. What reason did Paul give for this visit to Jerusalem?—Revelation, divine command.

3. To whom did Paul preach privately?—To men of influence.

4. What was the nationality of Titus?—He was a Greek.

5. How did false teachers come in?—Privately, as spies.

6. Did Paul and his helpers yield to these false teachers?— They refused to yield for the shortest period of time.

7. What paradox do we find in verse 20?—That the Christian though crucified with Christ, lives, or rather Christ lives in him as the Source of life.

8. What will be the result of Christ living in believers now?— They will live eternally with him in heaven.

JUSTIFICATION BY FAITH.
(Gal. 3.)

1. What question did Paul ask the Galatians?—Why they had left the faith and were depending upon the law.

2. Who are justified?—They that believe.

3. What is the function of faith?—It unites to Christ, in whom there is fullness of justifying merit.

4. As sinners to what are we under condemnation and exposure?—To the curse of the law.

5. On what basis can the penalty of the law consistently be remitted?—In the fact that Christ was made a curse for us. 3:13.

6. What was the blessing of Abraham?—Justification by faith.

7. Does this blessing have any national limits?—No. It comes to the Jews and Gentiles alike.

8. Does such blessing have any limit?—It has an individual limitation to believers in Christ.

FREEDOM THROUGH CHRIST.
(Gal. 4.)

1. What did God do in the fulness of time?—He sent his Son.

2. Why did God send his Son? —To redeem them that had been under the law.

3. The Mosaic economy with its various ceremonies seemed to emphasize what?—Something better. To meet man's unsupplied needs God sent his Son.

4. What is the Christian's privilege?—To claim filial union with God, whereby he can say "Abba Father."

5. What causes sorrow to the true minister?—To be in doubt of those who profess to be Christians, especially those who have made profession under his ministry. 4: 19.

6. How may many of the Old Testament Scriptures be used?— To illustrate important truths in the New Testament.

7. What impressive contrast do

we have?—The bondage of the law and the freedom of the Gospel.

8. We should be thankful for what freedom?—The freedom from our sins through Christ the great spiritual emancipator; for whom "the Son shall make free shall be free indeed." John 8:36.

FRUIT OF THE SPIRIT.
(Gal. 5.)

1. What does Paul urge the Galatians to do?—To stand fast.

2. To stand fast in what?—In the liberty (faith and hope of the Gospel) of which Christ is the author.

3. What is the most powerful principle known to the human heart?—Faith.

4. How does such faith function?—Through the heart its influence promotes all of the activities of the Christian life.

5. What is the danger when false doctrine is introduced into the church?—It may corrupt the entire membership. 5:9.

6. What is a safe guard against fulfilling the desires of the flesh?—To walk in the Spirit. 5:16.

7. What should be of utmost importance?—To inherit the kingdom of God.

8. Where do we find a list of the works of the flesh?—In Galatians 5:19, 20, 21.

9. What is the fruit of the Spirit?—Love, joy, peace, long-suffering, gentleness, goodness, faith, meekness, temperance. 5:22, 23.

BROTHERLY LOVE.
(Gal. 6.)

1. How should the Galatians deal with a brother in fault?—Mildly.

2. What should they do further?—Restore him.

3. They should do this with what kind of spirit?—The spirit of meekness.

4. What were they to consider?—Themselves—lest they also be tempted.

5. What is the law of Christ?—His new commandment, requiring his disciples to love one another. John 13:34, 35.

6. To what does such love lead?—To bear one another's burdens. 6:2.

7. Are there also individuals?—Yes, every man shall bear that which his own sins brings on him.

8. What universal law does Paul give in verse 7?—Be not deceived, God is not mocked: for whatsoever a man soweth, that shall he also reap.

9. Is there any degree of spirituality beyond the reach of temptation?—No, all should ever keep in sight verse one, "lest thou also be tempted."

10. How do the acts of life decide eternal destiny?—Whatsoever a man soweth.

11. Of what then should we be careful?—To select the right kind of seed.

12. Opportunities to do good create what?—Obligations to do good.

13. In what should all Christians glory?—The cross of Christ.

14. What proofs did Paul give of his loyalty to Christ?—The marks of the Lord Jesus honorable scars received for his sake while fighting under his banner.

15. What was Paul's benediction?—Brethren, the grace of our Lord Jesus Christ be with your spirit. Amen.

EPHESIANS INTRODUCTION.

1. When was the book of Ephesians written?—About the year 63.

2. Where was it written?—Probably during Paul's first imprisonment at Rome.

3. Where was Ephesus?—A celebrated city of Asia Minor.

4. Of what was it the capital?—Of what is known in history as proconsular Asia.

5. What did this embrace?—The western part of the Peninsula of Asia Minor.

6. How was the district governed?—By proconsul under the jurisdiction of Rome.

7. What made Ephesus a place of commercial importance?—It was situated on the highway from Rome into the continent of Asia.

8. What object was Ephesus renowned for as one of the seven wonders of the world?—The Temple of Diana.

KNOWLEDGE OF CHRIST.
(Eph. 1.)

1. The rich blessings of God are bestowed upon his people by whom?—By Jesus Christ.

2. From whence do these blessings come?—From heavenly places.

3. They prepare the recipients for what?—The heavenly places where they will be enjoyed in perfection.

4. Why is the Gospel properly termed the Gospel of salvation?—Because it reveals the way of salvation.

5. What further reason?—Because it is the power of God unto salvation; to every one that believeth.

6. What startling fact do we find in verse 22?—That he who died on Calvary and was buried in the tomb, is head over all.

GRACE.
(Eph. 2.)

1. The state of impenitence is described as what?—Dead in trespasses and sin.

2. Does this mean physically and intellectually dead?—No.

3. What kind of death is it?—They are dead spiritually, dead to God, to holiness, and to their best interest.

4. What doctrine is suitable to the condition of the lost sinners?—The doctrine of salvation by Grace, through faith.

5. Is there any other doctrine that can save such?—There is none other that sheds a ray of light on their darkness.

6. The phrase, "the blood of Christ" means what?—It presents his death in its aspects of sacrifice and expiation.

7. What should we ever remember?—That Christ died to make atonement for sin.

8. What is one of the great blessings of the death of Christ?—Its harmonious union between Jews and Gentiles who believe on his name.

9. The true Church has what kind of foundation?—Jesus Christ as its foundation.

MYSTERY MADE PLAIN.
(Eph. 3.)

1. What did Paul mean by, "for this cause"?—For the reason that the Gentiles have been made partakers of the blessings of the Gospels.

2. What is the meaning of "prisoner of Jesus Christ"?—Imprisoned because he was the servant of Jesus Christ.

3. What does "for the Gentiles" mean?—Paul was called by special commission to preach to the Gentiles.

4. What did Paul mean by "the Grace of God"?—The Grace given in his Apostleship. 3:2.

5. What was the mystery of Christ? 3:4.—The fact that the Gentiles were to be saved through Christ.

6. What are the unsearchable riches of Christ?—The treasures of Grace so great as to defy search. We have at the most only a superficial knowledge of what they mean.

7. Will we ever be able to comprehend the love of Christ in its vast dimensions?—Maybe, not on earth.

8. What should we do toward obtaining such knowledge?—Keep on striving.

9. The inflowing of the fullness of God into the soul is regulated by what?—By the extent of our knowledge of the love of Christ.

190

UNITY.
(Eph. 4.)

1. Paul exhorts the Ephesians to exercise what spirit?—The spirit of unity.

2. How should Christians live?—Consistently with their calling.

3. The heart is the seat of what?—Depravity.

4. What does the hardness of the heart affect?—The intellect by darkening the understanding.

5. What should the consecration of Christians include?—The tongue.

6. Why?—Because what they have to say should be edifying.

7. God exercises his forgiveness and mercy for whose sake?—For Jesus' sake.

8. What is the reason for this?—Because Christ bore our sins in his body. 1 Pet. 2:21.

RIGHTEOUS LIVING.
(Eph. 5.)

1. Did the sacrifice of Christ please the Father?—It was well-pleasing to him.

2. Why?—Because the atonement by means of that sacrifice possesses the value which the Father's approval can give it.

3. The tongue is referred to in Scripture sometimes as what?—As man's glory. Psalm 30:12.

4. How else is it used?—To man's shame. James 3:5, 6.

5. How do professed Christians sometimes desecrate the tongue?—By foolish talking and jesting.

PRE-EMINENT CHRIST.
(Eph. 6.)

1. How should those of all ages seek to serve God?—By doing that which is right in his sight.

2. What is our warfare against?—Most powerful interests for time and eternity.

3. How can we win against such formidable foes?—By being strong in the Lord and in the power of his might.

4. What does prayer accomplish?—It unites the poor, weak creature to the strong Creator.

5. What is the prevailing characteristic of all Christians?—That they love and serve the Lord Jesus Christ.

6. Where do we find Christ pre-eminent in exaltation?—In Eph. 2:6.

7. Where is Christ pre-eminent in separation?—In Eph. 3:6.

8. Where is Christ pre-eminent in education?—In Eph. 4:13.

9. Where is Christ spoken of as pre-eminent in ullumination?—In Eph. 5:8.

10. Where does it refer to Christ as pre-eminent in occupation?—In 6:6, 7.

11. Where is Christ spoken of as the head of the Church?—In 1:22.

PHILIPPIANS INTRODUCTION.

1. Where did Philippi derive its name?—From Philip King of Macedon.

2. When did it become a Roman colony?—During the reign of Augustus.

3. What kind of city was it considered?—The chief city of that part of Macedonia in which it was situated. Acts 16:12.

4. What first led Paul to Macedinia?—A vision.

5. What was the result of Paul's visit to Macedonia?—The preaching of the Gospel first in Europe.

6. Who were among the converts?—Lydia and her family.

7. Who were converted when Paul and Silas were imprisoned?—The jailer and his household.

8. What was the result of these conversions?—A church was formed.

9. Where was this letter written?—From Rome.

10. When was it written?—Toward the close of Paul's first imprisonment. Acts 30:31.

11. What is the date of its writing?—About the year 63.

BLESSED TRUTH.
(Phil. 1.)

1. For what was Paul thankful?—For the fruits of their faith, and fellowship in his suffering.

2. What caused the Apostle to rejoice?—The state of the Church. 1:4.

3. What did Paul mean by "the Day of Jesus Christ"?—The day of his second coming. 1:6.

4. Spiritual knowledge leads to what?—Spiritual discernment. 1:9.

5. The fruits of righteousness lead to what?—The glory and praise of God. 1:11.

6. What did Paul mean "to live in Christ"?—To him life was nothing apart from Christ.

7. What was the meaning of "to die is gain"?—The great advantage in death to the Christian. 1:21.

8. What is the meaning of "an evident token of perdition"?—Their persecutors became their adversaries and God's enemies, an indication that they were on their way to perdition. 1:28.

9. What was "the same conflict" to which Paul referred?—That which they witnessed when he was in Philippi. Acts 16:22-24. This also continued with him in Rome.

HUMILITY.
(Phil. 2.)

1. What gives the Gospel its saving value?—The Diety of Christ.

2. Where is such clearly taught? —In the Word of God.

3. Where do we find great condescension?—In verses 7 and 8.

4. From what depth did Christ rise to the height of his glory?— The depth of humiliation.

REJOICE.
(Phil. 3.)

1. What is the keynote of this Epistle?—Joy.

2. Of what should all Christians seek to know more?—To know and feel more keenly the power of his resurrection.

3. What distressing words do we find in verse 18?—Enemies of the cross of Christ.

4. What does the word conversation mean in this connection?—Citizenship. The community heavenly—such should be the conduct. Their names are written in heaven. Luke 10:20.

CONTENTMENT.
(Phil. 4)

1. Why is the peace of God so precious?—Because it passeth all understanding.

2. What Paul learned in respect to want?—In whatever state therewith to be content—satisfied and patient. Verse 12.

3. Of what two states of life was he familiar?—A. How to be abased, so as to have nothing. B. To abound, so as to have all he should want. 3:12.

4. How could Paul do all things?—Through Christ who gave him strength.

COLOSSIANS.
INTRODUCTION.

1. What was Colosse?—One of the principal cities of Phrygia, a province of Asia Minor.

2. Where was it located?—Not far from the cities of Laodicea and Hierapolis, mentioned in the Epistle, 4:13.

3. Had Paul visited Colosse?— It is clear from chapter 2:1, that the Colossians had never seen Paul.

4. When was this Epistle written?—About the year 63.

5. Where was it written?—In Rome during Paul's first imprisonment.

6. Why was it urgent to write this Epistle?—Judaism and Oriental philosophy caused diffusion of error.

THE TRUE CHRIST.
(Col. 1.)

1. For what did Paul thank God?—For their faith.

2. What is the great object of Christian hope?—Complete salvation.

3. How did Paul meet the heresies that minimized Christ?—By presenting the Eternal Christ, Creator and Head of all beings. 1:1-16.

4. What did Paul do to combat the reliance on forms?—He tells of Christ in you as the great mystery and gift.

WALKING WITH CHRIST.
(Col. 2.)

1. How should they, who have received Christ, walk?—They should walk in him. 1:6.

2. Is it now necessary to beware of false teachers?—From the Apostolic age until now it has been necessary for Christians to be on the alert and beware of the false teachings of human philosophy.

3. In what did the Mosaic law abound?—Types and shadows.

4. In whom are these types fulfilled?—In Christ.

WHAT WE SHOULD SEEK.
(Col. 3.)

1. What things should we seek?—Those things which are above. 3:1.

2. Christ is "all, and in all" to whom?—To those of all nations.

3. What is the word of Christ?—The word of truth. Therefore we should believe it.

4. What else is the word of Christ?—It is precept and therefore we should obey it.

5. What further is the word of Christ?—It is the word of salvation, therefore we should love it.

6. The word of Christ is what else?—It is the word of promise, therefore let us rejoice in it. 3:16.

7. How should we perform our daily tasks?—Whatsoever ye do, do it heartily, as to the Lord, and not unto men.

8. What is a man's character?—It is what he is.

9. How does God deal with man?—According to his character.

PRAYER.
(Col. 4.)

1. What is a very important duty of Christians?—Prayer.

2. What is the accompaniment of prayer?—Watching (Matt. 26:41).

3. How should Christians walk?—In wisdom, wisely, discreetly.

4. How are the opinions of men of the world influenced by Christians?—By their conduct.

5. What then is of utmost importance?—That those who name the name of Christ show to the world that they are righteous in all their transactions.

6. What touching words do we find at the close of this Epistle?—Remember my bonds.

7. What do they suggest?—The value of the Gospel which in Paul's judgment was not only worth suffering for but was also worth dying for.

LAST THINGS.
(1 Thess. 1.)

1. Under the Roman rule Macedonia was divided into how many parts?—Four parts.

2. What was the chief city of the second part?—Thessalonica.

3. What type of city was it in the first century?—A city of commercial importance.

4. What was the date of the writing of these Epistles?—Probably near the end of the year A.D. 52 or the beginning of 53.

5. Following the Acts of the Apostles, where did Paul go after his liberation from the Philippian prison?—To Thessalonica where there was a synagogue of the Jews.

6. While there where did Paul preach and carry on his labors?—In the synagogue.

7. What was the result of his work there?—Both Jews and Greeks were converted.

8. What further results of success grew out of these meetings?

193

—A church was formed, composed of believing Jews and Gentiles.

9. Persecution compelled Paul to do what?—To escape with his life. (See Acts 17:1-10).

10. Paul was conducted by the brethren to what places?—To Berea and thence to Athens.

11. What happened at Athens?—Paul delivered his great discourse on "Mars Hill. . . ."

12. With what do these two Epistles deal?—The last things.

13. What do the first three chapters review?—Their receiving the Gospel, and Paul's personal anxiety and comfort in them.

14. What do the last two chapters of the first Epistle teach?—Doctrinal and practical matters.

15. What is the doctrinal subject?—The second coming of Christ.

16. How will Christ come to believers?—See I Thess. 4:13-18.

17. How will he come to unbelievers?—See 1 Thess. 5:1-4.

SECOND THESSALONIANS.

1. What was the reaction to the first Epistle?—Some had the wrong impression of the second coming of Christ.

2. Why did Paul write the second letter?—To correct the views of those who had derived wrong impressions.

3. These two Epistles contain the fullest teachings on what subject?—The second coming of Christ.

4. What are we to do?—To wait and hope for it. 1 Thess. 4: 10.

5. What is then given?—Crown of Glory. 1 Thess. 2:19.

6. What is our comfort in the loss of friends?—The second coming. See 1 Thess. 4:13-18.

7. To whom will it come unexpectedly?—To the world. 1 Thess. 5:1-6.

PASTORAL EPISTLES.

1. What are the Pastoral Epistles?—First and Second Timothy, Titus, and Philemon.

2. These were written to whom?—To ministers associated with Paul.

3. Where was Paul when he wrote to Philemon?—In prison, the first time.

4. When did Paul write First Timothy and Titus?—After being released from prison.

5. Where was he when he wrote Second Timothy?—In prison, the second time.

6. Who was Timothy?—One of Paul's converts who afterward became an assistant. He was very faithful and was greatly beloved by Paul.

7. What seemed to be the special work for Timothy?—An evangelist. Paul wrote to him in his last letter, "Do the work of an evangelist." 2 Timothy 4:5.

8. Where was Timothy when Paul wrote the first letter to him?—In Ephesus where Paul had spent much time.

9. With what does the first chapter deal?—Doctrine. The use of law.

10. Chapter 2?—Public services, especially prayer.

11. Chapter 3?—Officers of the church.

12. Chapter 4 comprises what?—Errors and personal exhortations.

13. What classes are mentioned in chapter 5?—Various classes, such as elders, widows, servants.

14. With what does chapter 6 deal?—Errors and greed, and the closing charge.

SECOND TIMOTHY.

1. What is this Epistle considered to be?—The last message that we have from Paul.

2. Where was Paul when he wrote it?—In prison at Rome, awaiting execution.

3. What were the last words of Paul, as far as recorded?—For I am now ready to be offered, and the time of my departure is at hand. I have fought a good fight, I have finished my course, I have

kept the faith: henceforth there is laid up for me a crown of righteousness, which the Lord, the righteous judge, shall give me at that day: and not to me only, but unto all them also that love his appearing. . . . The Lord shall deliver me from every evil work, and will preserve me unto his heavenly kingdom: to whom be glory for ever and ever. Amen. 2 Tim. 4:6-8, 18.

4. Chapter 1 contains what?—Personal recollections of Timothy.

5. Chapter 2 comprises what?—Paul's charge to Timothy.

6. What does Chapter 3 deal with?—Foretelling of coming evils in the Church.

7. With what does Chapter 4 deal?—Paul's last message and testimony.

TITUS.

1. What was the personal relationship between Paul and Titus?—Titus was more like a companion to Paul while Timothy was as a son.

2. What is the Epistle of Titus like?—Letter of instructions.

3. This book treats of what?—Ordination of elders, how to deal with the Cretans. Various classes such as women, young men, and servants.

4. What else does it discuss?—Subjection to rulers and industry.

PHILEMON.

1. What is the book of Philemon?—Personal letter to Philemon about a runaway servant who came to Paul and was converted. Paul sends the servant back to Philemon with a plea for kindness. This beautiful book of one chapter gives a fine illustration of Christ's intercession for us.

HEBREWS.

1. When was this Epistle written?—Probably in the year 64 from Italy.

2. By whom was this epistle written?—Some difference of opinion exists but from century to century the sentiment has been that Paul wrote it. It is not certain who wrote it.

SUPERIORITY OF CHRIST.
(Heb. 1.)

1. What is the chief design of the Epistle?—To exalt the Lord Jesus Christ and show his superiority to Moses, Joshua, angels, and all other beings.

2. What three words bring us a magnetic message?—"God has spoken," 1:2. He has spoken unto us by his Son.

3. How did God speak to us previously?—By the Prophets. 1:1.

4. What great proof do we find in verse 3?—Conclusive proof of Christ's Deity. Of none other but Christ could it be said, "He is the brightness of the Father's glory, and the express image of his person."

5. What other great truth do we find in verse 8?—The stability and eternity of the Messiah's throne.

6. What great truth is in verse 14?—Christians, because of their relationship with Christ are greatly honored—angels are their servants. 1:14.

OBEDIENT TO CHRIST.
(Heb. 2.)

1. How should we treat this message?—We should give earnest heed to these things and be obedient to Christ.

2. What great sin, if persisted in, renders escape from the wrath of God impossible?—To neglect the great salvation that the Gospel reveals.

3. The suffering and death of Christ were followed by what?—Triumphant resurrection and exaltation.

4. Who is the captain of our salvation?—Christ who was made perfect through sufferings. 2:10.

5. What does "all of one" mean in verse 11?—All of one blood. Of one family.

6. What should be a source of great joy to Christians?—That Christ is not ashamed to call us brethren.

7. How can we be delivered from the fear of death?—Through Christ, for he alone can take away sin, which is the sting of death.

8. What should be our encouragement in the hour of temptation?—That Christ is able to succor them that are tempted.

CHRIST WORTHY OF GLORY
(Heb. 3.)

1. What does Paul call Christ in the first verse?—Apostle and High Priest of our profession.

2. Why was Christ counted worthy of more Glory than Moses?—Because of Christ's superior greatness.

3. How is this superiority illustrated?—By the difference between the builder of a house and the house itself.

4. What difference do we have in verses 5 and 6?—The servant and the Son.

5. What was the difference between Moses and Christ?—Moses was a servant and Christ was a Son.

6. What is the day of provocation?—The day when the Israelites provoked God. (See Numbers 14: 11.)

7. What always follows refusal to hear the voice?—Hardness of heart.

8. The sin of unbelief is the source of what?—Of other sins.

9. Why is unbelief the sin of sins?—Because it means the rejection of Christ, the Saviour of sinners.

REST.
(Heb. 4.)

1. How is the Christian's rest attained?—By faith.

2. What kind of rest remains for the people of God?—Repose from all labors and sorrows, and trials of this life.

3. How does this rest differ from the rest Christ now gives us?—The rest that Christ now gives us is only the beginning and an assurance of the rest to follow.

4. How is the Word of God represented as living and energetic?—The Word of God is quick and powerful.

OUR HOPE.
(Heb. 5.)

1. What does "Who" refer to in verse 7?—To Christ.

2. With strong crying and tears refer to what event?—The Gethsemane scene.

SUPERIOR GOSPEL.

1. What had been the temptation of the Hebrew Christians?—To fall back into the Judaistic belief and customs.

2. What is the aim of this Epistle?—To show the superiority of the Gospel to all that went before, especially the Old Testament teaching and practice of the law.

3. What are the recurring words?—"Better" "Hold Fast."

SUPERIOR PERSON.

4. Where do we find Christ superior in his person?—In chapter 1:4, better than Prophets, and even Moses.

SUPERIOR IN OFFICE.

5. Where do we find Christ superior in his office?—As High Priest; is better than Aaron and his offerings. Chapter 5:7.

SUPERIOR WORK.

6. Where do we find him superior in his work?—Christ's work reaches heaven and the inmost heart of men. Chapter 8:10.

SUPERIOR RELIGION.

7. Wherein is he superior in his religion?—The effect is faith Chapter 11. Hope Chapter 12. Love Chapter 13.

TITLES.

8. What are some of the titles of Christ given in this Epistle?—Son of God, Captain of our salvation, head of his house, High Priest, our forerunner, mediator of the New Covenant, intercessor, our sacrifice. The Great Shepherd of the sheep.

TEACHING OF THE BOOK.

9. What is the teaching of the whole?—That Christ is sufficient for all the needs of the believer.

FAITH.

10. What does the chapter on faith tell us?—What was done by believers in secular and temporal matters.

TYPES AND CEREMONIES.

11. What were the types and ceremonies of the law?—Shadows and copies; heavenly things which the believers now enjoy in Christ.

GENERAL EPISTLES.

1. What are the general Epistles?—James: 1, 2 Peter: 1, 2, 3 John; Jude.

2. Why are these many times grouped together?—Because they are alike in that they are not addressed to any particular church.

3. They were written by whom?—James, Peter, John, and Jude.

4. The Epistle of James was written to whom?—"To the twelve tribes scattered abroad"; that is, Jews throughout the world converted to Christ.

5. What is its teaching?—Christian morality rather than doctrines.

6. What does it discuss?—Trials, temptations, respect of persons, dead faith, the tongue and its misuse, strife and worldliness, oppression and patience, the prayer of faith.

PATIENT SUFFERING.
(1 Peter 1.)

1. To whom did Peter address his Epistles?—To the same dispersed Jews as James.

2. What is the general theme of the Epistles?—Patience in suffering.

3. What else is taught?—Holiness of life.

4. What further do we find in 1 Peter?—Glory to come at the revelation of Christ. Our royal state and the example of Christ. Exhortations to servants, wives, husbands. The suffering of Christ and the blessing of fellowship with him. To the elders.

WARNINGS.
(2 Peter.)

1. The subjects in this Epistle are what?—Exhortation, progress, and confidence. Attests his presence with Christ on the Mount of Transfiguration and refers to Christ's prediction of his death. Warns against false prophets, their fate. Cites the flood. Sodom and Balaam.

2. This Epistle foretells the destruction of the world. How?—By fire.

3. What does it foretell with regard to heaven and earth?—A new heaven and earth.

CONFIRMED FAITH.
(1 John.)

1. Are the Epistles of John like the previous ones?—They are different from all others.

2. When were they written?—After the destruction of Jerusalem and the death of all the Apostles.

3. What is the theme?—To confirm the faith of the believers.

4. What do we find in the first Epistle?—Assurance.

5. What else does it emphasize?—Inner spiritual states such as, fellowship, holiness, love.

6. What word occurs often?—Know.

7. Second John deals with what?—It is a private letter to a lady of rank.

8. What does he write?—A warning of false teachers who will come.

9. Third John is what?—A similar letter to Gaius.

10. Of what does he warn him?—Warns of a certain false Christian.

FALLEN ANGELS.
(Jude.)

1. Of what does the book of Jude warn?—It warns against apostates.

2. What else does it discuss?—The fall of angels and their state.

3. What strong terms does he use of false members in the Church?—Hidden rocks, selfish shepherds, clouds without water, etc.

THE REVELATION OF ST. JOHN THE DIVINE.
INTRODUCTORY.

1. Who is the author of the book of Revelation?—Undoubtedly the Apostle John.

2. What is the Greek title of this book?—The Apocalypse.

3. What do we learn from the first verse?—Revelation of Jesus Christ. God gave it and it was communicated to the author by an angel.

4. How many other Apostles were living at this time—None. John was the only living Apostle.

5. What happened to his brother James?—He had fallen more than fifty years before by the sword of Herod Agrippa.

6. Where was John at the time of this writing?—He was an exile on the Island of Patmos.

7. Why was he exiled?—For preaching the Gospel, and for his testimony for Jesus Christ.

8. To whom were the seven letters written?—To the seven churches of Proconsular Asia.

9. What did these letters contain?—Instructions to Christians of all ages.

10. How was John favored?—With heavenly visions.

11. What was the nature of these visions?—A panoramic view of the struggles, conflicts, defeats, and ultimate triumphs of Christianity.

12. What was the date of the writing?—Probably about A.D. 96.

13. By whose order had John been banished?—By Domitian, the Roman Emperor.

SEVEN SPIRITS.
(Rev. 1.)

1. What is this book called?—The Revelation of Jesus Christ.

2. The angel was especially commissioned to do what?—To make known to John this revelation.

3. Where in another chapter do we find reference to this angel?—Rev. 22:16.

4. What is the meaning of "keep these things"?—These things were to be observed.

5. The message came from One who embraced what?—All the present, all the past, and all the future.

6. Who were the seven spirits?—Seven with the Hebrews signified completeness. The seven spirits therefore denote the Holy Spirit in the many and fulness of his operations.

7. Why is Jesus called the faithful witness?—Because his is true and credible testimony.

8. Why is Jesus called the first begotten of the dead?—The first who rose from the dead.

9. Where was Patmos?—A rocky island in the Aegean sea, the prison home of John.

10. What was John's attitude on the Lord's day?—He was in the spirit.

11. When John heard the voice and turned what did he see?—Seven golden candle sticks. 1:12.

12. In the midst of the candle sticks what else did he see?—One like unto the Son of man, the Lord Jesus.

PORTRAIT OF CHRIST.

13. How was the Master dressed?—In priestly attire. A garment to the feet. A golden girdle about his breast. Priestly

distinction. 1:13.

14. What was the color of his hair?—White as snow, denoting the purity of his character.

16. What were his eyes like?—Expressive as a flame of fire. O just think of the Omniscient scrutiny of Christ!

17. What were the feet like?—Fine brass. Intensely bright.

18. What of his voice?—Commanding, loud and majestic. As the sound of many waters.

19. Seven stars were symbols of what?—The angels or rather the pastors of the seven churches.

20. What came from his mouth?—A sharp two-edged sword.

21. What of his countenance?—It was resplendent with Glory. It was as the sun.

22. Then what happened?—He laid his right hand upon me saying, fear not; "I am the first and the last." 1:17.

23. The seven stars represent the seven pastors. What do the seven candle sticks represent?—The seven churches.

MESSAGES TO THE CHURCHES. (Rev. 2.)

1. What was written to the church of Ephesus?—I know thy works, and thy labor, and thy patience, and how thou canst not bear them which are evil: and thou hast tried them which say they are apostles, and are not, and hast found them liars. 2:2.

2. For what else were they commended?—And hast borne, and hast patience, and for my name's sake hast labored, and hast not fainted. 2:3.

3. For what were they condemned?—They had left their first love. Their love had lost its original ardor.

4. What is the meaning of "the first and the last"?—Supreme Deity.

5. What was the message to the church of Smyrna?—I know thy works, and tribulation, and poverty, but thou art rich. 2:9.

6. How could this church be in poverty and at the same time rich?—It was rich in spiritual things.

7. What was against the church of Pergamos?—Because they had in their midst those who taught the doctrine of Balaam. 2:17.

8. What was against the church of Thyatira?—Because of a wicked woman by the name of Jezebel who claimed to be a Prophetess. Her purpose however was to lead them astray in doctrine and practice.

9. What was the promise to the one who overcame?—"I will give him the morning star." That is he would give himself. Chapter 22:16. "I am the bright and morning star."

NOMINAL PIETY.
(Rev. 3.)

1. What was there against the church of Sardis?—They had a name to live but were dead. See 3:1. Nominal piety only.

2. Was the whole church dead?—No. There were a few faithful ones who would walk in white with the Lord.

OPEN DOOR.

3. What was the great promise to the church at Philadelphia?—Behold I have set before thee an open door, and no man can shut it: for thou hast a little strength, and hast kept my word, and hast not denied my name. Verse 8.

4. What was the trouble with the church of the Laodiceans?—They were lukewarm, indifferent.

5. Who stands at the door?—Christ.

6. What should we do?—Open the door to show that he is welcome.

THE THRONE OF GOD.
(Rev. 4.)

1. What did John see through

the open door of heaven?—The throne of God in heaven, and one sitting on the throne.

2. Who sat about the throne?—Twenty-four elders, representing God's people in all ages.

3. What was before the throne? the sea of glass, clear as crystal.

4. What else was there before the throne?—Four beasts. The translation should be, "four living creatures."

5. What is the meaning of "full of eyes"?—Intelligence, vigilance.

6. What does "like a lion" mean?—Majestic, powerful.

7. What is the meaning of "like a calf"?—Patient.

8. What is the meaning of "a face as a man"?—Rational nature. Instinct with intelligence.

BOOK. SEVEN SEALS.
(Rev. 5.)

1. What is referred to in chapter 5?—The book sealed with seven seals.

2. Who only could open the book?—The lion of the tribe of Judah. The Messiah, descended from Judah, and like a lion in majesty and strength.

3. What is the substance of the new song?—Thou art worthy to take the book, and to open the seals thereof: for thou was slain, and hast redeemed us to God by thy blood out of every kindred, and tongue, and people, and nation.

OPENING OF THE SEALS.
(Rev. 6.)

1. What do we find in this chapter?—The opening of the seals.

2. When the first of the seven seals was opened, what did John see?—A white horse and rider.

3. What is the meaning of this?—Conquering.

4. Upon the opening of the next seal what did John see?—Red horse and rider. War takes peace from the earth.

5. When the third seal was opened what did he see?—Black horse and rider.

6. What did this denote?—Oppression, sorrow and lamentation.

7. What did the rider of the black horse have in his hand?—A balance, showing that food was to be carefully weighed because it would be scarce.

8. When the fourth seal was opened what did he see?—A pale horse and rider. Sword, famine, and pestilence.

9. What was the name of the rider of the pale horse?—Death. He was riding this pale horse and doing his terrible work.

10. Upon the opening of the fifth seal what did he see?—He saw the martyrs and heard their cry.

11. When the sixth seal was opened what did John see?—Signs in sun, moon, heavens. The great day of wrath.

WHITE ROBED MULTITUDE.
(Rev. 8.)

1. After John had witnessed the opening of the six seals what did he see?—The sealing of the one hundred and forty-four thousand. The great white robed multitude.

SEVEN TRUMPETS.
(Rev. 8.)

1. When the seventh seal was opened what happened?—There was silence in heaven for a half hour.

2. What was the seventh seal?—Seven trumpets.

3. When the first trumpet was blown what happened?—Hail, fire. Third part of trees and grass destroyed.

4. What happened when the second trumpet was sounded?—A burning mountain in the sea. Third part of life destroyed.

5. When the third trumpet was blown what happened?—A burning star. Rivers became worm-

wood.

6. When the fourth trumpet was sounded what happened?—The sun, moon, stars were smitten in the third part.

7. When the fifth trumpet was blown, what do we have?—Woe 1. Locusts from the abyss. Torment five months. Fallen star.

8. Woe 2?—Sixth trumpet. Satanic horsemen from the Euphrates. Repented not.

SEVEN THUNDERS.
(Rev. 10.)
9. In chapter 10 what do we have?—John. The angel with the little book. Seven thunders.

TEMPLE MEASURED.
(Rev. 11.)
10. In chapter 11 what do we find?—The Temple measured, two olive trees, witnesses.

HEAVENLY CHORUS.
(Rev. 12.)
11. In chapter 12?—Woe 3, seventh trumpet, heavenly chorus, sun clothed woman. Man child dragon, flight.

BEASTS.
(Rev. 13.)
12. In chapter 13?—Beasts from the sea. Beast from the earth. Blasphemy. Persecutions.

GLORIFIED THRONG.
(Rev. 14.)
13. In chapter 14, we have the glorified one hundred forty-four thousand, warning angels, harvest, winepress.

VIALS OF WRATH.
(Rev. 15.)
14. In chapter 15, what do we have?—We have the seven vials of wrath.

VIALS POURED OUT.
(Rev. 16.)
15. In chapter 16, what do we have?—The seven vials poured out.

16. What was in the first vial?—Sores on man and beast.

17. What did the angel do with the second vial?—Poured death on sea.

18. What was done with the third vial?—Poured on rivers turned to blood.

19. What was done with the fourth vial?—Poured on the sun. Men scorched. Repented not.

20. What did the fifth angel do with his vial?—Poured it on the throne of the beast. Torment. Repent not.

21. What did the sixth angel do with his vial?—Poured it on the river Euphrates, Kings of the East, three unclean spirits.

22. What happened when the seventh vial was poured out?—The angel poured it out into the air. "It is done." Great city divided. Cities fall. Men blaspheme.

SCARLET WOMAN.
(Rev. 17.)
23. Of what do we read in chapter 17?—The scarlet woman and her fate.

FALL OF BABYLON.
(Rev. 18.)
24. Was the fall of Babylon cause for world lament?—It was. See chapter 18.

CONFLICT.
(Rev. 19.)
25. What do we find in chapter 19?—Heavenly chorus over the fall of Babylon. The word and the white horse army. Conflict with the beast. Victory.

SATAN BOUND.
(Rev. 20.)
26. In chapter 20 what is discussed?—Satan bound a thousand years. Apostasy. Final conflict. Judgment of the great white throne.

NEW HEAVENS—NEW EARTH.
(Rev. 21.)

27. What is discussed in chapter 21?—New heaven and a new earth.

RIVER OF LIFE.
(Rev. 22.)

28. What is discussed in chapter 22?—The river of life. Closing words.